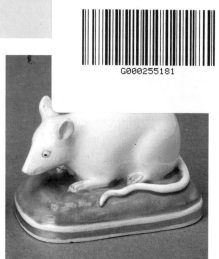

Colour Plate 24a (left). Rockingham shepherdess and sheep, 6¾ in. (17.1cm) high, and b (right) shepherd and dog, 8½ in. (21.6cm) high, each incised 'No 4' and impressed with the griffin mark. 1826-30.

English Porcelain Animals

of the 19th century

D.G. RICE

Antique Collectors' Club

ISBN 1 85149 085 X

Published for the Antique Collectors' Club
by the Antique Collectors' Club Ltd.

British Library CIP Data

Rice, Dennis
    English porcelain animals of the 19th century.
    1. English porcelain, 1745-1870 — Collectors' guides
    I. Title
    738.2'0942

Printed in England by
the Antique Collectors' Club Ltd.
Woodbridge, Suffolk

Contents

continued

Contents continued

Colour Plates

Acknowledgements

I am much indebted to Sotheby Parke Bernet and Co. and to Christie Manson and Woods Ltd. for their generous provision of photographs of animals which have, over the years, passed through their salerooms, and for their permission to reproduce them and to quote from their sale catalogues. I am also indebted to those dealers who have kindly made photographs available to me for reproduction, notably Mr Geoffrey Godden, Mr Stafford Lorie, Mr Bryan Bowden, Messrs Graham and Oxley and Mr Ron Beech.

I appreciate the help I have received from Mr H.E. Frost, Curator of the Dyson Perrins Museum, in obtaining for me photographs of certain items in his museum and the help of Ms Joan Jones, Curator of the Minton Museum, Royal Doulton Tableware Ltd., in supplying copies of the drawings from the Minton factory's drawing book. I am also indebted to Mr C. Miller, managing director of Royal Worcester Spode Ltd., for allowing me to reproduce the animal drawings in the Grainger Lee pattern book. I am likewise grateful for the assistance rendered by the staff of the Yorkshire Museum in allowing me to illustrate two of their animals, and for the help received with photographs from Mr T.A. Lockett and Mrs Audrey Dudson. Mr Anthony Oliver was kind enough to vet the accuracy of a general paragraph I had written on Staffordshire figures. Mr Henry Sandon, a former curator of the Dyson Perrins Museum, provided me with interesting information relating to Worcester figures of the second half of the nineteenth century. Mrs Pat Halfpenny, Keeper of Ceramics, of the City Museum and Art Gallery, Hanley, Stoke-on-Trent, and Ms Amy de la Haye, Assistant Curator of the Hove Museum and Art Gallery, gave me details of certain items in their respective museums. I am also grateful to John Murray (Publishers) Ltd. for their permission to quote from the diary of Elizabeth Moulton-Barrett (later Browning) published for the first time in *The Barretts at Hope End* (ed. by Elizabeth Berridge).

My acknowledgements would not, however, be complete without my recording the help and general encouragement in writing this book that I have received from my wife, to whom the subject matter has always presented a particular appeal.

Preface

It is the purpose of this book to study, not a particular English porcelain factory, but rather a particular type of product emanating from a variety of different factories. The items in question are the numerous porcelain animals manufactured in this country during the nineteenth century, a hitherto neglected subject. Such animals were turned out in their thousands, both by the great contemporary factories such as Rockingham, Derby, Worcester and Minton, but also by the numerous, and for the most part wholly unidentified, factories operating in Staffordshire during the period 1830-50. After the end of the first half of the nineteenth century small porcelain animals fell out of fashion, and the animals of the period 1850-1900 tended to be large, sculptured in form, and more suited as decorative objects for the home than as the contents of the collector's cabinet.

Encouraged by the absence of any significant public collections, I have endeavoured to illustrate, both in colour and black and white, a representative selection of English porcelain animals of the nineteenth century, and to describe and discuss them in the context of the output of the relevant factories. So far there has been no monograph directed to the study of English porcelain animals of the nineteenth century, and insofar as they are referred to at all in the various standard works concerned with individual factories (and for the most part they are not), they have received treatment very much as subsidiary items. I have endeavoured to bring conveniently within the confines of a single volume a survey of porcelain animals of the nineteenth century factories, including illustrations of most of the known Rockingham models. Of course, this survey is not, nor does it purport to be, exhaustive of the subject. In covering what is a broad field, I have had to be selective in what I have included. I have, however, endeavoured to present a reasonably comprehensive selection. It is perhaps useful to remember that such selection has had to be made from those nineteenth century English porcelain animals that have survived to this day, which are only a small fraction of those actually produced, and so may or may not fairly represent the factories' original output.

Introduction

English porcelain animals of the nineteenth century have previously been a largely neglected field of study. Moreover, no public collection of any consequence at present exists, so that the opportunities for study of these minor, but nevertheless fascinating figures, have always been circumscribed. An attempt is made in this book to remedy the position by illustrating and describing a representative selection of animals, both from the leading factories known to have made them, and also from certain minor unidentified manufacturers operating at the time in Staffordshire. However, of the principal factories it is interesting that no animals have so far been ascribed to Flight Barr and Barr, Worcester, Spode, Nantgarw, Coalport, H. and R. Daniel or Ridgway.[1]

CLASSIFICATION

The animals I have described and illustrated are grouped under certain broad headings: animals of the home — cats; animals of the home — dogs; animals of the farm; animals of the English countryside; animals from abroad and birds. However there is nothing sacrosanct about this grouping; it is entirely a matter of convenience.

Some species of animals are only occasionally found in porcelain during our period; others are reasonably prolific. For instance, dogs are legion, whilst in relation to them cats are rare. Nevertheless, some breeds of dog are only occasionally encountered, and viewed as an individual breed, are rarer than cats as a species. The respective rarity of different types of porcelain animals will be commented upon.

REVERSING OF MODELS

Sometimes animals have survived in pairs; but more often a particular animal appears as a single item. Where a companion model in reverse has not so far been recorded, the question immediately arises whether it was originally a single model or one of a pair. In some instances no great difficulty presents itself. A stag was normally produced to go with a matching hind (though sometimes stags in reverse were made to form pairs) and a ram with a matching ewe. Where a dog or other animal is modelled in such detail that it can be determined whether it is male or female, it was almost certainly made to go with an animal of the opposite sex modelled in reverse. Difficulties arise where an animal's sex is not easily determinable by the modelling, e.g. cats, squirrels, rabbits, mice,

---

1. However, Ridgway & Robey (1837-40) issued portrait figures, and William Ridgway, Son & Co. (c.1838-45) suffered a burglary at their factory in February 1842 when there were included, among other items stolen, 'china figures' and 'large china figures — The Seasons and The Brigands'. (See G.A. Godden's *The Illustrated Guide to Ridgway Porcelain,* p.38). Perhaps animals were produced, and any survivors have not been identified.

giraffes and elephants. Where there is only one surviving specimen, whether there was a companion model cannot be certain. Moreover, even when three or four survivors are recorded, the fact that they all face in one direction does not prove that the factory did not also produce a companion model in reverse. Three or four specimens are too small a sample to enable us to reach a reliable conclusion. The matter is not resolved where a factory's models are illustrated in a surviving master drawing book. Although a particular model may be illustrated looking in one direction, instances have come to light where an example of that same model appears in reverse (see page 71).

Accordingly, where it is known that a particular model was reversed I have so remarked. However, where I have not stated this, it does not necessarily follow that there was never a reverse. It may be that an example has so far simply not materialised (there is, I consider, a bias in favour of such a conclusion in view of the increased marketability of pairs).

GILDING

Gilding appears as a regular decorative feature of porcelain animals at least of the first half of the nineteenth century. However, it was a very expensive process. This is vividly revealed by the sharp increase in the selling price of a Derby cat with a gilt collar as against one without this minor adornment. The factory price doubled from 6d. to 1s. (See Haslem's list at page 215). Moreoever, this increase would appear to have operated irrespective of any enamel decoration, so that a white cat with a gilt collar would still seem to have cost double that of a similar enamelled animal without a gilt collar. The expense of enamelling a cat — and where gilding was not employed, the animal might have been given a coloured collar as well as coloured markings on the body — would appear to have been so small in relation to the cost of gilding that, in fixing the factory sale price, such extra expense could safely be disregarded.

Confirmation of the cost of gilding can be found in the Chamberlain Worcester factory documents of 1791.[1] Admittedly, they relate to a period slightly before that with which we are directly concerned, but they serve to indicate a situation which also obtained in the nineteenth century. The Chamberlain Worcester factory in 1791 was buying figures from outside suppliers but gilding them itself. Among other items, there is a reference in the documents to:

---

1. See G.A. Godden's *Chamberlain Worcester Porcelain* at p.56.

	China			Gilding		
	£	s	d	£	s	d
2 Greyhounds, killing hare		3	0		1	6
40 Pointer dogs, enamelled	1	10	0	1	0	0
3 French Tarriers, enamelled		2	3		1	6

BISCUIT ANIMALS

What is perhaps surprising to discover is that the most expensive animals were those left in the biscuit state, that is, without glaze or decoration of any sort, enamel or gold. One might, on the contrary, have expected such animals to have been the cheapest.

The reason why this was not so was that a biscuit specimen, if it was to find a ready market, had to be perfect for there was nothing to take the eye from the unadorned ceramic body. There could be no question of any defect being camouflaged by enamel painting or gilt decoration. The number of pieces which left the kiln in a perfect condition was of course limited, and as a result they commanded a disproportionately high price. Even the cost of gilding could not offset the rarity value of 'perfection'. The various lists of Derby figures published by Haslem, which reveal a higher factory price when a figure was sold in the biscuit state than when it was sold enamelled and gilt, establish the matter beyond doubt. The following examples are taken from the list of figures modelled by Edward Keys:

	Enamelled and gilt			Biscuit		
	£	s	d	£	s	d
'Paris cries', Set of six Figures	1	4	0	1	16	0
Peacock	0	2	0	0	3	6
Bucks and Does	0	4	0	0	7	0

It is interesting to note the reference to the following animals in the records of the Chamberlain Worcester factory:[1]

---

1. See G.A. Godden's *Chamberlain Worcester Porcelain*, p.214.

	Biscuit		
	£	s	d	
A toy biscuit poodle		5	0	[Sept. 1828]
A pug dog		2	6	[Jan. 1829]
Elephant		2	6	
To a biscuit poodle and shade[1]		15	0	[Feb. 1829]

The most expensive items are those in biscuit. Although there is no direct comparison between a particular biscuit animal and its enamelled and gilt counterpart, and we do not know the comparative sizes of the animals listed above, nevertheless the first item is described as a toy, suggesting something particularly small. As explained below, strictly speaking *all* small animals of the first half of the nineteenth century were described in contemporary language as 'toys', and accordingly to make a special point of distinguishing a particular animal as being 'a toy' in relation to the others, is to suggest something of truly diminutive size. This nomenclature has for convenience been adopted in this book to describe animals of truly minute proportions (e.g. colour plate 2, figures 2, 39a, 88, 107, 130, 133 and 137). The evidence, then, points to Chamberlain Worcester animals left in the biscuit state as being more expensive than those enamelled and gilt.

THE SALES MARKET

In the first half of the nineteenth century small animals in porcelain were generally referred to as 'toys', but it does not follow from this that they were necessarily made exclusively for children. Miniature objects of all kinds are, of course, attractive to children, but often, particularly where they are of fine quality and expensive, they were made for adults, usually women. What was the ultimate destination of small porcelain animals during the period 1800-50 is problematical. After 1850 porcelain animals tended to be large, and as such fulfilled the function of ornamental objects placed about the house.

Hugh Owen in his book *Two Centuries of Ceramic Art in Bristol,* published in 1873, refers on page 290 to 'Mrs James (mother of the late well-known Bristol dealer in curiosities)' as 'employed [at the Bristol china works] in modelling children's toys — lambs, &c.' The Bristol porcelain factory operated from 1770 to 1781, and if its animals should be regarded as children's toys, so too presumably should the animals of later factories, including those functioning in Owen's lifetime. Confirmation of this can

---

1. Biscuit figures, not being glazed, and therefore partially porous, absorbed the impurities of the air and were frequently protected against this by means of a 'shade', i.e., a glass dome.

be found in *The Connoisseur,* September 1922, p.37, where an interesting account is to be found of how a small dog there illustrated had been given to a relative of the writer sometime prior to 1836, when the former was four years old. In contrast a similar dog had been presented to the relative's sister and had been broken within a few days.

In relation to the sale price of tableware and figures generally, small animals were comparatively cheap, and there is nothing intrinsically absurd in supposing that the primary market for them was children. Presumably china animals were normally only given to children able to appreciate the delicate material of which they were made, and the more expensive animals went to children in more comfortable circumstances. Even so, fatalities must have been colossal, and perhaps this explains the paucity of surviving specimens. However, there was absolutely nothing to stop an adult who liked a particular animal from buying it, and doubtless many a lady did.

DATING

The exact dating of porcelain animals of the nineteenth century is fraught with difficulty, and it is generally necessary to apply fairly wide bands. One of the problems is that even when a particular model is known to have been first produced at a specific date, it does not follow that all examples of that model were turned out shortly thereafter. Needless to say, some models soon fell out of fashion, but this was not invariably the case. Sometimes the form of the mark, where it appears, helps with the dating, but if, as in the case of the 'Chamberlain(s) Worcester' mark in script, the period covered is extensive, the assistance given by it is severely limited. Happily, however, where Rockingham animals are concerned, we can be relatively precise. They were all modelled between 1826 and 1830, and for the reasons set out in Appendix A all, or nearly all, of them were also produced during this short period.

Less precise are the periods indicated by the written mark 'CB' (Charles Bourne) — 1817-30, the name 'GRAINGER LEE AND CO, WORCESTER' impressed in capitals — 1812-37, and the factory mark of Copeland and Garrett — 1833-47, but nevertheless these marks do establish the time bands within which manufacture must have taken place. Again, the Derby mark in the form of a Crown over crossed batons, dots and a 'D', all in red, is helpful to the extent that the relevant item cannot have been made after about 1825. Animals made in the second half of the nineteenth century sometimes have a date mark, e.g. colour plate 29 and figure 22.

Marks are not the only means of dating. Thus, the Minton factory book, which has survived, reveals that that particular factory's animals were not turned out before 1830. Again certain of the records of the Chamberlain factory, which are also extant, suggest that, although some animals were produced from the beginning of the nineteenth century (and even earlier) onwards, the peak period was 1820-30, followed by a sharp decline in the succeeding decade. Although according to G.A. Godden the records do not mention any order received after 1840, nevertheless the form of the mark used on the small biscuit poodle illustrated in figure 39 indicates that there must have been exceptions. (See also the dog sold at Sotheby's on 25 February 1986, lot 345.) It is also interesting to note that the distinctive dry blue ground colour, which often features on the base of Chamberlain animals, is not mentioned in the factory records before 1820.

Broadly speaking, most small animals emanating from the 'great' factories can be attributed to the period 1820-40, whilst most small animal models from the minor Staffordshire concerns were made during the slightly later period 1830-50. After 1850 small porcelain animals fell completely out of fashion. Parian became the vogue, and most animals produced in this medium tended to be somewhat large. So too were the glazed animals from the Royal Worcester and Copeland factories. However, at the end of the nineteenth century the Royal Worcester factory was responsible for some delightful toys (colour plate 29).

I. Animals of the Home

Cats

'Cruel, but composed and bland,
Dumb, inscrutable, and grand;
So Tiberius might have sat,
Had Tiberius been a cat'
　　　　(Matthew Arnold)

In the natural history books published before the twentieth century, the cat received a poor press. However, 'pussy' has always succeeded in insinuating himself into the affections of a large proportion of the human population, as is evident from his constant appearance in paintings throughout the centuries. It is not surprising, then, to find him represented in porcelain during the nineteenth century.

Cats are far more rarely seen in porcelain than dogs. Unlike the latter, which consist of a variety of different breeds, cats in the last century comprised essentially one kind, the modern day, ever present, 'moggie'. Such sophisticated felines as the Siamese, the Persian, the Burmese or the Abyssinian have no place in porcelain during the nineteenth century. Although a particular breed of dog may prove rarer in porcelain than cats generally, the fact still remains that the totality of porcelain dogs produced vastly exceeds the entire output of cats.

Although cats are occasionally found in biscuit,[1] normally they are glazed, appearing in white with gilt embellishments, usually on the base and collar (figures 1, 3, 5, 6, 7, 9b and 11) or in enamel colours and gold. In the latter case, tortoiseshell cats (with a preponderance of white) are by far the most common (colour plates 1, 2 and 6). Less frequent are black and white cats (figure 10a) and rarer still by far are the tabbies (colour plate 7a and figure 8). Rarest of all are the ginger cats (figure 12a) and black cats (colour plate 5b and figure 2). Although the decoration necessary to represent a tabby or ginger cat was considerable, so that the rarity of such models is readily understandable, this was not the case with black cats. Their decoration presented no difficulty, and their scarcity is all the more puzzling. Presumably for some reason the real black cat was out of fashion. Perhaps, like the black pug, it was thought unlucky.

Usually porcelain cats are found as individual animals, either sitting upright or lying recumbent, on a variety of different bases, a cushion with tassels being particularly popular. Sometimes, however, they are modelled with a single kitten (colour plates 6, 7 and 8, and figures 14, 15a, 17b and 18) and occasionally with a litter of kittens (colour plates 3 and 9b and figures 6, 7 and 8). Sometimes a cat appears as part of a figure group (colour plate 4a).

---

1. See the Rockingham example shown at p.142 (illustration 5) of *The Connoisseur Year Book*, 1962.

Figure 1. Three Rockingham white and gilt cats seated on tasselled cushions, each incised 'No 77'. 1826-30. a (left). Height 2⅜ in. (6cm), Cl 1 (note that this model also appears 2½ in. (6.4cm) high, colour plate 1b). b (centre). Height 2⅛ in. (5.4cm), incised '2 size' in script. Impressed 'ROCKINGHAM WORKS'. c (right) Height 1¾ in. (4.4cm). Incised '2', Cl 1. Impressed mark.

Figure 2. Rockingham toy black cat seated on a green and white tasselled cushion, 1⅜ in. (3.5cm) high. Cl 2. 1826-30 (cf. the three Rockingham toy cats of colour plate 2).

ROCKINGHAM

The cats turned out at the Rockingham factory in Swinton, Yorkshire, were beautifully modelled. Apart from the cat playing with an apple in the hat of a kneeling girl, which is included in the group shown in colour plate 4a (No 40)[1], there are only four Rockingham cat models so far recorded. (The examples are normally, though not invariably marked, and almost always incised with the relevant model number.) In the case of the first model (No 77), the cat is sitting upright, usually on a tasselled cushion (colour plates 1b and 2, figures 1 and 2), but occasionally on an oval scroll base of restrained rococo design (colour plate 1a, figure 3).

Examples on the cushion base are recorded as being of the following heights, namely 2⅜ in (6cm), 2⅛ in (5.4cm), 1¾ in (4.4cm), and 1⅜ in (3.5cm). Some of these, in addition to the incised number, have likewise incised under the base '1 size' (colour plate 1b) or '2 size' (figure 1b) or just the numeral '2' (figure 1c). Strangely '3 size' or '3' is so far unrecorded, and it is somewhat confusing, then, to find that the smallest and middle size cats in figure 1 are both described under the base as being the second size. Perhaps at the time each was made there were only two sizes being produced, apart from the toy 1⅜ in (3.5cm) high, and it would then have been accurate to say that each of the two cats in question was the smaller version.

The three examples with tortoiseshell markings shown in colour plate 2, being only 1⅜ in (3.5cm) in height, are clearly toys. They bear no mark, nor even an incised 'No 77'. However, their modelling, their paste

18

1. A biscuit version is illustrated opposite page 33 of H. Boswell Lancaster's *Talks on Pottery* [1949].

Colour Plate 1a (left). Rockingham cat on an oval scrolled base 2¼ in. (5.7cm) high. Incised '1 size' in script and 'No 77'. Cl 2. 'BRAMELD' impressed. 1826-30. b (right). Rockingham cat on a tasselled cushion base, 2½ in. (5.7cm) high. Incised '1 size' in script and 'No 77'. Impressed mark. 1826-30.

and glaze, and, most important of all, the correspondence of their crimson or green bases with identically coloured bases of marked or numbered examples establish their Rockingham provenance beyond doubt. Interestingly, the same model in the same size sitting on a green

Colour Plate 2. Three Rockingham toy cats, each seated on a tasselled cushion base, 1⅜ in. (3.5cm) high. 1826-30 (See figure 2 for a black example).

Figure 3. Rockingham white and gilt cat seated on an oval scroll base, 1⅞ in. (4.7cm) high. Incised '2' in script and 'No 77'. Impressed mark. 1826-30. (Note the different base to that appearing in figures 1 and 2).

base — but this time the cat is black — likewise has no incised number, but it does have a 'Cl 2' mark in red (figure 2), establishing beyond any doubt that all these toy cats do emanate from the Rockingham factory.

Rockingham cats incised 'No 77' but seated on the oval scroll form of base (colour plate 1a, figure 3) are recorded as being of two sizes, namely 2½ in. (6.4cm) and 1⅞ in. (4.7cm) in height respectively. It is to be noted that all the examples of model No 77 illustrated here, on whichever base they sit, look in one direction. So do all the others I have ever seen, suggesting that no reverse model was ever made.

It is worthwhile mentioning that although the impressed mark appears frequently on examples of model No 77, a single instance has been recorded where the printed red mark has been used — in respect of a black cat 2½ in. (6.4cm) high seated on an oval scroll base appearing as lot 585 of Sotheby's sale of 'British and Irish Ceramics', 22 May 1984. Interestingly, the usual incised number was missing from that particular specimen. It is a reasonable inference from this that this model was issued before the numbering system had started (see page 270) and was therefore one of the first animals to be produced at Swinton.

The Rockingham factory also manufactured a cat lying in a recumbent position (No 104). It would seem to have been made in one size only, namely 2¾ in. (7cm) long. Three examples are shown here (colour plate 4b, figure 9). One is white and gilt, the other two are enamelled with patches of black and yellow. No reverse of this model has so far been recorded, but presumably, as the Derby and Chamberlain equivalents are found in pairs, a reverse model was in fact made. Support for this view can be found in the fact that this same model *in reverse* appears as the central figure in the cat and kittens group, No 107, described below.

A third model of a Rockingham cat is shown in figure 5. It is very rare; indeed, the example illustrated is the only one I have ever seen. The same model, however, appears in figure 84 of Margaret Vivian's *Antique Collecting* (published in 1937). Dr Vivian writes amusingly of that cat and how she came to acquire it. She explains that it was offered to her by 'a runner' for £10, but after considerable haggling was obtained by her for £5, which at the time she considered a fair price. Like the cat of figure 5 it was white and gilt, printed with the red griffin mark, and seemingly without an incised number. The model, which is 2½ in. (6.4cm) high, must have been issued before the numbering system was adopted (see page 270). Needless to say, no reverse has been recorded.

It is interesting to note that the above is the only known Rockingham animal to have a base (figure 4) whose underside is glazed and slightly recessed, in contrast to the normal Rockingham base where the underneath is left flat and unglazed, and, save for a centrally located hole,

Figure 4. The base of the cat shown in figure 5. (Note that the base is recessed in contrast to the normal type of Rockingham base shown in figure 76).

Figure 5. Rockingham white cat seated on an oval scroll base flecked with gold, 2½in. (6.4cm) high. Unnumbered. Red griffin mark. 1826-27.

is completely closed-in (figure 76). Possibly the explanation for this is that this particular model was produced before the usual Rockingham form of base construction had been introduced from Derby, in which event it must have been an extremely early model indeed. The scarcity of examples of it suggests that it was soon discontinued and replaced by model No 77.

The final cat model to be recorded as coming from the Rockingham

Figure 6. Rockingham white and gilt cat and kittens on a rectangular paved base, 4¼in. (10.8cm) long. Incised 'No 107'. Cl 1. Impressed mark. 1826-30. (Note the saucer located on the left.)

Figure 7. Rockingham white and gilt cat and kittens group on a rectangular paved base, 4¼in. (10.8cm) long. Incised 'No 107'. Cl 1. 1826-30. (Note the saucer located this time on the right; cf. colour plate 3b.) *Sotheby's.*

factory is No 107. It is a group consisting of a recumbent cat (the same model as No 104) with three kittens lying on a rectangular paved base. The group is found in two sizes, namely 3⅞in. and 4¼in. long respectively. Two of those illustrated here are white and gilt (figures 6 and 7), the other three are decorated with enamel colours and gold (colour plate 3, figure 8). An interesting feature of this particular model is that sometimes a saucer of milk is included as part of the group. Its absence, however, from the examples in colour plate 3a and figure 8 is, I hasten to point out, not due to damage; the saucer was never included at the time of manufacture. No reverse model has been found.

Figure 8. Rockingham cat and kittens, the cat striped grey, the kittens grey and ochre, on a rectangular paved base, 4¼in. (10.8cm) long. 1826-30. Note the total absence of a saucer (cf. colour plate 3a).

Figure 9. Rockingham recumbent cats, 2¾in. (7cm) long. a (left). White with black and yellow markings, but no collar. 1826-30. b (right). White and gilt. Incised 'No 104'. Cl 1. Impressed mark. 1826-30. (Presumably a reverse model was also made.)

DERBY

As has been explained earlier, the similarity between certain Rockingham and Derby animals is so remarkable that it defies coincidence. There must be a connecting link, seemingly the simple pirating by the Rockingham factory of the Derby designs. The similarity in modelling is nowhere more dramatically illustrated than in the case of the two Rockingham model Nos 77 and 104, and their Derby equivalents.

Figure 10. Derby recumbent cats, 2¾in. (7cm) long. a (left). Black and white. Mark Bloor Derby within a circular band encompassing a crown, c.1830. b (right). White with tortoiseshell markings. Incised '1', c.1830. (These cats are almost identical to the Rockingham cats of figure 9.)

Figure 11. Pair of Derby white and gilt cats, 2¾ in. (7cm) long, c.1830. *(Sotheby's)*

At pages 216 and 217 there is a list of Derby animals set out, modelled by Edward Keys, and it includes:

	Enamelled and gilt	
	s	d
Cats on Cushions, large...each	2	0
Cats on Cushions, small...each	1	6

Are the 'cats on cushions' the Derby equivalent of the Rockingham model No 77? A Derby example of a cat sitting upright on a tasselled cushion has come to light and is illustrated in colour plate 5b. It is a black cat on a pink base, with gilt tassels. Like most Derby animals of the first half of the nineteenth century it is unmarked and, of course, has no incised number (see page 213). The base, in a way typical of Derby animals, is closed in underneath save for a small hole centrally located to allow occluded gasses to escape during manufacture. Of course, it might be objected that this form of base is also that adopted at the Rockingham factory, suggesting the possibility that the animal is not in fact a product of the Derby factory, but rather a Rockingham cat, and that it is without a mark and without an incised number, for occasionally Rockingham animals are found lacking both. However, the height is 2in. (5.1cm), which does not appear to correspond to that of any Rockingham model, and the pink enamel colour applied to the base, although a common enough feature of Derby cats (colour plate 6), has not so far been applied to the base of any cat that is indisputably Rockingham. More importantly, the modelling of the cushion base is not quite as sharp and well defined as that of the Rockingham cushion base, particularly as regards the tassels. There can be little doubt that the cat illustrated in colour plate 5b has a Derby provenance, and must surely be one of the 'Cats on cushions' included in the list of Edward Keys' works. Whether it is a large or small cat is problematical. Unless and until one has two examples different in size, it is impossible to say.

The list of animals, said by Haslem to have been made from the 'Bow and Chelsea models', includes:

	s	d
Cat lying down	0	6
Ditto with gold collar	1	0

The description and price suggest identification with the model illustrated in figures 10 and 11. It measures 2¾ in. (7cm) in length,[1] and is almost indistinguishable from the Rockingham model, No 104. The only slight difference is that the Derby cat is somewhat fuller in the face. The Derby cats of this shape appear in white and gold (figure 11) and in enamel colours and gold (figure 10). Normally they are unmarked. However, the cat illustrated in figure 10a is interesting for the fact that it is printed under the base with the red Bloor mark, thereby establishing, if there had been any doubt, an unchallengeable Derby provenance. This model was produced in reverse. Presumably these cats were originally sold as pairs. All the Derby 'lying down' cats shown here have a gilt collar, which had the effect of doubling the price at which they were originally sold. An interesting Derby cat of this model is recorded having a blue collar with a bow. Presumably it sold originally for only 6d. The cost of the cats with gilt collars lay in the gold.

It is interesting to note the reference by Bemrose in his list of Derby moulds and models in existence in 1795 to: 'Pair laying cats, 2 sizes'. The accuracy of the reference to '2 sizes' is confirmed by surviving specimens. In addition to the normal sized cat, which incidentally sometimes has under the base an incised '1' to indicate that it was the larger of the two models, the factory occasionally produced a smaller version, 2in. long, sometimes incised with a '2'. An example of the latter is recorded, so incised, which is decorated with elaborate tortoiseshell markings, and has no collar, either gold or painted. The second size cat is slightly differently proportioned from the first size.

It is to be remarked that Haslem's list of 'Bow and Chelsea' models includes: 'Large Sitting Cat' [no price given]. I have seen three examples (each from the nineteenth century) of a large Derby cat, 4¾ in. (12.1cm) high, sitting on a tasselled cushion, similar in form (though larger in size) to the Derby cat already described and illustrated in colour plate 5b. On the basis of their size each must have been sold by the factory for a sum well in excess of 2s, so that on no footing could they be the larger version

---

1. Sometimes in sale catalogues it appears as 2¼ in. long. This would appear to arise from the base alone being measured, not the cat.

of the 'Cats on Cushions' modelled by Edward Keys. They must be examples of the 'Large Sitting Cat', a conclusion supported by the reference in Bemrose's list of moulds and models existing in 1795 to: 'Pair large siting [sic] cats'.

The three cats with tortoiseshell markings, each lying on a rectangular base with gold braid, which appear in colour plate 6, though not mentioned in any of Haslem's lists, are undoubtedly from the Derby factory. Apart from each having a Derby-type base — flat and closed-in save for a small central hole — the centre specimen carries the factory mark, a crown over crossed batons and dots and a 'D' in red script. Each cat is 1⅝ in. (4.1cm) long and 1⅛ in. (2.8cm) wide, with similar colouring, and lies on a pink base.[1] An interesting feature of one of the cats shown in colour plate 6 is that the hole on the underside of the base has almost disappeared — what remains is no more than $^1/_{16}$ in. (0.15cm) in diameter. The point is important in helping to attribute to Derby the cat and kitten group of colour plate 7a. For the latter group, which measures 1⅝ in. (4.1cm) by 1½ in. (3.8cm), has no hole at all under its base, and in this respect is identical to the Chamberlain group shown in the same colour plate. The fact that the normal hole has almost disappeared from one of the Derby cats of colour plate 6 indicates that its total absence from the group of colour plate 7a is no bar to a Derby attribution. The general quality of the group, the modelling, the palette, the paste and the glaze are all consistent with a Derby attribution. Moreover, though in size and design it appears virtually identical to the Chamberlain cat and kitten group of colour plate 7b (the edging, however, is moulded slightly differently), it does not have the grey paste invariably associated with the latter factory. However, the remarkable similarity in mouldings suggests that either there was a common modeller or one of the two factories pirated the other's design.

The Derby cat and kitten group, like the individual cat model of which three examples are shown in colour plate 6, is not included in any of Haslem's lists, but what are included (being attributed to Edward Keys) are 'New Cats with prey', each priced at 1s. 6d. However, no examples have been discovered.

It is to be noted that all the recorded examples of the cat of colour plate 6 and the cat and kitten group of colour plate 7a are looking in the same direction. One would expect reverse models to have been made, but so far no instances have come to light.

---

1. As do two other examples that have come to my attention. All look in the same direction.

Figure 12. Pair of Chamberlain Worcester cats, 2½ in. (6.4cm) long, both marked 'Chamberlains Worcester', written in script inside the hollow body. a (left). Ginger with blue collar, b (right) tortoiseshell with red collar, c.1820-40. (Although outwardly these cats appear similar in shape to those of figures 9-11, they do not have a base that is closed in save for a centrally located hole, but are entirely hollow.)

CHAMBERLAIN, WORCESTER

Reference has already been made to the Chamberlain cat and kitten group of colour plate 7b. Both animals are white with gilt collars, and they lie recumbent on a green base. The group is incised 'Chamberlain' in script. The base measures 1⅝ in. (4.1cm) x 1½ in. (3.8cm). No reverse model has been recorded. The model was probably produced more or less contemporaneously with the Derby model illustrated beside it. Another model, with the same type of base consists of a cat sitting upright, whilst a kitten lies recumbent beside it. An example is illustrated in G.A. Godden's *Chamberlain Worcester Porcelain* (plate 249). It measures 2½ in. (6.4cm) in height, and has the written mark 'Chamberlains Worcester' in script. (Another example is illustrated on p.79 of Katharine McClinton's *Antique Cats for Collectors*.) Presumably this cat and kitten group or the one of colour plate 7b is of the same kind as the group referred to in the factory papers of April 1826,[1] namely

	s	d
1 cat and kitten	3	6

Doubtless the cat of each of these two groups was also made as an independent model. This is certainly true of the kitten. An example on

---

1. G.A. Godden, *Chamberlain Worcester Porcelain*, p.214.

a matt-blue oval base appeared at the Grosvenor House Antiques Fair 1986 on the stand of Klaber & Klaber.

The Chamberlain factory also produced a cat, somewhat similar to the Rockingham model No 104 and to the Derby equivalent illustrated in figures 10 and 11, but when it is turned upside down the Chamberlain version, unlike the corresponding Rockingham or Derby cat, is seen not to be closed-in but to have been left completely hollow. The mark is written on the inside of the animal. A pair of such cats are illustrated in figure 12. The one with its head turned slightly to the left is decorated with mottled tortoiseshell markings and a red collar, whilst the reverse with its head turned slightly to the right has ginger markings and a blue collar. Each is 2½ in. (6.4cm) long and has the written mark in script 'Chamberlain Worcester'. Conceivably, they are the same model as the eighteen cats priced at £1-7-0 referred to in the factory documents of 1822[1] or the '12 cats, sorted at 1s. 6d' (presumably each) mentioned in the papers as having been supplied in 1820 to certain Cheltenham dealers.[2] It is perhaps convenient at this juncture to point out another reference in the factory documents,[3] namely to:

		s	d
Tortoiseshell cat	[February 1821]	2	0

However, once again the shape of the cat is unknown.

At a sale of European ceramics conducted on 26 July 1977 by Sotheby's, a certain number of English porcelain animals were auctioned. It is interesting to note that lot 229 reads: 'A Chamberlain's Worcester Figure of a white Cat crouching upon a rectangular base, picked out in dark-blue, 1 in. 'Chamberlain's Wor' inscribed in puce; another Figure of a Cat with tortoiseshell markings, seated on his haunches, 1⅓ in., and a Figure of a recumbent Cat, similarly marked, 1⅓ in., all about 1815-25'

Presumably the measurements relate to height. The last figure of lot 229 may represent the cat modelled on its own, from the cat and kitten group of colour plate 7b — the height is the same in both cases — and the first 'Figure' may be a smaller version. The remaining cat, as it is seated on its haunches and measures only 1⅓ in. (3.4cm), must be a toy. It may represent a small version of the cat from the cat and kitten group illustrated in G.A. Godden's *Chamberlain Worcester Porcelain,* plate 249.

In Katharine M. McClinton's *Antique Cats for Collectors,* page 79, there is a tabby cat sitting upright on a pink elliptical base edged with a

---

1. G.A. Godden, *Chamberlain Worcester Porcelain,* p.214.
2. Ibid., p.137.
3. Ibid., p.214.

Colour Plate 3a (left). Rockingham cat and three kittens on a paved rectangular base, 4¼ in. (10.8cm) long. Incised 'No 107'. Cl 2. 1826-30. b (right). Rockingham cat and three kittens on a paved rectangular base, 4¼ in. (10.8cm) long. Incised 'No 107'. 1826-30. (Note the addition of a saucer on the right).

Colour Plate 4a (left). Rockingham girl playing with a kitten, 3¾ in. (9.5cm) high. Incised 'No 40'. Impressed mark. 1826-30. b (right). Rockingham recumbent cat, 2¾ in. (7cm) long. Incised 'No 104'. Cl 2. 1826-30.

continuous gilt line. The author attributes the model to Worcester, presumably the Chamberlain factory. I have no reason to doubt her attribution.

Finally, it is interesting to note that the factory records show that in December 1816, six cats together with other animals were sent to the London shop.[1] What sort of cats these were it is now impossible to say. The same is true of 'A pair cats   3s 0d.[2] included in a selection of the firm's products sent to Humphrey Chamberlain who was apparently, at the time, in Birmingham.

1. G.A. Godden, *Chamberlain Worcester Porcelain,* p.214.
2. Ibid., p.138.

GRAINGER, LEE & CO., WORCESTER

Amongst the animals appearing in the factory's pattern book (see chapter 6) is a cat which lies recumbent on a rectangular base with rounded corners (see page 233). The centre of the edge of the base is banded with a moulded rope. No example of this model has so far been recorded, but I consider that it is unlikely that there are no existing examples. It is rather that an example has simply not come to light. The animals appearing in the pattern book are in no way exhaustive of the factory's output, as is clear from the fact that there are various Grainger Lee porcelain animals not recorded there (for example, those appearing in figures 86 and 92 illustrate items not in the factory pattern book). Whether or not there was any cat model or models produced by the Grainger Lee factory other than the one already mentioned is unknown.

ROYAL WORCESTER

Certainly the Royal Worcester factory modelled cats. In the factory list there appear a group of cats and rat (item 24 in the factory list, modelled in 1862), a kitten (item 328, modelled in 1873) and a group of cats (item 518, modelled in 1875).[1]

1. See Henry Sandon's *Royal Worcester Porcelain,* Appendix 1.

MINTON

Like the factories already referred to, the Minton factory was one of the great porcelain producers of the period with which we are concerned. It is somewhat surprising, then, to find that the drawing book (see Chapter 6) of the factory's figure production makes no mention of any cat, at least as an independent model. However, a cat sitting upright appears as part of a group described as being from 'Tom Jones' and numbered 87 in the drawing book. A porcelain example of this group, 7½in. (19.1cm) high, is illustrated in G.A. Godden's *Minton Pottery and Porcelain,* plate 144. The group itself is in the possession of the Glasgow Art Gallery and Museum.

COPELAND

An example of a late cat, bearing the impressed Copeland mark, is shown in figure 22. It is large, as animals of the second half of the nineteenth century were apt to be, measuring 14in. (35.6cm) in height. It has glass eyes and is glazed all over in turquoise. The date code used shows it to have been made in 1872.

CHARLES BOURNE

The Charles Bourne factory was very much a minor concern in relation to the factories already mentioned. It is distinguishable from the general run of minor Staffordshire producers of good quality porcelain by the practice (not normally adopted elsewhere in Staffordshire) of marking its output. Charles Bourne's products are frequently painted with the letters 'CB', and this has enabled us to identify a few animals as belonging to the factory, including a recumbent cat lying on a high cushion base with tassels. It measures 2½in. (6.4cm) long, and an example,[1] painted grey and black with a dark red collar, sitting on a cushion with black tassels, is to be seen in the City and Museum Art Gallery, Stoke-on-Trent. The mark takes the form of $\frac{CB}{209}$ painted in red.

---

1. Illustrated in G.A. Godden's *An Illustrated Encyclopaedia of British Pottery and Porcelain,* colour plate 1.

SAMUEL ALCOCK

By sheer good fortune a representative cache of Samuel Alcock's various products, including his animals, was buried under the new factory's

Colour Plate 5a (left). Derby black pug on an oval scroll base, 2½ in. (6.4cm) high. Incised '2' c.1800-10. (Note the similarity of this model to the Rockingham version shown in colour plate 12.) b (right). Derby black cat on a tasselled cushion, 2in. (5.1cm) high. c.1810-30.

Colour Plate 6. Three Derby cats, each recumbent on a rectangular base, 1⅝ in. (4.1cm) long; the one in the centre marked with a crown over crossed batons, dots and 'D' in red, c.1810-25.

Figure 13. Samuel Alcock cat, with tortoiseshell markings, lying recumbent on a yellow mound base, 2¾in (7cm) long. Impressed '9' or '6', c.1830-45.

foundation stone laid on 24 April 1839, and as a result it has proved possible to identify other animals turned out by the factory (see page 256). Such a model is the cat illustrated in figure 13, lying recumbent on a rocky base typical of the factory. The cat is white with patches of black and ochre. Under the pale yellow base, 2¾in. (7cm) long, can be seen an impressed 9 or 6 (depending on which way up the animal is held).

Illustrated in figures 14 and 15a is a Samuel Alcock cat and kitten group, 2½in. (6.4cm) high, the cat sitting upright, the kitten rising from a recumbent position, both decorated with similar markings to those appearing on the cat of figure 13. The underneath of the hollow base, moulded on top with raised scrolls, carries an impressed '2'. The base is recorded both in pale yellow and in green. The same cat, but without the kitten, is shown in figure 68 of Anthony Oliver's *Staffordshire Pottery*.

The Samuel Alcock factory also turned out a toy cat seated upright on a high mound base, octagonal in form, measuring 1⅝in. (4.1cm) high in all. The example shown in figure 15b is white with black markings, whilst the base is green, edged with gold. In the case of other examples the base is coloured pale yellow instead of green. The cat of figure 15b is impressed with the number '4', but probably the correct number should be '94'. For the latter number appeared on an example of that same model (similarly decorated but with a pale yellow base) sold at Sotheby's on 25 February 1986 (lot 345). It would seem that the figure '9' was simply omitted from the impressed number of the cat shown in figure 15b.

An interesting Samuel Alcock group comprising a cat playing with a

Figure 14. Samuel Alcock cat and kitten group, with tortoiseshell markings, on a yellow mound base, 2½in. (6.4cm) high. Impressed '2', c.1830-45.

Figure 15a. (left). Samuel Alcock cat and kitten group, with tortoiseshell markings, on a green mound base, 2½in. (6.4cm) high. Impressed '2', c.1830-45. b. (right). Samuel Alcock kitten, with tortoiseshell markings, seated on a green octagonal mound base, 1⅝in. (4.1cm) high. Impressed '4' (seemingly an error for '94'), c.1830-45.

Figure 16. Samuel Alcock cat and poodle group on a yellow mound base, 3½in. (8.9cm) high. Impressed '239', c.1830-45.

seated poodle is illustrated in figure 16. It measures 3½ in. (8.9cm) in height, the pale yellow base being impressed with the number '239'.

MINOR STAFFORDSHIRE FACTORIES

A great number, if not most, of the porcelain animals produced during the first half of the nineteenth century came from a diversity of unidentified small factories operating in Staffordshire. These animals, though more crudely modelled than the corresponding products of the great concerns such as Rockingham, Derby and Minton, nevertheless have a verve and charm that confer on them a particular attractiveness, and render them so typically English. Among such animals are to be found various cat models.

The two cat and kitten groups shown in colour plate 8 are interesting for the distinctive yellow and black markings with which the animals are decorated. (One group is, of course, the reverse of the other and both take the form of a cat sitting upright with a kitten lying recumbent next to it, on a rectangular base with rounded corners.) A single cat, similarly coloured, sitting upright on a high mound base, more or less square, but with canted corners, is illustrated in Katharine McClinton's *Antique Cats for Collectors* (between pages 72 and 73) and clearly comes from the same factory. The two groups shown in colour plate 8 are not a pair. One has a thin scroll moulding on the base, and although of the same overall height, namely 2⅝ in. (6.7cm), has a slightly longer base than the other, measuring 2⅞ in. (7.3cm) as against 2½ in. (6.4cm). Two other examples of the model (one the reverse of the other) with the thin scroll moulding are illustrated in Katharine McClinton's book, but this time the markings are different. The cat and kitten are still tortoiseshell in decoration, but the hand responsible is quite different (more akin to that appearing on the group of figure 17b) thereby indicating that the factory employed at least two artists. The same group is to be seen in white and gold in plate 68 of Anthony Oliver's *Staffordshire Pottery* together with a white and gilt version (in reverse) of the single cat described above as appearing in *Antique Cats for Collectors*. Unfortunately, it has not been possible to identify the particular Staffordshire factory responsible for these animals.

The cat and kitten of figure 17b, 2⅜ in. (6cm) high, is similar in modelling to the group of colour plate 8 except that the animals, which are tortoiseshell in colouring, lie on an elliptical-shaped base. The palette employed serves to link the group with the toy cat or kitten illustrated in figure 17a. The latter is white with black and ochre markings, and sits upright on a square mound base, measuring 1⁹/₁₆ in. (4cm) high in all. Under the base are some indistinct markings, which might conceivably

Figure 17. a (left). Staffordshire kitten, with tortoiseshell markings, seated on a square mound base, 1⁹/₁₆ in. (4cm) high, c.1830-45. b (right). Staffordshire cat and kitten group, with tortoiseshell markings, on an oval mound base, 2⅜ in. (6cm) high, c.1830-45. (These animals would seem to be from the same factory.)

Figure 18. Staffordshire cat and kitten group painted with patches of black and yellow, the kitten turned away from the cat, on a green rectangular base with rounded corners, 2½ in. (6.4cm) high, c.1830-45.

consist of an asterisk and the number 4, in which event a Samuel Alcock origin might suggest itself. However, the markings are not readily decipherable and the group of figure 17b certainly is not impressed with any numeral. Accordingly, no attribution can confidently be given beyond the general description 'Staffordshire'.

A particularly interesting Staffordshire cat and kitten group, 2½ in. (6.4cm) high is illustrated in figure 18. The animals are tortoiseshell in decoration, seated on a green rectangular base with rounded corners. The kitten, like the cat, is sitting upright, but the distinctive feature is that the head of the kitten is turned away from the adult animal — a most unusual pose. Presumably both this group and that of figure 17b were produced in reverse. All the Staffordshire cats described above have particularly attractive facial markings.

Three toy cats, respectively 1¹/₁₆ in. (2.7cm), 1⅛ in. (2.8cm), and 1¼ in. (3.2cm) long, are illustrated in figure 19. Each is in a recumbent position, one lying on an unusual cushion shaped base closed-in underneath, and another lying on a green rectangular base heavily banded with gold. Two of the cats are plain white, whilst the other is decorated with black and ochre markings. Each cat would seem to emanate from a different factory. They would appear to have been made around 1830 to 1845.

Another interesting cat model of the same date is also illustrated in figure 20. Not a toy, the cat is white with tortoiseshell markings and wears a red collar. It lies recumbent on a rectangular base with a gold band, 3in. (7.6cm) long.

Figure 19. Staffordshire toy cats, c.1830-45, each lying recumbent. a (left). on a rectangular base, edged with a gilt line, 1¹/₁₆ in. (2.7cm) long. b (centre). on a green rectangular crinkled base, edged with a gilt line, 1⅛ in. (2.8cm) long. c (right). on a 'pillow base', with black and orange markings, 1¼ in. (3.2cm) long.

A charming group, 4in. (10.2cm) high, comprising a cat with two kittens (white with tortoiseshell markings) in a round wicker basket covered with a green cloth is shown in colour plate 9b. The companion model, 3½ in. (8.9cm) high, has, instead of a cat and kittens, a spaniel bitch and two puppies (figure 65). The identity of the Staffordshire factory that was responsible for these two groups is unknown, but manifestly, from the quality of its products it ranks decisively over and

Figure 20. Staffordshire cat with tortoiseshell markings and red collar, lying recumbent on a rectangular base edged with a gold band, 3in. (7.6cm) long, c.1830-45.

Figure 21. Staffordshire cat with tortoiseshell markings, seated on a green and white stool with four white and gilt legs, 4¼ in. (10.8cm) high, c.1830-45.

above the general run of Staffordshire porcelain manufacturers. It also issued a somewhat larger version of the above two models, where the basket is rectangular with rounded corners and where the number of kittens or puppies, as the case may be, is three instead of two. Figure 67 shows the bitch and three puppies. Interestingly, the factory also produced the mother cat, 4¼ in. (10.8cm) high, and the spaniel bitch, 4⅛ in. (10.5cm) high, as separate models, each sitting on a stool (figures 21 and 66).

Katharine McClinton in her *Antique Cats for Collectors* illustrates in colour between pages 72 and 73 a variety of Staffordshire cats belonging to our period. They include a pair with rather large pointed ears and tortoiseshell markings, each sitting upright on a rectangular base with canted corners, together with a single example of the same shape and similar colouring, a further pair of cats similarly decorated but this time

Figure 22. Late Copeland cat with glass eyes, glazed in turquoise, seated on an oval base, 14in. (35.6cm) high. Impressed mark and date code 1872. *(Sotheby's)*

Figure 23. William Brownfield & Son group of two Parian cats playing with a bowl or vase, 9½ in. (24.1cm) high. Design registered 31 March 1875. *(Godden of Worthing Ltd.)*

each sitting on a tasselled cushion (similar to the Rockingham cat of colour plates 1b and 2 (No 77), but much cruder in modelling), a group of two white and gilt kittens playing with a ball on a more or less elliptical base encrusted with coloured moss, and a pair of black, white and orange cats with large ears, each surmounting a green inkwell standing on four rococo style legs. In addition, she shows a well-modelled tortoiseshell cat lying recumbent on a green rectangular cushion with yellow tassels, and an interesting tortoiseshell cat on a pink cushion base with tassels, the quality of moulding of which falls far short of the corresponding Rockingham and Derby base. This last model would seem to come from the same factory as was responsible for the small poodle of figure 50b. It has the same pink cushion with tassels.

Finally, mention should be made of a late Parian group. It consists of two cats playing around a bowl or vase on a circular base, 9½ in. (24.1cm) high (figure 23). It is the product of William Brownfield & Son, the design having been registered by them on 31 March 1875.

Colour Plate 7a (left). Derby cat and kitten recumbent on a rectangular base, 1⅝ in. (4.1cm) long, c.1820-30. b (right). Chamberlain Worcester cat and kitten recumbent on a rectangular base, 1⅝ in. (4.1cm) long. Incised 'Chamberlains' in script, c.1820-30.

Colour Plate 8a (left). Staffordshire cat and kitten on a rectangular mound base with rounded corners and moulded scrolls, 2⅞ in. (7.3cm) long, c.1830-45. b (right). Reverse model, but without the moulded scrolls on the base, 2½ in. (6.4cm) long, c.1830-45.

Dogs

Not surprisingly, dogs feature prominently among the animals produced by the various porcelain factories operating during the nineteenth century, though mongrels do not appear to have been modelled. Presumably, the market for porcelain dogs was from among those who wished to have a replica of a pure thoroughbred and not the offspring of some chance encounter. Unfortunately, it is not now always easy to identify the specific breed which a particular model is intended to represent. Sometimes a modern breed has undergone significant genetic changes since the period with which we are concerned. Accordingly, recourse has, on occasion, had to be made to contemporary engravings, but even reliance on information derived from this quarter is not without danger. As was said by Gordon Stables in *Our Friend the Dog* (1895):

> 'It is a common thing for writers on dogs to refer to old pictures or engravings, in order to obtain information regarding the style of any breed of dog that obtained in by-gone times. But such information is often very misleading, for the simple reason that the artist, although a good painter, may have known nothing at all about the points of dogs. Few even of the brethren of the brush of now-a-days could tell a Setter from a Sheepdog.
>
> For instance, the dog that stands for a Setter at page ninety of Youatt's book is a disgrace to the text; he resembles a Landseer Newfoundland, with bad legs and stern; he is stilty in fore-legs and wears a Collie's head with a Spaniel's ears.'

In the nineteenth century, particularly in the first half, breeds of dogs were less numerous than they are today. They can conveniently be divided into two groups, working dogs and pets. The former group can be subdivided into sporting and non-sporting dogs. Sporting dogs were valued for their services in the field, and although doubtless some were also companionable, they lived, out of doors, in the kennel. They included the greyhound, the spaniel (springer, cocker and water), the setter, the pointer, the poodle (or rough water dog),[1] and, of course, the foxhound. The useful non-sporting dogs included the Great Dane (or Danish dog) and the Dalmatian, both of which were employed to accompany and watch over carriages, the Newfoundland and the mastiff, both guard dogs (the former with a remarkable ability to rescue people from drowning), and the all-important sheepdog (or, as it was originally called, the shepherd's dog). Pet dogs included the Italian greyhound, the King Charles spaniel (sometimes called 'the comforter'), the pug and the

---

1. The unclipped poodle accompanying the boy of colour plate 14 may, by reason of its size in relation to the boy, have been intended to represent the sporting poodle, rather than a pet.

poodle. The poodle appears in both classifications i.e. as a sporting dog and as a pet, but it is in the latter capacity that it was normally modelled in porcelain during the period with which we are concerned.

There were other breeds existing in the nineteenth century e.g. the lurcher, the cur, the turnspit, the Maltese dog, but these do not seem to appear in porcelain and therefore need not concern us. One breed, however, which seems never to have been produced in porcelain is worthy of remark — the bulldog, an animal, incidentally, quite different in shape from its modern-day counterpart. Unlike today's bulldog it was, in the period with which we are concerned, noted for its ferocity and tenacity. It received a bad press, William Youatt speaking of it in the following terms:[1]

'The round, thick head, turned-up nose, and thick and pendulous lips of this dog are familiar to all, while his ferocity makes him in the highest degree dangerous. In general he makes a silent although ferocious attack and the persisting powers of his teeth and jaws enable him to keep his hold against any but the greatest efforts, so that the utmost mischief is likely to ensue as well to the innocent visitor of his domicile as the ferocious intruder. The bull-dog is scarcely capable of any education and is fitted for nothing but ferocity and combat'.

Not surprisingly, the breed, with its association with bull-fighting, did not command itself to those most likely to purchase porcelain animals, namely, children and ladies. No factory will produce what it cannot sell easily. There were other breeds of dogs intrinsically more acceptable to the market, and the various porcelain manufacturers preferred to direct their attention to this more inviting field.

The most common breeds to be found in porcelain during our period are the greyhound, the spaniel, the pug (up to shortly after 1830) and the poodle (mainly from about 1830 onwards). Other contemporary breeds are found, but less frequently, and some breeds are rarely encountered at all. We will consider each breed of dog in turn.

---

1. *The Dog* p.98.

Colour Plate 9a (left). Minton greyhound (model no. 30) standing on a deep oval base, 2⅜in. (6.7cm) high, c.1830-40. b (right). Staffordshire cat and two kittens on a cloth in a wicker basket, 4in. (10.2cm) high, c.1830-45.

Colour Plate 10. Pair of Copeland and Garrett greyhounds, each lying recumbent on a mound base, 5in. (12.7cm) long. Factory mark. 1833-47.

GREYHOUNDS

Greyhounds have been in this country for centuries and can be traced back to the time of the Roman occupation. In 1496 the qualities to be looked for in a greyhound were expressed in verse by Wynkyn de Worde in *The Treatise perteyning to Hawkynge, Huntynge, &c, emprynted at Westmestre:*

> 'A greyhound should be headed lyke a snake,
> And neckyd lyke a drake,
> Fotyd lyke a cat,
> Tayled lyke a ratte,
> Syded like a teme,
> And chyned like a bream.'

During the eighteenth century, the greyhound was improved. Although it enjoyed good looks, it lacked speed and stamina, qualities essential for hare-coursing for which it was required. The strain of other breeds was introduced including in particular that of the bulldog, noted for its ferocity and tenacity.

Greyhounds were much prized by sportsmen and the first tomb erected for a dog in this country commemorated an eighteenth century 'Snowball', one of a litter of three outstanding examples of the breed. Major Topham of the World Cottage, Yorkshire wrote an epitaph for 'Snowball' commencing:

> 'He who out-bounded time and space
> The fleetest of the greyhound race
> Lies here! At length subdued by death
> His speed now stopped and out of breath.'

Greyhounds normally hunted the hare in pairs. The technique employed is described by Youatt in *The Dog*.[1]

'In the "Sportsman" for April 1840, is an interesting account of the chace of the hare. It is said that, in general, a good greyhound will reach a hare, if she runs straight. He pursues her eagerly, and the moment he is about to strike her she turns short, and the dog, unable to stop himself, is thrown from ten to twenty yards from her. These jerking turns soon begin to tell upon a dog, and an old well-practised hare will seldom fail to make her escape. When, however, pursued by a couple of dogs, the hare has a more difficult game to play, as it frequently happens that when she is turned by the leading dog she has great difficulty in avoiding the stroke of the second.

'It is highly interesting to witness the game of an old hare. She has generally some brake or thicket in view, under the cover of which she

---

1. *The Dog*, p.36.

means to escape from her pursuers. On moving from her seat she makes directly for the hiding-place, but, unable to reach it, has recourse to turning, and, *wrenched* by one or the other of her pursuers, she seems every moment almost in the jaws of one of them, and yet in a most dexterous manner she accomplishes her object. A greyhound, when he perceives a hare about to enter a thicket, is sure to strike at her if within any reasonable distance. The hare shortens her stride as she approaches the thicket, and at the critical moment she makes so sudden, dexterous, and effectual a spring, that the dogs are flung to a considerable distance, and she has reached the cover and escaped.'

Mention must also be made of the Italian greyhound, a miniature of the greyhound just described, but with a more arched neck and with a high stepping action, rather like that of a well-trained carriage horse. As the name suggests, the breed was imported into this country from Italy. Italian greyhounds are not suited to kennel life but require comfort and companionship: they are lap-dogs, not sporting dogs. Bewick in his *History of Quadrupeds* speaks (on p.296) of the breed as being, 'not common in this country, the climate being too rigorous for the extreme delicacy of its constitution.' Taplin[1] gave the breed an even more damning press: 'this diminutive breed...seems only calculated to soothe the vanity, and indulge the frivolities of antiquated ladies... They are so deficient in the spirit, fortitude and self-defence of every other sort of the canine race, as not to be able to officiate in the services of domestic alarm or protection, and in consequence are dedicated only to the comforts of the tea-table, the fire-side carpet, the luxurious indulgencies of the sofa, and the warm lap of the mistress.'

Modern writers have pointed out that the Italian greyhound is perfectly suited to this climate and have challenged the accuracy of much of Taplin's criticism, but, be that as it may, the breed was popular in this country as a lap-dog at the end of the eighteenth century, vying with the pug dog for the affections of the ladies. (A specimen is to be seen in the famous painting of the 'Ladies of Llangollen' returning from riding.) Italian greyhounds were said to be only suitable for women; hence the restriction on the numbers bred. Nevertheless, they were still popular during the 1830s (see the engraving of 1835 reproduced in Hutchinson's *Dog Encyclopaedia,* p.1003).

The frailties of the Italian greyhound are vividly remarked upon by Mrs Sherwood (1775-1851) in her diary:[2]
'My little greyhound at the time filled too much of my thoughts, and

---

1. In *The Sportsman's Cabinet,* (1803).
2. See *The Life and Times of Mrs. Sherwood.* Ed. by F.J. Harvey Darton at p.166.

Figure 24. Rockingham silhouette group of two white greyhounds on a white and gilt rectangular base, 2$^{13}/_{16}$ in. (7.2cm) long, C.1, Red griffin mark.1826-30.

caused me to throw too many kind affections, which would have been far better employed on a poor fellow-creature. This beautiful little animal suffered so terribly from the cold, and had so many contrivances to warm itself, that it was impossible not to pity it. When we walked out it crept into my muff, and there it lay with its head only looking out. It often crept into my pocket or on my lap under my work, or into my work-basket, and when in the kitchen it always sat on the back of Lion, our great Newfoundland house-dog. I loved my little Bonne [the animal's name] so much that I resolved, after I lost her, never to make a pet of any animal.'

The importance of the greyhound as a sporting dog and a lap-dog is reflected in the frequency with which this particular breed of dog is represented in porcelain.

ROCKINGHAM

The most important factory associated with animal production during our period is the Rockingham factory at Swinton, Yorkshire. This particular concern was responsible for a variety of different breeds of dog, but so far no greyhound has been recorded. It is inconceivable that the factory should have produced such comparative rarities as mastiffs (colour plate 20) and Great Danes (colour plate 19) and neglected the greyhound, for which there must have been a wide and ready market. We know from the numbering system employed at Swinton that certain animal models remain to be discovered, and amongst these must surely be the greyhound.

In any event, what is recorded as having emanated from the Rockingham factory is a silhouette or flat-back figure of a pair of greyhounds, the bitch standing, the dog lying recumbent. A very rare example, in white and gold, 2$^{13}/_{16}$in. (7.2cm) long, with the red griffin mark, is illustrated in figure 24.

Figure 25. a (top left). Derby squirrel eating a nut, in natural colours on an oval mound base, 3¼in. (8.3cm) high. Incised '3', c.1810-30. (Cf. figure 131 for a white and gilt example.) b (top centre). Derby fox in natural colours seated on a rectangular base edged with two gilt lines, 4¼in. (10.8cm) high, c.1810-30. (This is the reverse of the fox of colour plate 26). c (top right). Derby pug dog, with gilt collar and pale brown markings, seated on an oval scroll base, 2¾in. (7cm) high. Incised '2', c.1810-30. d (below). Pair of Derby greyhounds, one with black and grey, the other with brown patch markings, lying recumbent on a shaped rectangular base applied with flowers, 4¼in. (10.8cm) long. Late 18th or early 19th century. *(Christie's)*

DERBY

Somewhat surprisingly, there is no greyhound model listed among the creations of Edward Keys or any other Derby modeller of the nineteenth century. However, there is an entry in Haslem's list of 'Bow and Chelsea models', though no example is recorded.

	Enamelled and gilt	
	s	d
London Pointer and Greyhound, each	1	6

A fine pair of Derby greyhounds are illustrated in figure 25d. They are described in Christie's sale catalogue of 15 June 1970 (lot 173): 'A FINE AND RARE PAIR OF DERBY FIGURES of recumbent greyhounds, their tails curled up round their hind legs, one with black and grey and the other with brown patch markings, the shaped rectangular mound bases applied with flowers — 4 ¼ in. (11cm) *wide.'* It is interesting to note that this same greyhound model appears lying at the feet of the Derby figure 'Diana the huntress', a figure originally produced in the eighteenth century (nos. 65 and 120 in Haslem's numbered list), but carried on into the nineteenth century. Whether the greyhound as an independent model was also made in the nineteenth century is not known for certain. The pair appearing at Christie's in 1970 could from the description have been from either the eighteenth or nineteenth century, but regardless of the date of that particular pair, it is reasonable to assume that, in accordance with its normal practice where eighteenth century animals were concerned, the factory continued producing these greyhounds into the nineteenth century. It is to be noted that Bemrose in his list of moulds and models existing in 1795 refers to: 'Pair greyhounds with ground pedestal.'

KING ST. FACTORY, DERBY

This small factory is known to have turned out a pair of recumbent greyhounds, 5 ¼ in. (13.3cm), for such a pair, with the Sampson Hancock mark, indicating an origin subsequent to 1862, were sold at Sotheby's on 24 February 1987, lot 250.

Figure 26. Chamberlain Worcester greyhound, with crossed front legs, lying recumbent on a rectangular dry-blue base with rounded corners, 4in. (10.2cm) long. Mark 'Chamberlain Worcester' written in script, c.1820-40. *(Godden of Worthing Ltd.)*

CHAMBERLAIN WORCESTER

The Chamberlain Worcester factory produced a greyhound model lying recumbent with crossed front legs on a rectangular base with rounded corners, some 4in. (10.2cm) long. An example with a matt-blue base, a colour typical of the factory, is illustrated in figure 26. Doubtless, it was one of a pair. Another Chamberlain model is referred to in Sotheby's sale catalogue of 20 December 1977 (lot 175): 'A Chamberlain's Worcester Figure of a white Greyhound sitting on a stepped canted-rectangular base washed in pink, 3⅛ in. 'Chamberlain's Worcester' in red script...'

It should also be noted that greyhounds are mentioned in the factory documents:[1]

4 Greyhounds and oak trees		[December 1813]
2 Greyhounds at	4-0	[July 1824]

1. *Chamberlain Worcester Porcelain,* pp.213, 214.

Figure 27. Pair of Grainger Lee white and gilt greyhounds, couchant, 4½in. (11.4cm) long. Impressed 'GRAINGER LEE & CO WORCESTER' in capitals, 1820-37.

Figure 28. Copeland and Garrett greyhound bitch lying recumbent on a rectangular base with shaped corners, 11in. (27.9cm) long. Factory mark. 1833-47. *(Godden of Worthing Ltd.)*

GRAINGER LEE & CO., WORCESTER

The pair of white and gilt greyhounds, 4½in. (11.4cm) long, shown in figure 27, came from the Chamberlain factory's rival at Worcester, the Grainger Lee factory. They are charmingly modelled, one of them recumbent with crossed legs, the other with head raised. They measure respectively 1½in. (3.8cm) and 2½in. (6.4cm) in height and are both impressed with the words 'GRAINGER LEE & CO, WORCESTER'. They are illustrated in the factory's pattern book (see chapter 6, page 234).

ROYAL WORCESTER

Early in its life the Royal Worcester factory produced a group of greyhounds chained. It is item 33 in the factory's list.[1]

---

1. See Henry Sandon's *Royal Worcester Porcelain*, Appendix I.

COPELAND AND GARRETT

A large Copeland and Garrett greyhound bitch lying recumbent on a rectangular base with concave corners, 11in. (27.9cm) long, is illustrated in figure 28. It bears under the base the printed mark consisting of the words 'Copeland and Garrett' within a wreath surmounted by a coronet. The reverse must have been a greyhound dog. The pair of marked greyhounds shown in colour plate 10 also came from the factory. They each measure 5in. (12.7cm) in length, and are grey and black respectively. The factory mark appears on each.

51

MINTON

The Minton factory produced, c.1831, a greyhound lying recumbent on a tasselled cushion, 4in. (10.2cm) long. It is no. 18 in the drawing book (see page 248). Manifestly, this particular model was not intended to represent an animal whose life was spent out of doors coursing hares. The element of comfort and luxury implicit in the tasselled cushion indicates that a lap-dog was meant, and accordingly this must have been the Italian greyhound. This conclusion is reinforced by the fact that other animals which the Minton factory modelled on a tasselled cushion, that is to say, a King Charles spaniel (one version lying recumbent, another standing begging), a pug and two different versions of a poodle were in every case lap-dogs and not sporting dogs. However, sometimes the factory was inconsistent in that its setter (model no. 29), a purely sporting dog, is made in one version to lie on a tasselled cushion rather than a plain rectangular base with scrolled decoration moulded around the edges, compare figure 78 with colour plate 17.

In contrast, the dog of colour plate 9a would appear to be the sporting version of the greyhound. It would seem to be of Minton origin and in fact an example of model no. 30 in the factory drawing book (see chapter 6, page 243). Unfortunately, no actual illustration accompanies the bare description in the drawing book 'standing dog', so that complete certainty is impossible. However, the construction of the underside of the base is identical to that appearing on all other contemporary Minton dogs, i.e. it is flat and closed-in save for a small central hole. Admittedly, this particular form of base construction is also used to support Rockingham and Derby dogs, but the paste, glaze and palette are different. Moreover, the deep oval base of the dog is similar to the bases of the other Minton figures e.g. Sancho Panza (an example of which is shown in plate 129 of G.A. Godden's *Minton Pottery and Porcelain*). The animal is also in a standing position, thereby corresponding with the drawing book description. Accordingly, on the balance of probability, it is a rare example of a Minton dog model until now unidentified. It is grey in colour and stands on a green base with reddy brown splashes.

An interesting animal appearing in the Minton drawing book is no. 120, a greyhound sitting upright on a high mound, 6½ in. (16.5cm) high in all. An example of that particular model is shown in figure 29. It is in fact in Parian, although the model was originally produced in biscuit porcelain. Notwithstanding that, in the original drawing book, model no. 120 is entitled simply 'greyhound', in the later Parian list of models, dated 1852, it is more specifically described as 'Italian greyhound'. Clearly once again the factory opted to produce a lap-dog rather than the larger sporting animal.

Colour Plate 11. Three Rockingham pugs, each seated on an oval scroll base; the two dogs (left and right) are each 2⅝ in. (6.7cm) high, the bitch (centre) is 2½ in. (6.4cm) high. Unnumbered. 'Cl 2' under the base of each of the dogs, red griffin mark under the base of the bitch, 1826-30.

Colour Plate 12. Two Rockingham pugs, each seated on an oval scroll base. The dog on the left is 2⅝ in. (6.7cm) high, the right hand dog is 2⅛ in. (5.4cm) high. Incised 'No 76'. Cl 2. Impressed mark. The smaller pug is also incised '2' to indicate the second size. 1826-30.

Figure 29. Minton greyhound in Parian seated on a high rocky base, 6½ in. (16.5cm) high (no. 120 in the factory drawing book), c.1850-70.

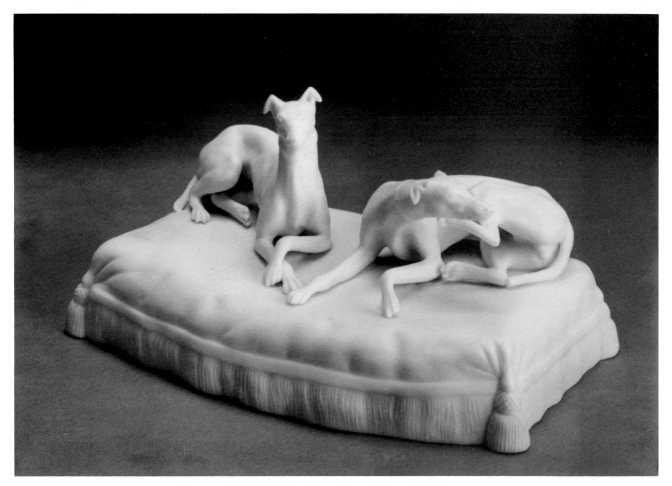

Figure 30. Samuel Alcock model of a group of 'Chained Greyhounds' consisting of a bitch elegantly posed, and a scratching dog lying recumbent on a tasselled cushion and linked together with a chain (now missing), 7¼ in. (18.4cm) long (no. 55 in the factory list), c.1850-70.

However, there is no reason to suppose that the large coloured greyhound crouching on a scroll base (no. 130) shown in plate 190 of *Staffordshire Porcelain* side by side with the corresponding factory drawing is other than the ordinary English coursing greyhound. The same goes for the two greyhounds illustrated as item 229 in the factory list (see page 248).

SAMUEL ALCOCK

The Samuel Alcock factory produced a finely modelled greyhound group comprising an elegantly poised bitch and a scratching dog recumbent on a tasselled cushion and linked together with a chain attached to their respective collars. This group was manufactured in biscuit, and in parian (figure 30). A biscuit example from the Victoria and Albert Museum has an impressed 55 under the base. The group appears in the 1851 Exhibition Catalogue,[1] and it is clear from this that it was modelled by S.W. Arnold. The comparatively low number appearing on the model

---

1. Unless the group in the Exhibition was a later version of the same subject.

Colour Plate 13. Lloyd Shelton poodle standing outside its kennel on a rectangular base with rounded corners encrusted with moss, 3⅛ in. (7.9cm) long, c.1835-40.

Colour Plate 14. Pair of Staffordshire groups consisting of a boy with an unclipped poodle (left), and a girl with a goat and kid (right), 5½ in. (14cm) high. c.1835-40.

suggests that it was made before April 1839 when the foundation stone of the new factory was laid. It will be remembered that the animals buried under the foundation stone were numbered 36 and 86 (or 98) respectively. Accordingly, model no. 55 must already have been in existence, and it is impossible to avoid the conclusion that it was made long before the 1851 Exhibition. The fact that the two animals are lying on a tasselled cushion indicates that they are intended to be pet dogs, and therefore Italian greyhounds.

A pair of greyhounds are recorded in an identical pose to those mentioned above, but modelled separately, each completely white on a claret cushion base with gilt edges and tassels. One is 2¾in. (7cm) high, the other 2¼in. (5.7cm), and both bases measure 5in. (12.7cm) in length. The factory of origin is unknown. Another pair of greyhounds, again in the same pose, appear on page 37 of *The Connoisseur,* September 1922 (illustration no. 5). They are described as being 'of exquisite modelling and pose... They are pure white porcelain on bases enamelled an apple green'. Whether these greyhounds belonged to the same factory as was responsible for the other pair mentioned here is uncertain. The models are probably based on unidentified marbles or bronzes.

SWANSEA

W.D. John in his definitive work *Swansea Porcelain* illustrates in plate 48B what purports to be a biscuit greyhound, 4in. (10.2cm) long, from the Swansea factory. However, the animal was not marked and was never seen by John himself. He relied for its authenticity on the opinion of two other persons who found the animal in a private collection. From the illustration the dog looks identical to the Minton greyhound. I consider that John's attribution should be treated with extreme scepticism.

MINOR STAFFORDSHIRE FACTORIES

Greyhounds were produced in profusion throughout Staffordshire during the period 1830-50. An above-average quality model lying recumbent on a flower-encrusted mound base is illustrated in plate 126 of B. & T. Hughes' *Collecting Miniature Antiques.* An interesting group, 4⅔in. (11.7cm) long, consisting of a pair of coursing greyhounds with a dead rabbit, on a dark green rocky base, is to be seen in the Schreiber Collection in the Victoria and Albert Museum. The factory responsible for this group is distinctive, but so far unidentified. It would seem to have produced a variety of different animals with the same distinctive dark green rocky base including a recumbent greyhound (doubtless one of a pair) and the lioness and cub group of colour plate 31.

Figure 31. Derby white and gilt pug-dog seated on an oval scroll base, 2¼ in. (5.7cm) high, incised '3', c.1810-30.

PUGS

Pugs, which seem to have originated in China, were brought over to this country from Holland by William and Mary in 1688 and hence were initially called 'Dutch dogs'. They were popular throughout Europe in the eighteenth century, being, incidentally, the badge or symbol of Mopsorden or the Order of the Pug (an institution that replaced the Order of Freemasons, membership of which was forbidden by the Pope in 1736 on pain of excommunication). Not surprisingly, pugs were produced in porcelain in considerable quantities by the Meissen and other Continental factories. They were also made in this country during the eighteenth century at Chelsea, Bow, Derby and elsewhere. However, as is clear from Bewick's *History of Quadrupeds,* first published in 1790, they had grown out of favour by the end of the eighteenth century. Why this should have been is not altogether clear. A pug bitch and her puppy from a drawing by Philip Reinagle are illustrated in the *Sportsman's Cabinet,* published in 1803, and the comments made by its author, William Taplin, may have done something to accelerate the breed's decline:

'...in the whole catalogue of the canine species, there is not one of less utility, or possessing less powers of attraction than the pug dog... applicable to no support, appropriated to no useful purpose, susceptible of no predominant passion, and in no way whatever remarkable for any extra emminence, he is continued from era to era for what alone he might have been originally intended, the patient follower of a ruminating philosopher, or the adulating and consolatory companion of an old maid.'

Whatever the reason for the decline in the pug's popularity, the breed seems to have fallen out of favour at least by 1830. Save in connection with cropping, pugs were not even mentioned by William Youatt in his book *The Dog* and this fall from grace is reflected in the disappearance of porcelain models from shortly after 1830 till much later in the century,[1] to be replaced by poodles.

However, during the first thirty years of the nineteenth century interest in the pug was still sufficiently strong to ensure that the breed was well represented in porcelain in this country. The modern reader will be struck by the difference in shape between the pug of the nineteenth century and the pug of today, the proportions being quite different. The earlier version stood higher, was smaller in the scull, lighter in the bone, longer in the muzzle, and not so wide in the front. Pugs of the period with which we are concerned were usually fawn.[2] From time to time black

---

1. They were modelled at the Royal Worcester factory in 1862, 1872, 1873 and 1875.
2. However Hogarth illustrates a black pug in his *The House of Cards.*

Figure 33. Minton white pug-dog, with blue and gilt collar, lying on a cushion with gilt tassels, 4¼ in. (10.8cm) long, c.1830-40.

puppies were thrown up in a litter, but they were normally drowned at birth, being regarded as unlucky. Indeed, black pugs were not taken seriously by breeders until about 1886, although twenty years earlier Lady Brasey had exhibited one at the Maidstone show, and it was only after 1918 that outstanding black pugs were bred.

Figure 32. Chamberlain Worcester fawn-coloured pug-dog seated on a green base, 2½ in. (6.4cm) high. Mark 'Chamberlain Worcester' written in script, c.1820-40.

Figure 34. Minton pug-dog, fawn-coloured with black features and black and gilt collar lying recumbent on a rectangular gilt banded base, 3¾ in. (9.5cm) long, c.1830-40.

ROCKINGHAM

The Rockingham factory turned out a pair of pugs, a dog and bitch (in reverse) in two different versions. The earlier models are shown in colour plate 11. Neither the dog nor the bitch is numbered, but the bitch has the red painted griffin mark. The later version, which was modelled in at least two sizes, is incised 'No 76'. Examples of the dog (as distinct from the bitch) are shown in two sizes in colour plate 12. Each has the impressed mark, and is almost identical to the model produced at the same time at Derby (see colour plate 5a and figures 25c and 31). The Derby model was made in three different sizes (see page 61) and according to Haslem the modeller was William Còffee. As there would seem to be a connection between William Coffee and the Rockingham model of a small curled-up setter on a rectangular base (No 91) (colour plate 16b and figure 73a), the possibility suggests itself that William Coffee might be the modeller of the pair of pugs numbered 76. Incidentally, the earlier Rockingham models of a pug dog and bitch would seem to be from a wholly different hand. All coloured Rockingham pugs recorded so far are found to be fawn.

With the exception of the Chelsea model of Hogarth's pet, Trump,[1] an interesting feature of the Rockingham models (and, as far as I am aware, of *all* pugs produced in this country during the eighteenth and nineteenth centuries) is that their ears are cropped. The bitch and puppy appearing in the engraving (after Reinagle) referred to above have suffered this form of mutilation, and the porcelain animals merely reflected the treatment undergone by the real animals. Why pugs should have been mutilated in this way is not immediately obvious. The motive for cropping is to prevent a fighting dog, e.g. a bulldog or mastiff, being taken by the ears by its opponent, but as the pug was only a lap-dog, never a fighting dog, the need for cropping never existed. Sad to say, the malpractice was in deference to the dictates of fashion. William Youatt denounced the practice observing:[2]

> 'Mr Blaine very naturally observes, that, "it is not a little surprising that this cruel custom is so frequently, or almost invariably, practised on pug-dogs, whose ears, if left alone to nature, are particularly handsome and hang very gracefully".'

---

1. The suggestion has been made that this dog is not a pug but some form of mastiff. The animal is in fact modelled after a terracotta by Roubiliac of Hogarth's dog lying in a recumbent position. The terracotta was sold after the death of the painter's widow in 1789 and was illustrated in an engraving in Samuel Ireland's *Graphic Illustrations of Hogarth,* published in 1799. It has since vanished. That 'Trump' was a pug is manifest from his portrait alongside his master in Hogarth's painting of 1745, now in the Tate Gallery, although in fairness it may be that the animal was not pure-bred but contained an element of mastiff. Hogarth had three pug dogs in succession, one of which actually answered to the name of 'Pugg' — see the advertisement inserted by Hogarth on 5 December 1730 in *The Craftsman* seeking the dog's return and offering a half-a-guinea reward.
2. *The Dog,* at p.166.

DERBY

Included in Haslem's list of unnumbered figures are:

	Enamelled and gilt	
	s	d
Large Pug Dogs, per pair, Coffee	4	0
Less Ditto, ditto, ditto	3	0
Small Ditto, ditto, Coffee	2	0
Begging Pugs, ditto, Chelsea	2	0

On the face of it, the last entry looks like a reference to a known eighteenth century model, but, be that as it may, nineteenth century examples undoubtedly exist. One was illustrated in Sotheby's sale catalogue of 25 March 1974 (lot 169). It was naturalistically coloured and it wore a gold collar. It stood on a green mound base, 3in. (7.6cm) overall. The other pug models would also appear to be eighteenth century in origin, as they are attributed to Coffee who commenced modelling circa 1794, and there are included in Bemrose's list of moulds, models etc belonging to William Duesbury in 1795, 'Pair large pug dogs, 3 sizes' However, all the surviving examples of these models seem to belong to the nineteenth century. They are in three sizes, approximately 3¼in. (8.3cm), 2⅜in. (6.7cm) and 2¼in.(5.7cm) high respectively. It would appear that Coffee actually copied earlier eighteenth century models, for Derby dogs of the same design are recorded dating from circa 1758 onwards. Examples of Coffee's models are shown in colour plate 5a and figures 25c and 31. Sometimes the sizes, in descending order, are indicated by an incised 1, 2 or 3 as appropriate. An interesting example, seated on a green base edged with gilt scrolls 2¼in. (5.7cm) overall, appeared as lot 584 of Sotheby's sale of 'British and Irish Ceramics', 22 May 1984. The noteworthy feature of this particular animal was that it carried the Bloor Derby mark under the base. Another example, this time 3in. (7.6cm) high, was sold by Christie's on 15 October, 1973 (lot 147), with 'iron-red mark'. It is rare indeed for an example to be marked. Normally coloured Derby pugs were fawn, but a rare black specimen (size 2), 2½in. (6.4cm) high, is shown in colour plate 5a, demonstrating that real black pug dogs were occasionally preserved and not all of them drowned at birth. It is interesting to note the appearance of 'A black pug dog 10s' in Christie's 'CATALOGUE of The Remainder of the Valuable Stock of the CHELSEA Porcelain Manufactory' sold on 5 May 1778. It should also be mentioned that Coffee's pug is recorded in biscuit.

Included among the models of Edward Keys are:

	Enamelled and gilt	
	s	d
New Sitting Pugs, on Cushions	1	6

No examples of the above models have so far been identified. However, a marked Derby pug is recorded, seated erect on a low mound base supported in turn on a rectangular plinth. An example is illustrated and described in Sotheby's sale catalogue of 9 February 1971, lot 104: 'DERBY PUG…with a gilt collar and red rosette, its body of pale beige colour, the rectangular base with a gilt line border, 3¼ in. *crown, crossed batons and D mark in red and numeral 41.*' Moreover, the next lot in that same sale (also illustrated) appears to be the same dog in reverse, but this time the rectangular base is supported on four ball feet.

For completeness, it should be mentioned that a well-known Derby eighteenth century model consisting of a stocky pug with prominent studded collar seated erect on a rectangular mound base, 3½ in. (8.9cm) high (a pair are illustrated in *Derby Porcelain,* D. G. Rice, plate 77) was continued into the nineteenth century, and examples are occasionally to be found. One white and gilt example measures 2in. (5.1cm) high.

CHAMBERLAIN WORCESTER

The Chamberlain factory produced a pair of pug models and an example of one of them is shown in figure 32. It sits on a green rectangular base with rounded corners 2½ in. (6.4cm) high overall. It is marked under the base in script 'Chamberlain Worcester'.

It is interesting to note that a collection of animals sent in December 1816 from the factory to the London shop included '2 Pugs'. Pug dogs appear to have been among the earliest animals produced by the Chamberlain concern. For there is a reference in the factory documents of November 1802[1] to:

	s	d
8 Pug doggs, coloured proper at	3	0

Pugs must have continued up to at least January 1829, for in a document of that date there is mention of:

	s	d
A pug dog[2]	2	6

---

1. See G.A. Godden, *Chamberlain Worcester Porcelain,* p.213.
2. Ibid, p.214.

Figure 35. Worcester dogs. a (top left). Sitting pug (item 267 in the factory list), 3½in. (8.9cm) high, in unglazed ivory porcelain (trial piece). First modelled in 1872. b (top centre). Skye terrier (item 374), 5½in. (14cm) high. In unglazed earthenware. First modelled in 1873. c (top right). St. Bernard (item 444), 6¾in. (17.1cm) high. In glazed ivory porcelain. First modelled in 1874.* d (below). King Charles spaniel (item 387), 6½in. (16.5cm) high. In glazed earthenware. First modelled in 1874. *(The Trustees of the Dyson Perrins Museum.)*
*Although this dog looks nothing like a St. Bernard, the Museum's records indicate that this *was* the factory's St. Bernard.

GRAINGER LEE & CO., WORCESTER

Surprisingly, so far no pug model has been recorded as emanating from the Grainger Lee factory. However, it is difficult to believe that it did not produce at least one model, for at the time it was turning out animal models the pug was still a popular breed. Doubtless in due course a model will come to light.

ROYAL WORCESTER

The researches of Henry Sandon, based on the factory records, have revealed that in 1862 the Royal Worcester factory modelled a group of pugs (item 109 in the factory list), in 1872 a pug seated (item 267) a pug standing (item 268), and in 1873 a life size pug standing (item 355), and in 1875 a pug bitch (item 506). The sitting pug is illustrated in figure 35a and the life size pug in figure 36.

63

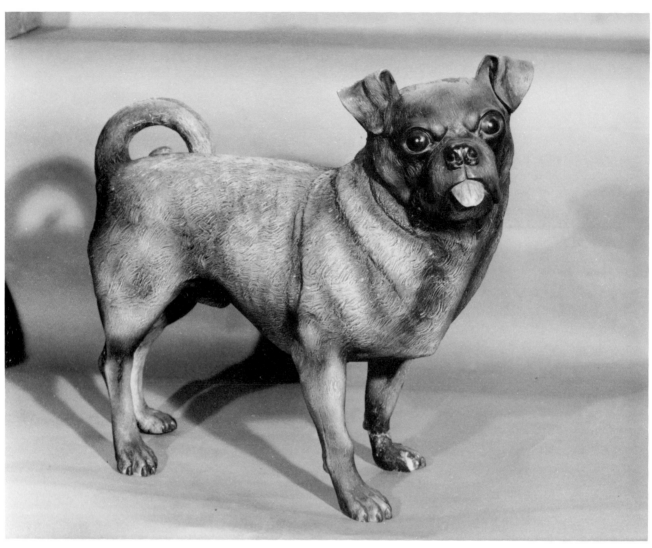

Figure 36. Royal Worcester standing pug (item 355), 15in. (38.1cm) high, life size. Naturalistically coloured in a matt finish on an earthenware body, date code for 1900, first modelled in 1873. (*The Trustees of the Dyson Perrins Museum.*)

MINTON

The white pug, with blue and gilt collar, lying on a tasselled cushion, 4¼in. (10.8cm) long, shown in figure 33 comes from the Minton factory. It corresponds with illustration no. 20 in the drawing book (page 244). This same model also appears in colour and in biscuit.

Interestingly, the pug of figure 34 seems to be the same dog but it has a plain rectangular base instead of one in the form of a tasselled cushion. The underneath, however, is flat and closed-in save for a small round hole centrally located. The dog would appear to be of Minton origin — the factory sometimes varied its bases (compare the setter of colour plate 17 with that of figure 78). The animal is fawn with black features and with a black and gilt collar, and the base, which is 3¾in. (9.5cm) long, is banded with gold.

CHARLES BOURNE

This factory is known to have produced a pug dog lying recumbent on an oblong base. However, it is very rare.

SAMUEL ALCOCK and the minor Staffordshire factories

No pug model attributable to the Samuel Alcock factory has so far been recorded, though this does not prove that no such model was ever made. However, it may be that, by the time the Samuel Alcock factory came to manufacture animals on any scale, the pug dog had fallen out of favour, and the management considered that it was not worthwhile producing replicas of this particular breed. This may also have been the view of the numerous minor Staffordshire factories operating in the period 1830-50; for I cannot recollect ever having seen a Staffordshire pug of this period; the poodle had completely taken over.

POODLES

It is a matter of dispute whether the poodle originated in France or Germany, though it is found in all parts of the Continent and even further afield. It is a dog of considerable antiquity, being mentioned by Gesner in 1524. To begin with, it was employed as a gun-dog for duck shooting, and was called a 'water dog' or 'rough water dog'. What is clearly an unclipped poodle, and referred to as a 'water dog', is illustrated in William Taplin's *Sportman's Cabinet* published in 1803. It is there distinguished from the water spaniel. A similar animal, likewise unclipped and called the 'large rough water dog' appears in Thomas Bewick's *General History of Quadrupeds,* first published in 1790. However, notwithstanding these illustrations, the poodle was normally trimmed with what came to be known as the 'lion-clip'. Interestingly, a print entitled 'The Dog Barbers', published by Bretherton in 1771, shows poodles in France being clipped. A later print dated 1819 depicts two Frenchwomen energetically clipping poodles with enormous scissors on the Pont Neuf in Paris, and the entry in the diary of Mary Browne (1807-1833) for 7 May, 1821, contains the comment '...we crossed the Seine by the Pont Royal...on the bridge were several women clipping poodles...'[1] The reason for subjecting the animal to the lion-clip was to enable it to shake off the water, when it was being used for retrieving ducks. The area of its body which contained the vital organs or which might be susceptible to rheumatism, e.g. the knees, was protected by leaving the hair untrimmed.

---

1. *The Diary of a Girl in France in 1821,* Mary Browne, 1905.

Figure 37. Rockingham poodle seated on a deep rocky base, 3in. (7.6cm) high, incised 'No 82'. 1826-30.

Although poodles started off as gun-dogs, soon many of them became simply pets. Thus, a mezzotint, published in 1780 from a series entitled 'Jack on a Cruise' and sub-titled 'Avast, there! Back your mainsail', shows a sailor trying to attract the attention of a young lady who is accompanied by a small gambolling poodle trimmed with the traditional lion-clip. In this country by the beginning of the nineteenth century and thereafter, the poodle came to be predominantly a pet and not a gun-dog. However, its popularity seems not to have really taken off until after about 1830. It was only after that date that porcelain replicas came to be produced in quantity.

It should also be mentioned that poodles are remarkably intelligent, and as a result have always been regular performers in travelling circuses and similar forms of entertainment. In 1700 a troupe of poodles in an act called 'The Ball of Little Dogs' performed before Queen Anne. Somewhat later in the eighteenth century a troupe of eighty miniature poodles performed a unique act in which they sat at a banquet and were waited upon by other dogs of inferior breed. During the nineteenth century poodles regularly appeared throughout the country as entertainers, jumping through hoops, dancing, performing somersaults, and undertaking all manner of tricks. Doubtless it was their entertainment qualities which contributed to their popularity among the public at large.

ROCKINGHAM

In view of the fact that the Rockingham factory was for many years best known to the public for the numerous poodles erroneously attributed to it,[1] it is ironic that only one single example has so far been discovered which can properly be identified with it, and even this did not come to light till February 1988. It sits on a deep oval rocky base 3in. (7.6cm) high overall, and is incised 'No. 82'. It is illustrated in figure 37. Whether the factory produced any other poodle models is unknown.

1 See D.G. Rice, *Rockingham Ornamental Porcelain*, pp.45-47, although I now consider that most of the Staffordshire porcelain poodles were made prior to 1850 and not in the mid-Victorian period.

DERBY

In the list of so-called 'Bow and Chelsea models' compiled by Haslem are to be found

	Enamelled and gilt		Biscuit	
	s	d	s	d
Poodle Dogs and Fleecy Sheep, each	-		5	0

Figure 38. Pair of Derby white and gilt poodles lying recumbent on elaborately scrolled bases, 4½ in. (11.4cm) in length. Crown over 'D' mark in red, c.1825-35.

'Biscuit' is always more expensive than 'enamelled and gilt', so that a coloured version might cost (say) 3s 6d. The pair of poodles with rococo bases illustrated in figure 38 could conceivably be nineteenth century white and gilt examples of the above 'Poodle Dogs'. However the selling price for their size seems somewhat high (they are 4½ in. (11.4cm) long), and it is remarkable, bearing in mind that the original rococo style gave way to the classical around 1770, that no eighteenth century examples are recorded. (That the dogs illustrated are nineteenth century is established beyond doubt by the 'Crown over a D mark' printed in red under the base.) More likely, they are examples of John Keys'.

Figure 39. a (left). Derby toy poodle in biscuit, begging, 1¼ in. (3.2cm) high, c.1830-45. b (right). Chamberlain Worcester poodle in biscuit, standing 1⅞ in. (4.7cm) high on a base 2in. (5.1cm) long. Impressed under a completely closed-in base 'CHAMBERLAINS'. 1847-52.

	Enamelled and gilt	
	s	d
New Poodle Dogs...each	2	0

The elaborate bases may perhaps be early instances of the neo-rococo style just coming into fashion, in which event they were probably modelled immediately before Keys left the factory in 1826. However the neo-rococo style did not generally manifest itself until after 1830, and one wonders whether the pair of poodles of figure 38 are examples of models executed by some artist other than John Keys.

Illustrated in figure 39a is a toy poodle in biscuit, a mere 1¼in. (3.2cm) high (with a flat closed-in base save for a central hole). Doubtless it was made in the town of Derby, but whether it was turned out at the great Derby factory is problematical. Conceivably, it was a nineteenth century toy version of one of the

	Enamelled and gilt	
	s	d
Begging French Dogs, per pair Chelsea	2	0

More likely it was made by the same factory as was responsible for the two sheep shown in figure 107, and these were more probably produced by George Cocker or Robert Blore.

CHAMBERLAIN

The Chamberlain factory turned out at least four different poodle models. The first comprises a poodle lying on a tasselled cushion, its hind quarters upraised, with a basket in its mouth. An example in biscuit is shown in figure 40; others are known in white and gold and in enamel colours and gold.[1] The example measures 4in. (10.2cm) in length and has under the hollow base the words incised in script 'H. Chamberlain and Sons, Worcester'. A similar model is illustrated in figure 41. It too measures 4in. (10.2cm) in length, but it has a somewhat different mark incised in script under the base. It reads 'Chamberlains Royal Porcelain Manufacturers'. The really interesting feature of this particular model is that, although the dog seems to be a poodle — like almost all poodles of

---

1. An interesting specimen holding a basket of fruit and lying on a blue cushion with the elaborate printed Royal arms mark and the New Bond St address appears in Colour Plate XIII of G.A. Godden's *Chamberlain Worcester Porcelain*.

Figure 40. Chamberlain Worcester poodle in biscuit lying on a tasselled cushion base, with a basket in its mouth and with its hind legs upraised, 4in. (10.2cm) long. Incised in script under the recessed base 'H. Chamberlain and Sons Worcester', c.1820-40.

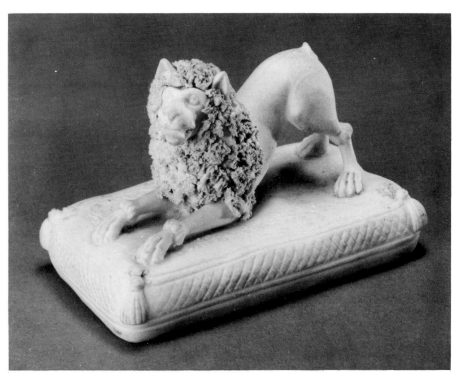

Figure 41. Chamberlain Worcester poodle in biscuit with pricked ears and with its hind legs upraised, lying on a tasselled cushion, 4in. (10.2cm) long. Incised in script under the recessed base 'Chamberlains Royal Porcelain Manufacturers', c.1820-40.

our period it has the distinctive lion-clip — it has, instead of the normal pendulous ears, the short pricked variety (see also the Samuel Alcock poodles of figure 44a and c).

The third Chamberlain model consists of a poodle standing 1⅞in. (4.7cm) high on a base 2in. (5.1cm) long. An example in biscuit is illustrated in figure 39b. Under the hollow base is impressed in capitals the word 'CHAMBERLAINS'. From the form of the mark, this particular animal would appear to have been manufactured after 1846.

The fourth model comprises a seated poodle on an oblong base with rounded corners. An interesting feature is that the wool is depicted by the moulding of the porcelain and not, as in the case of the other models mentioned, by the application of thin threads of porcelain. An example of this model is illustrated in figure 42a. It stands on a matt-blue base under which is written in script 'Chamberlain Worcester'. It is 2¾in. (7cm) high overall.

It is interesting to note that poodles are mentioned in the following factory documents:[1]

	s	d	
2 new Poodles at	3	0	[June 1824]
2 Poodles on blue cushions at	2	6	
A toy biscuit poodle	5	0	[Sept 1828]
To a biscuit poodle and shade	15	0	[Feb 1829]

The price of the last item suggests that it was very large, a view supported by the reference to the preceding much cheaper poodle as a 'toy'.

1. See G.A. Godden, *Chamberlain Worcester Porcelain*, p.214.

GRAINGER LEE & CO., WORCESTER

A poodle appears in the Grainger Lee drawing book belonging to the Dyson Perrins Museum, Worcester. The animal, with its hind-quarters upraised, lies on a rectangular tasselled cushion supported by four bun feet (see chapter 6, page 233). No porcelain example of this model has so far been recorded.

MINTON

The Minton factory produced two poodle models. They appear in the original drawing book as illustrations 19 (see page 242) and 33 (see page 245) respectively. One of them (no. 33) holds a basket in its mouth. The pose of both is similar to that of the Chamberlain model shown in figure 40. Each lies on a tasselled cushion, 4in. (10.2cm) long. An example of

Figure 42. a (left). Chamberlain Worcester white poodle seated on a dry-blue base 2 ¾ in. (7cm) high. Marked 'Chamberlain Worcester' in script, c.1820-30. b (right). Chamberlain Worcester grey mouse lying on a dry-blue oval base, 1 ⅝ in. (4.1cm) long. Marked 'Chamberlains' in script, c.1820-40.

model no. 19 (said to be after a Vincennes model), appeared at the 'Exhibition of Staffordshire Porcelain 1740-1851' organised by the Northern Ceramics Society in 1979, and is illustrated in plate 119 of the catalogue. The base was purple and yellow. The two illustrations appearing in the drawing book are the reverse of each other, so that conceivably they could have been sold as a pair. However, it is more likely each separate model was produced in reverse, and pairs were made up accordingly. Certainly, the poodle appearing at the 'Exhibition of Staffordshire Porcelain' was the reverse of illustration 19 in the drawing book, and a fine pair of poodles in reverse of model no. 33 in biscuit were in the possession of Mercury Antiques Ltd. in 1986, still in their original glass display boxes.

SAMUEL ALCOCK

One of the three animals buried under the foundation-stone of the new Samuel Alcock factory opened in April 1839 was a poodle with upraised hind quarters. Only part of that particular example has survived, but a more satisfactory specimen is shown in figure 43. Like the buried animal, it is impressed with number '36'. The yellow base measures 3 ¼ in. (8.3cm) in length.

Another Samuel Alcock poodle, 3 ½ in. (8.9cm) high appears in the group of figure 16. A companion cat is seen playing with it. It is in a seated position and is particularly interesting for the fact that the lion-clip is represented by moulding, and not by the application of porcelain threads or granules. The group is impressed '239' and presumably, in view of the high number, was modelled after 1830, by which time poodle

71

Figure 43. Samuel Alcock poodle lying recumbent, with upraised hind quarters, on a yellow mound base, 3¼ in. (8.3cm) in length. Incised '36', c.1830-45.

wool (as well as sheep wool) was not normally represented by means of moulding.[1] We have here an unusual return to the original technique. An interesting pair of unclipped poodles with pricked ears are illustrated in figure 44a and c. Unfortunately the impressed number is indecipherable. The factory also produced a poodle lying recumbent on a rocky mound base impressed '22'. Once again the fur is represented by moulding, but this time was presumably, by virtue of the low number, an early one. An example is recorded lying on a yellow base, 3⅝ in. (9.2cm) long.

The following poodles described in various sale catalogues would appear to be further Samuel Alcock models:

'A Staffordshire Figure of a white Poodle — seated upon a pale yellow oval base, 3½ in *impressed numeral 312'*. (Sotheby's, 17 January 1978, lot 159)

'A Rockingham Group of a Poodle and its Puppy, lying on a green and cream coloured cushion with tassels at the corners, 4¼ in *impressed numeral 330'*. (Sotheby's, 3 October 1972, lot 28)

1. See in addition to the poodle number 36, the sheep of figures 108-110.

LLOYD SHELTON

The poodle of colour plate 13 stands in front of a white and gilt kennel (the floor of which is strewn with straw) on a rectangular rocky green and yellow base with rounded corners 3⅛ in. (7.9cm) long. A particularly attractive feature is the bowl of bones placed at the entrance to the kennel. Although the piece is unmarked, it probably emanates from the Lloyd Shelton factory. This attribution is founded on a similarity in shape and decoration to the base of a marked Lloyd Shelton figure illustrated in

Colour Plate 15. Copeland and Garrett King Charles spaniel recumbent on an elaborately scrolled base, 4½in. (11.4cm) long. Factory mark, 1833-47.

Colour Plate 16a (left). Rockingham setter lying recumbent on a rectangular base, 4¼in. (10.8cm) long. Incised 'No 94'. Cl 2. 1826-30. b (right). Rockingham setter lying curled up on a rectangular base, 2⅜in. (6.7cm) long. Incised 'No 91'. 1826-30.

Figure 44. a and c (left and right). Pair of unclipped Samuel Alcock poodles, with pricked ears, standing on green bases edged with a gilt line, 2¾ in. (7cm) high. Impressed numerals indecipherable, c.1830-45. b (centre). Samuel Alcock group of rabbits playing on a grassy mound in front of hollow tree trunks, 4½ in. (11.4cm) high. Impressed '135', c.1830-45. *(Sotheby's)*

Figure 45. Lloyd Shelton white poodle emerging from a grey kennel, the white rectangular base (with rounded corners) encrusted with moss and decorated with a rich continuous gilt line, 3⅛ in. (7.9cm) long, c.1835-40.

colour plate 3 of Anthony Oliver's *The Victorian Staffordshire Figure*. A similar model, but this time with the poodle emerging from its kennel, is shown in figure 45. The kennel is grey, whilst the moss-encrusted base is left white, save for a rich continuous gilt line around the edges.

A Lloyd Shelton attribution can still more confidently be given to the delightful toy white and gilt poodle, 1⅝in. (4.1cm) high, illustrated in figure 46, notwithstanding that it too is unmarked. Apart from the quality of the gilding, a particular feature of the products of John and Rebecca Lloyd, identification with the Lloyd Shelton factory is unequivocally established by the appearance of the same poodle model on the base of the Lloyd Shelton figure of 'The Woodman', an example of which is illustrated in plate 157 of Anthony Oliver's *Staffordshire Pottery*. The thin white and gilt base of both the figure and the independent poodle model of figure 46 is substantially the same in form and decoration. Moreover, the dog's tail turns back in a distinctive way in the case of both the animal that accompanies 'The Woodman' and the dog appearing in figure 46. The Lloyd Shelton model of 'The Woodman' is based on a Bartolozzi engraving after a print by Thomas Barker of Bath. Ironically, the dog

Figure 46. Small Lloyd Shelton white poodle, with tail flicked back over its body, standing on a thin rectangular base edged with gold, 1⅝in. (4.1cm) long, c.1835-40.

Figure 47. Lloyd Shelton white poodle with black markings on the muzzle, holding a black hat in its mouth and standing on a rectangular base with a continuous gilt line around the edges, 2¼in. (5.7cm) long, c.1835-40.

Figure 48. White poodle, with black markings on the muzzle, lying recumbent on a white mound supported in turn by a white rectangular base, 2in. (5.1cm) long. Possibly Davenport, c.1830-40.

accompanying 'The Woodman' in the engraving would appear to be a lurcher; it is certainly not a poodle. Doubtless the factory found it more convenient to substitute the more fashionable breed. The same model as that shown in figure 46 appears in figure 47. The dog is somewhat larger standing 2¼ in. (5.7cm) high overall. Interestingly, it holds in its mouth a black hat, of the shape incidentally worn by 'The Woodman'.

A further poodle model, this time a large one, standing 8in. (20.3cm) high with a basket in its mouth, has been attributed to Lloyd Shelton by Anthony Oliver in his *Staffordshire Pottery,* plate 155.

DAVENPORT

The 2in. (5.1cm) long base of the well-modelled poodle of figure 48 is rectangular supporting an oval mound and bears a remarkable resemblance in shape to that of the King Charles spaniel of figure 62. Moreover, the pose of the two animals is similar, as is their sense of movement, all of which suggests the same modeller. If the spaniel comes from the Davenport factory (see pages 253-255), conceivably the poodle does as well. However, the decoration is not as rich, as the poodle is left in white save for a continuous gilt line around the edge of the base and black markings to the face. Although the Davenport factory might possibly have turned out animals of different qualities, a more likely explanation is that some minor unknown Staffordshire factory simply copied the finer model.

MINOR STAFFORDSHIRE FACTORIES

Poodles were turned out in profusion during the period from 1830 to 1850, and most of them came from the various minor Staffordshire factories operating at the time. These poodles far exceeded in quantity any other breed of dog. Why this should be so is mystifying. Perhaps the real dogs assumed a unique popularity among the public, which was reflected in a corresponding demand for porcelain replicas. Perhaps interest in the breed was stimulated to an abnormal extent by the appearance of poodles at travelling circuses and other places of entertainment, which made them particularly appealing to children, and doubtless this was the primary market.

The porcelain models of the period 1830-50 clearly represent pet or circus dogs, not the sporting animal. Sometimes they appear in comic situations, e.g. holding a black hat in their mouth (figure 47),or wearing a dunce's hat on their heads, presumably after circus animals. Staffordshire poodles in different poses, e.g. lying recumbent (flat or with

Figure 49. Staffordshire white glazed poodle, with upraised hind legs, lying recumbent on a shaped base, 3⅜in. (8.6cm) long, c.1830-40.

hind quarters raised), standing or seated, sometimes with baskets in their mouth, sometimes not, are here illustrated. A particularly attractive dog lies on a pink square cushion with tassels, 1½in. (3.8cm) across (figure 50b). It comes from the same factory responsible for a cat on a similarly decorated and shaped base illustrated in Katharine McClinton's *Antique Cats for Collectors*.[1] The group appearing in figure 51 is noteworthy for the fact that the bitch is accompanied by three puppies. The animals lie on a light yellow cushion, 3½in. (8.9cm) long, with blue tassels. The pair of boxes, each with a 'poodle and puppies' lid, illustrated in figure 52, are rare. One of these flower-decorated boxes is porcelain, the other pottery. Manifestly, the factory responsible turned out toys both in

1. Between pages 72 and 73, bottom row of the fourth illustration.

Figure 50. a (left). Staffordshire group of two poodles, one seated, the other lying recumbent on a shaped base, decorated in gros bleu 2½in. (6.4cm) long, c.1830-50. b (right). Staffordshire poodle lying on a square pink tasselled cushion, 1½in. (3.8cm) long, c.1830-50.

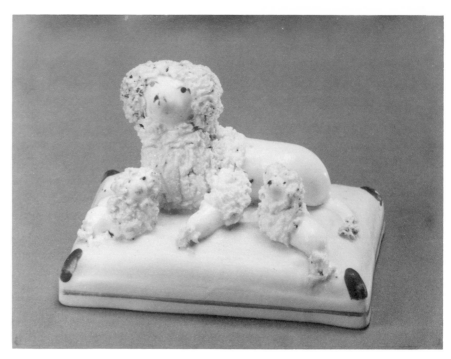

Figure 51. Staffordshire poodle bitch with three puppies on a yellow cushion base with blue tassels, 3½in. (8.9cm) long, c.1830-45.

Figure 52. Pair of Staffordshire flower-decorated boxes, with orange cushion lids surmounted by a poodle with puppies 3½in. (8.9cm) long, one of the boxes porcelain, the other earthenware, c.1840-50.

Figure 53. Staffordshire black-spotted poodle seated on a tapering rectangular plinth with a stiff leaf border between two gilt lines, 9½ in. (24.1cm) high, c.1830-40. *(Sotheby's)*

porcelain and earthenware. The model of a white poodle, 3⅜ in. (8.6cm) long, with raised hind quarters, shown in figure 49, is also recorded with its front paw about to descend on a naturally coloured rat. The shaped base of the group of two poodles appearing in figure 50a is distinctive, and examples are not infrequently found. In the Derby Museum, and illustrated in plate 127 of Barrett & Thorpe's *Derby Porcelain* (where it is erroneously ascribed to the Derby factory), is a rather striking Staffordshire poodle, seated on a rectangular scroll base, 4¼ in. (10.8cm) high overall. Its companion is a bitch with three puppies. A pair was sold by Sotheby's on 25 March 1974, lot 160. Sometimes a poodle is seen in conjunction with a human figure (colour plate 14a[1], figure 54).

An interesting collection of poodles is illustrated in figure 95 of Margaret Vivian's *Antique Collecting*. Other examples appear in plates 134 and 136 of B. & T. Hughes' *Collecting Miniature Antiques*. The black-spotted poodle, which is illustrated in figure 53, seated on a tapering

---

1. Note the absence of the usual lion-clip.

Figure 54. Staffordshire seated girl with a pink dress feeding her poodle out of a deep bowl, on a shaped base, 3¾ in. (9.5cm) high, c.1830-45.

Figure 55 a (left). Staffordshire white and gilt sheep standing on a rectangular base with rounded corners edged with a gilt line, 2in. (5.1cm) long, c.1830-50. b (centre). Staffordshire poodle holding an orange basket and standing on a mound base edged with a gilt line, 2¼ in. (5.7cm) long, c.1830-50. c (right). Staffordshire poodle, with pink mask, standing on a rectangular base with rounded corners, 2in. (5.1cm) long, c.1830-50.

Figure 56. Pair of Staffordshire poodle groups, each group consisting of two poodles, one seated, the other recumbent, on a gros bleu shaped concave base, 2½in. (6.4cm) long, c.1840-50.

rectangular plinth with a stiff leaf border between two gilt lines, is well modelled and comes from an unidentified factory, presumably somewhere in Staffordshire. The model appears in two sizes, 9½in. (24.1cm) and 8in. (20.3cm) high respectively. On a different scale entirely is a pair of Staffordshire poodle groups, shown in figure 56. Each group consists of two poodles, one recumbent, the other seated, on a gros-bleu shaped convex base, 2½in. (6.4cm) long. See also the poodles illustrated in figure 55b and c.

Finally, reference should be made to the existence of black poodles. They are, however, very rare.

SPANIELS

King Charles Spaniels

Toy spaniels were known on the Continent from the fifteenth century onwards. They appear regularly on canvasses, from Titian's painting of the Duchess of Urbino, executed in 1538, onwards, and before that on tapestries (see the Arras tapestry 'The Offering of the Heart'). In a painting by Antonio Moro, executed in 1554 and now or formerly hanging in Woburn Abbey, a pair of spaniels are represented at the feet of Mary I, and her husband Philip of Spain. In 1563 a small dog accompanied Mary Queen of Scots at her execution, and this was thought to be a toy spaniel. A year earlier Steven Van der Meulen painted a portrait of a woman, probably Catharine Carey, Lady Knollys, (now in the Yale Centre for British Art, New Haven, Connecticut and reproduced in *Apollo,* November, 1987 p.328, plate 10). A toy spaniel is depicted standing prominently on a table in front of her. However, this breed of lap-dog is particularly associated with King Charles I, and even more so with his son King Charles II. Hence the name King Charles spaniel!

These dogs appear regularly in the works of Van Dyck, Watteau, Boucher and Greuze, invariably as a small animal with a flat head, long nose, soft fleecy coat, and curly tail, and always hyperactive. They were brown/white, black/white, or tricolour. In 1678 Peter Lely painted Lady Temple 'with her favourite spaniel' (she was an enthusiastic owner of many spaniels). He also executed a portrait of Miss Skipwith with an almost lifesize toy spaniel.

Pepys in his Diary refers to these dogs when on an occasion in September 1666 he visited the Council Chamber: 'All I observed was the silliness of the King playing with his dogs all the while and not minding the business.' In 1867 Stonehenge made an interesting reference to the association of King Charles II with his small dogs: 'The old President of Magdalen College, who died about 10 years ago in his hundredth year, was accustomed to say that when he was a little boy he had been told by an old lady that when she was a little girl she saw the King round the Magdalen walks with these little dogs.'

John Evelyn positively disliked King Charles' spaniels. In a posthumous assessment of the King he wrote: 'He took delight in having a number of little spaniels to follow him and lie in his bedchamber and where he often suffered his bitches to puppy and give suck which rendered it very offensive, and indeed made the whole Court nasty and stinking.' James II also adored these toy spaniels, but on the fall of the Stuarts the dogs went out of fashion and they were replaced in popularity by the pug.

However, the King Charles spaniel did not disappear altogether, and the young Queen Victoria was painted with her dog 'Dash'. (Indeed in early Victorian times porcelain replicas of the breed seem to have enjoyed something of a revival.) Later in her reign the breed underwent certain changes: the long nose shortened and the flat head become domed. Doubtless, a cross was introduced, probably by means of a pug-dog. The modified breed continues today. In the late Victorian period, the original version became virtually extinct, but in 1928 certain breeders decided to recreate it. It is now called 'the cavalier' and today both variants are bred. All the porcelain replicas of the non-sporting animal belonging to our period are of the dog in its original form.

Spaniels as Sporting Dogs:

The spaniel was more than a mere lap-dog. During the nineteenth century it was a particular favourite of sportsmen, having an origin going back to the fourteenth century. There were different varieties — springer spaniels, cocker spaniels and water spaniels, each with its own special qualities. Engravings of springer spaniels are to be found in, among other places, Daniel's *Rural Sports,* Taplin's *Sportsman's Cabinet* and J.G.

Figure 57. Rockingham white and gilt springer spaniel running, 3¼ in. (8.3cm) long. Incised 'No 83'. Cl 1. Impressed mark. 1826-30. This seems to be a three dimensional form of the spaniel in the plaque shown in figure 58.

Figure 58. Rockingham plaque depicting a spaniel chasing game; signed on the reverse by 'Bailey'. Length 5½ in. (14cm), height 4¼ in. (10.8cm). Red griffin mark. 1826-30.

Colour Plate 17. Minton setter lying recumbent on a rectangular base edged with two gilt lines enclosing a raised scroll moulding, 4⅛ in. (10.5cm) long, c.1830-40. (The same setter in biscuit on a tasselled cushion base is shown in figure 78).

Colour Plate 18. Trotting Minton pointer beside a supporting tree on a mound base, 3½ in. (8.9cm) long, (no. 31 in the factory list), c.1830-40.

Wood's *The Illustrated Natural History,* and Taplin observes of this breed that:

> 'it was delicately formed with ears long, soft and pliable, coat waving and silky, eyes and nose red or black, the tail somewhat bulky and pendulous, always in motion when actively employed.'

Springer spaniels derived their name from their inherent ability 'to spring, flush or start all the game before them, and they pursue, without preference, hare, pheasant, partridge, woodcock, snipe and quail'. The cocker spaniel (illustrated in J.G. Wood's *The Illustrated Natural History)* was in contrast smaller than the springer. It found the scent more easily and being shorter and more compact could push its way through low bushy cover. It was chiefly employed in woodcock shooting — hence its name 'cocker spaniel'. Water spaniels accompanied wildfowlers, and an engraving of one of them appears in the frontispiece of the *Sportsman's Cabinet.* The breed is now extinct.

ROCKINGHAM

The King Charles spaniel has so far not been recorded as a product of the Rockingham factory. However, it is unlikely to have been ignored by the Bramelds. It is clear from the numbering system adopted by the factory that several animals still remain to be discovered (see chapter 6, page 205), and it is very probable that a King Charles is one of them.

Be that as it may, the spaniel as a sporting dog is to be found among the animals turned out at Swinton. The white and gilt model (No 83) illustrated in figure 57 (2⅞ in. (7.3cm) high and 3¼ in. (8.3cm) long), would seem to be a springer spaniel and was clearly intended to be a three-dimensional version of the dog in the Rockingham plaque illustrated in figure 58.

The enamelled and gilt springer of figure 59 looks remarkably like the Rockingham white and gold dog of figure 57. It is decorated with brown patches, and stands on a rocky white and green base splashed, in a typical Rockingham way, with gilding. However, in fact it is a copy, being probably the work of Samson of Paris, who from around 1870 onwards reproduced everything that was then collectable in porcelain. It is made of hard paste and the underside of the base is not constructed in the Rockingham fashion, i.e. made flat and closed-in save for a centrally located hole, but instead is deeply recessed. Also, it carries the Chelsea gold anchor mark on the top of the base, adjacent to the dog's right back leg. It is puzzling why the copyist should have given the piece a Chelsea rather than a Rockingham mark. The most likely explanation is that he had an enamelled and gilt Rockingham example to copy from (hence the typical Rockingham decoration as well as the similarity of modelling), but

Figure 59. White and brown springer spaniel running, on a hollow base splashed with green and gold, 4⅛ in. (10.5cm) long. This is a copy of a Rockingham model made by Samson of Paris c.1870, and fraudulently marked with a Chelsea gold anchor.

Figure 61. Minton King Charles spaniel with brown patches, lying recumbent on a narrow rounded rectangular base encrusted with flowers and berries, 8½ in. (21.6cm) long. Interlaced Ls mark in blue, c.1830-40. *(Sotheby's)*

that the example did not carry the Rockingham impressed mark (if it had the 'Cl' mark alone, this would have probably meant nothing to the copyist), and in consequence, not knowing to which factory to attribute it, he flatteringly, but inaccurately, assumed it belonged to Chelsea. The copy is of particularly fine quality.[1]

In figure 140 of *Antique Collecting,* Margaret Vivian illustrates what she calls a snuffbox (it would appear in fact to be a patch box), impressed with the Rockingham griffin mark, the lid of which is surmounted by a small spaniel lying with its head over its paws, seemingly asleep. It seems to be a puppy and either a cocker or a springer spaniel. Perhaps this model was produced with an incised number independently of the patch box. However, so far no example has come to light.

1. Although the copy is somewhat larger than the dog of figure 57, it may be that the Rockingham factory also produced a bigger version (compare Nos. 76, 77, 107 and 142 where the model was produced in more than one size), and the copyist happened to have before him the larger version of the spaniel.

DERBY, NOTTINGHAM ROAD

Three eighteenth century spaniel models from Derby are recorded, attributable to a date around 1765. One is a delightful King Charles spaniel lying on a flower-encrusted base,[1] the other two are illustrated respectively in plate 75a and colour plate L of my *Derby Porcelain 1750-70.* However, despite this no nineteenth century model has so far come to light. Certainly, there is no reference to spaniel in any of the lists of models mentioned by Haslem. If the King Charles was not produced at Derby during the nineteenth century, nevertheless it is surprising not to find the factory making a replica of the sporting version of the dog. Perhaps one day an example will come to light.

1. A pair are illustrated in *The Connoisseur,* September 1922, p.37, illustration no 14.

KING ST. FACTORY, DERBY

Although no spaniel can be assigned to the Nottingham Road factory at Derby, a Sampson Hancock pair are recorded. A biscuit pair lying recumbent, 3¾in. (9.5cm) was sold at Sotheby's on 24 February 1987, lot 250. The Sampson Hancock mark appearing on them shows them to have been produced at a date subsequent to 1862.

Figure 60. A Rockingham toy setter, white with black and iron-red facial markings and a gilt collar seated on an oval mound base, 1¾in. (4.4cm) high. Incised 'No 96'. Cl 1. 1826-30. *(Sotheby's)*

CHAMBERLAIN

That the Chamberlain factory did turn out spaniels is established by the reference, contained in certain factory sale documents of January 1823,[1] to:

	s	d
3 small Spaniel dogs at	2	0

As no porcelain example has been recorded so far, it is impossible to say what Chamberlain spaniels actually looked like.

---

1. See G.A. Godden's *Chamberlain Worcester Porcelain*, p.214.

GRAINGER LEE & CO., WORCESTER

A spaniel appears in the factory's pattern book (see page 234). However, so far no porcelain example is recorded.

ROYAL WORCESTER

In 1874 the Royal Worcester factory turned out two separate models of a King Charles spaniel (items 387 and 410 respectively in the factory list). The former, which was 15in. (38.1cm) in length, is illustrated in figure 35d.

MINTON

Illustration no.22 in the Minton drawing book (see chapter 6, page 244) shows a King Charles spaniel lying recumbent on a cushion base with tassels. Examples are known in biscuit, in white and gold, and in enamel colours[1] and gold.

The model measures 4in. (10.2cm) in length. It was also made to lie on a narrow rounded rectangular base encrusted with flowers and berries to form a paper-weight (figure 61). The only other spaniel model known as coming from this factory is a King Charles standing on a tasselled cushion begging. It is numbered 32 in the drawing book (see chapter 6, page 245).

---

1. 'A Minton figure of a recumbent spaniel with brown fur markings on a magenta tasselled cushion... 4in. wide, circa 1830' (Christie's English Porcelain Sale, 11 December 1978, lot 219).

Figure 62. White and brown King Charles spaniel lying recumbent on a green mound supported in turn by a black rectangular base edged with a thick gold band, 2¹/₁₆in. (5.3cm) long. Probably from the Davenport factory, c.1830-45.

Figure 63. Samuel Alcock King Charles spaniel, with brown markings, seated on a mound base with gilt line, 3in. (7.6cm) high. Impressed '125', c.1830-45.

COPELAND AND GARRETT

The Copeland and Garrett factory produced at least one Spaniel model, a King Charles. A marked example is illustrated in colour plate 15. The brown and white dog, 2½in. (6.4cm) high, lies recumbent on an elaborately scrolled base, 4½in. (11.4cm) long.

DAVENPORT

Whether or not the great Davenport factory produced any porcelain animals is not certain (see pages 253-255), but if it did this would seem to be the most likely provenance of the King Charles spaniel bitch shown in figure 62. It is white and brown and lies recumbent on a green mound supported in turn by a black rectangular base, 2¹/₁₆in. (5.3cm) long, banded with gold. The modelling is fine, the gold rich and the piece generally heavy in weight. The glazing is affected by crazing. Doubtless there was originally a companion dog in reverse.

SAMUEL ALCOCK

The King Charles spaniel, seated on a yellow mound base 3³/₁₆in. (8.1cm) long, illustrated in figure 63, comes from the Samuel Alcock factory. It is impressed under the base with the number 125. Another King Charles spaniel from the factory is recorded, this time in a begging pose on a yellow base wearing a black hat, presumably inspired by a performing dog in a circus act. It is 4⅝in. (11.7cm) high in all and is impressed 329. Another model lies recumbent on a mound base with scroll mouldings, 3in. (7.6cm) long and impressed '18'. Two examples, each on a yellow ground, are illustrated in figure 64.

In the sale of the Boothman Smallwood Collection, conducted by Christie's South Kensington on 26 and 27 April 1989, two Samuel Alcock

Figure 64. Two Samuel Alcock King Charles spaniels, each white and black on a yellow mound base with scroll mouldings, 3in. (7.6cm) long. Impressed '18' or '81'. c.1830-45.

models of a spaniel made their appearance. One pair, 5in. (12.7cm) high, with black and grey patches, sitting on yellow shaped mound bases edged with a gilt line, were impressed '121'. The other pair, 3⅛in. (7.9cm) high, with brown and black markings, seated on oval mound bases enriched in apricot and with a gilt line, were impressed with the number '183'.

STAFFORDSHIRE

Spaniels of various kinds were turned out prolifically by the minor Staffordshire factories during the period 1830-50. It is not known what concern was responsible for the charming King Charles bitch and puppies group in a round cloth-covered wicker basket illustrated in figure 65, but it must have been one of the quality manufacturers operating in Staffordshire. The group was modelled as a companion to the cat and kittens group illustrated in colour plate 9b. The bitch was also produced in an independent model (figure 66), and, as one would expect, the companion in reverse was the cat (figure 21) of the afore mentioned cat and kittens group. The factory responsible for the foregoing also produced a variant bitch and puppies group, where the wicker basket is rectangular with rounded corners and where there are three puppies instead of two (figure 67). The companion group is a cat in a similar basket with three kittens.

Figure 65. Staffordshire group of a black and white spaniel with two similarly marked puppies, on a green cloth edged with orange lying on the top of a circular twin handled wicker basket, 3½in. (8.9cm) high, c.1830-45.

Figure 66. Staffordshire black and white spaniel seated on a green and white stool with four white and gilt legs, 4⅛in. (10.5cm) high, c.1830-45.

A particularly charming model is the spaniel seated beside its moss-encrusted kennel on a rectangular base with rounded corners, 2⅝in. (6.7cm) long (figure 68). Perhaps from the same factory is the group of two spaniels lying outside a kennel on a pale apricot triangular base, 2¼in. (5.7cm) long (figure 69). The same model was also produced in a larger size. An interesting King Charles lying recumbent on a scrolled base, 3¼in. (8.3cm) long, is illustrated in plate 134 of B. & T. Hughes' *Collecting Miniature Antiques*.

Although the minor Staffordshire factories turned out a variety of different spaniel models in porcelain, it is noteworthy that this particular breed of dog, or more accurately the King Charles, was, in the second half of the nineteenth century, to be immortalised in the form of countless pairs of Staffordshire pottery replicas made to stand on Victorian mantelpieces. Parian spaniels are also recorded. An example of a King Charles reclining on a cushion, 4in. (10.2cm) long, from an unknown factory, is shown in figure 70. It is incised 'July 19 1849'. Finally, illustrated in figure 71 there is a group of three spaniels from the Dudson factory found on the factory site. The group shown is actually in earthenware, but the model might have been produced in porcelain as well (see page 264).

RARER BREEDS

The breeds mentioned so far were represented in porcelain on a considerable scale. However, other breeds were produced in much smaller quantities. Porcelain replicas of these seem to have been

Figure 67. Staffordshire group of a spaniel with three puppies on a gros bleu basket, rectangular with rounded corners, and twin handles, 4½in. (11.4cm) high, c.1830-45. *(Sotheby's)*

manufactured at only some of the factories operative in the nineteenth century. Accordingly, only a limited number of factories will be mentioned in relation to each breed. However, the omission of a particular manufacturer does not necessarily imply that it never produced a model of the type of dog under consideration, only that an example has not come to light.

Figure 68. Staffordshire spaniel seated beside its moss-encrusted kennel on a rectangular base with rounded corners, 2⅝in. (6.7cm) long, c.1830-45.

Figure 69. Group of two Staffordshire spaniels, with brown patches, lying outside their pink-roofed kennel, on a pale apricot triangular base with rounded corners, 2¼in. (5.7cm) long, c.1840-50. (Possibly from the same factory as was responsible for the dog in figure 68.)

Colour Plate 19. Rockingham Great Dane lying recumbent on a rectangular base, 3 ¾ in. (9.5cm) long. Incised 'No 87'. Cl 2. Impressed mark. 1826-30.

Colour Plate 20. Rockingham mastiff with tongue hanging out, lying on a rocky base, 4 ⅝ in. (11.7cm) long. Incised 'No 90'. Cl 2. Impressed mark. 1826-30.

Figure 70. Parian spaniel lying recumbent on a cushion base, 4in. (10.2cm) long. Incised 'July 19 1849'. (*Godden of Worthing Ltd.*)

Figure 71. Dudson group of three red spaniels seated on a blue quill-holder base, 5in. (12.7cm) long, 5in. (12.7cm) high, c.1845. This group, excavated at the factory site, is in pottery, although the same model may well have also been produced in porcelain. (*Mrs Audrey Dudson*)

Of pre-eminent importance for sport were setters and pointers. They acquired their respective names from their individual approaches to game. J.G. Wood in his *The Illustrated Natural History* puts the matter: 'As the pointers derive their name from their habits of standing still and pointing at any game which they may discover so the SETTERS have earned their title from their custom of 'setting' or crouching when they perceive their game. In the olden days of sporting, the Setter used always to drop as soon as it found the game, but at the present day the animal is in so far the imitator of the pointer, that it remains erect while marking down its game.'[1]

Though completely different in appearance, these two breeds performed essentially the same function, and sportsmen were divided as to the superiority in the field of the one as against the other. William Youatt said of them: 'The setter is more active than the pointer. He has greater spirit and strength. He will better stand continued hard work. He will generally take the water when necessary, and, retaining the character of the breed, is more companionable and attached. He loves his master for himself, and not, like the pointer, for the pleasure he shares with him. His somewhat inferior scent, however, makes him a little too apt to run into his game, and he occasionally has a will of his own.'[2]

---

1. J.G. Wood, *The Illustrated Natural History,* p.290.
2. W. Youatt, *The Dog,* p.91.

SETTERS

The qualities of the setter are referred to by Thomas Bewick in his *A General History of Quadrupeds:* its exquisite scent, its great speed, its wonderful perseverance, its sagacity and its caution. He concludes[1] by quoting from Somervile:

> 'When autumn smiles, all-beautious in decay,
> And paints each chequer'd grove with various hues
> My Setter ranges in the new-shorn fields,
> His nose in air erect; from ridge to ridge
> Panting he bounds, his quarter'd ground divides
> In equal intervals, nor careless leaves
> One inch untry'd, at length, the tainted gales
> His nostrils wide inhale; quick joy elates
> His beating heart, which, aw'd by discipline

---

1. At p.313.

Colour Plate 21. Pair of Samuel Alcock mastiffs, each lying on a rocky base, 5½in. (14cm) long, one with its tongue hanging out, impressed '305', both with a painted cross in red under the base, c.1830-45.

Severe, he dares not own, but cautious creeps,
Low-cow'ring, step by step; at last attains
His proper distance; there he stops at once,
And points with his instructive nose upon
The trembling prey.'

An excellent engraving by J. Scott of an 'Old English Setter' appears in Daniel's *Rural Sports,* after a drawing by H.B. Chalon.

ROCKINGHAM

The Rockingham factory produced four different models of a setter. The first (No 94) lies recumbent on a rectangular base, 4¼in. (10.8cm) long. An example is shown here in biscuit (figure 73b), and another in colour in reverse (colour plate 16a). The white example, with black facial markings, on a coloured base illustrated in figure 72 is erroneously incised 'No 90'. Presumably the second model of a setter (No 91) was likewise made in pairs. It is much smaller than the previous model, the animal lying curled up on a rectangular base, 2⅝in. (6.7cm) long. Two examples are illustrated, in colour plate 16b and figure 73a respectively,

Figure 72. Rockingham setter lying recumbent on a rectangular base flecked with green, and edged with a gilt line, 4¼in. (10.8cm) long. Incised 'No 90' (an error for '94'). Cl 1. 1826-30. *(Christie's)*

the one in colour with a gilt-banded base, the other in biscuit. A companion model has been discovered (figure 74). It is somewhat larger than the animals of colour plate 16b and figure 73a, being 3⅛in. (7.9cm) long. This is not necessarily fatal to a Rockingham attribution, the factory frequently making models in more than one size, but for the reasons set out at page 220 it is not possible to ascribe a Rockingham provenance. A Derby origin is more likely. The Rockingham model may be connected with William Coffee (see page 220).

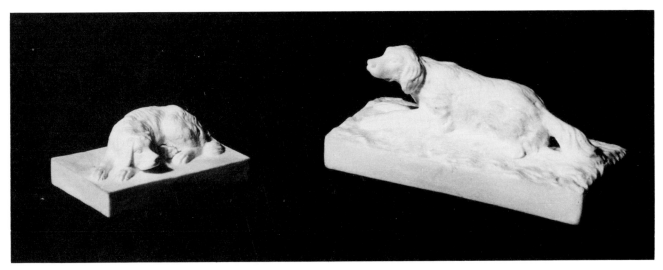

Figure 73a (left). Small Rockingham setter in biscuit, curled up on a rectangular base, 2⅝in. (6.7cm) long. Incised 'No 91'. Impressed mark. 1826-30. b (right). Rockingham setter in biscuit lying recumbent on a rectangular base, 4¼in. (10.8cm) in length. Incised 'No 94'. Impressed mark. 1826-30.

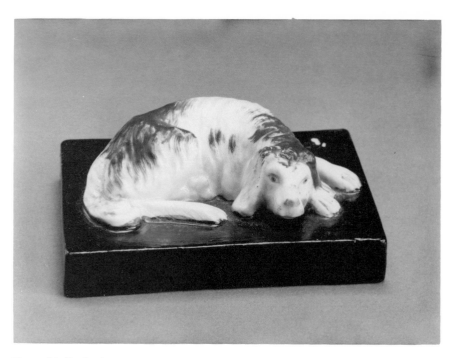

Figure 74. Derby brown and cream setter lying curled up on a black rectangular base, 3⅛in. (7.9cm) long, c.1820-40. (Cf. the Rockingham examples in reverse — colour plate 16b and in biscuit figure 73a).

Figure 75. Rockingham setter in biscuit, about to drink from a bowl, standing without support on a rectangular base, 3¾in. (9.5cm) long. Incised 'No 84'. Impressed mark. 1826-30.

Figure 76. Base of the dog in figure 75. Like the contemporary **Derby** and Minton animals, it is closed in save for a centrally located hole. It is incised with the model number and is impressed with the full griffin mark appropriate to the period 1826-30.

The third setter model to be turned out at Swinton (No 84), assumes a standing position (incidentally without any support, in contrast to model No 89 (figures 97 and 98) and is about to drink from a bowl. It is 3¾ in. (9.5cm) in length and 3¼ in. (8.3cm) in height. An example in biscuit, so far a unique survivor, is shown in figure 75. The base of the animal (figure 76) demonstrates the form of construction used on Rockingham (and, for that matter, contemporary Derby and Minton) animals. The Rockingham impressed mark and the incised model number can also be seen. The fourth Rockingham model of a setter (No 96) is illustrated in figure 60. It stands only 1¾ in. (4.4cm) high.

DERBY

The setter of figure 74, if it does not originate from the Rockingham factory, must necessarily have come from Derby. There is some evidence to suggest that this model is the work of William Coffee (see page 220).

A much larger setter (figure 77) with its nose close to the ground

Figure 77. Derby pointer (left) and companion setter (right) in natural colours. The pointer is trotting and the setter has his nose to the ground. Both are 6½ in. (16.5cm) long. Late 18th or early 19th century. (*Grosvenor Antiques Ltd. and Mary Wise Antiques*)

sniffing the scent, standing on a base some 6½ in. (16.5cm) long and with a pointer for a companion, was also modelled at Derby, but although it was undoubtedly made during the nineteenth century,[1] it would appear to have been an eighteenth century model. According to Haslem, the original model was the work of William Coffee made during the 1790s (see page 214).

---

1. An example is recorded with the Bloor mark. It is interesting to note that this model together with the companion pointer was also produced in pottery in Staffordshire (see the illustration in Sotheby's sale catalogue of 25 March 1974, lots 39 and 38).

MINTON

The biscuit setter shown in figure 78 emanates from the Minton factory. It has the same tasselled cushion base found in conjunction with the factory's King Charles spaniels (the one recumbent, the other begging), the two different poodle models, the pug, the greyhound and the Russian dog. Admittedly, there is no actual illustration in the factory drawing book of a setter on a tasselled cushion, or, for that matter, of a setter at all, but nevertheless the dog of figure 78 must be a porcelain representation of item no. 29, which is not illustrated but simply described 'Dog' (see chapter 6, page 243). The fact that the factory undoubtedly produced a pointer, illustration no. 31 in the drawing book (chapter 6, page 245), suggests that it would also have turned out a setter, as the two breeds are naturally linked, which serves to confirm the above view. Moreover, it is not without significance that item 30 in the drawing book is there described as 'Dog Standing' — once again there is no illustration. In the case of item no. 29 the absence of the word 'Standing' suggests that the animal referred to was not in a standing position, and was in all probability lying recumbent. What is puzzling is that the dog of figure 78 is recumbent on a tasselled cushion, a base wholly appropriate to a lap-dog, but quite unsuited to a sporting dog such as a setter.

It is of particular interest, then, to see in colour plate 17 the same dog, but on a totally different base, this time rectangular in form, 4⅛ in. (10.5cm) long, i.e. some ⅜ in. (0.9cm) shorter than the base of the dog of figure 78. The underneath is identical to that of the Minton tasselled cushion bases and the Rockingham and Derby animal bases: flat and closed-in save for a small centrally located hole. It is, however, heavier than the bases associated with Rockingham or Derby models, and is decorated in a style characteristic of the Minton artists — note the use of two single gilt lines running around the edges of the base enclosing a gilt

Figure 78. Minton setter in biscuit lying recumbent on a tasselled cushion, 4½in. (11.4cm) long, c.1830-40.

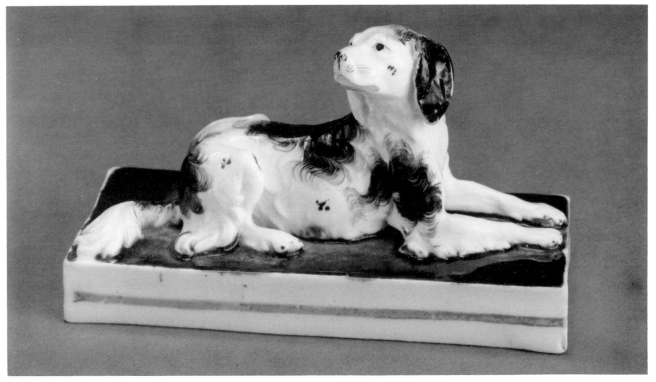

Figure 79. Staffordshire black and white setter lying recumbent on a gros bleu rectangular base edged in white and gold, 4⅜in. (11.1cm) long. c.1830-40.

101

Figure 80. Staffordshire finely modelled setter with chestnut brown patches, its head turned back and looking upwards, its right front paw and tail slightly overhanging the rectangular base, 4¾ in. (12.1cm) long, c.1830-40.

pattern (cf. plates 128, 129, 140, 142, 145 and 146 of G.A. Godden's *Minton Pottery and Porcelain*). More importantly, the top and bottom, where the two gilt lines appear, are slightly raised, as also is the distinctive scrolling picked out in gold. This raised moulding appears in identical form on the oval base of the Newfoundland dog shown in illustration numbers 25 and 26 of the factory drawing book. The base appearing in colour plate 17 seems more appropriate for a setter than the tasselled cushion version. Presumably, in the case of the latter base, the repairer, in the exercise of artistic licence, departed from reality simply to produce a pleasing composition. It is interesting to note that a well-known Ralph Wood pottery model of a setter was also made to sit on a cushion base (see, for example, the illustration in Sotheby's catalogue of 6 December 1977, lot 214), and that the records of the Chamberlain factory reveal that even stags were sometimes modelled on cushions (see page 159).

Illustration no. 119 in the drawing book (see chapter 6, page 246) shows a setter sitting upright on a high mound base. The model was in fact 7in. (17.8cm) high in all and was later replaced in Parian by a 'Persian Greyhound' (figure 96).

STAFFORDSHIRE

Setters were occasionally produced by unidentified factories operating in Staffordshire during the period 1830-50. A particularly charming example is that shown in figure 79. The animal, white and black, lies on a gros-bleu rectangular base, 4⅜ in. (11.1cm) long. A truly magnificent setter appears in figure 80, its modelling excelling its Rockingham, Derby and Minton counterparts. The head is turned back and looks upwards (presumably at game in flight, as depicted in some engraving from which the pose was surely taken) and the front right paw and the tail overhang the rectangular base on which it lies recumbent. It is decorated with chestnut brown patches and is 4¾in. (12.1cm) in length. It must have come from one of the larger concerns in Staffordshire, but so far it has proved impossible to assign it with any confidence to any particular factory.

POINTERS

There appears in Daniel's *Rural Sports,* an interesting engraving by J. Scott of a 'Spanish Pointer' after George Stubbs' painting. The Spanish pointer was brought to this country from Spain in the 1650s and was probably reintroduced after the Treaty of Utrecht in 1713. However, it was too slow to satisfy the needs of the nineteenth century sportsman, and was developed by cross-breeding into what became known as the 'English Pointer'. The latter, while retaining the 'nose' of the former proved to be a tireless hunter, a good stayer and swift enough to run down a leveret. Examples of English pointers in the form of the celebrated dog 'Dash' and the pair 'Pluto and Juno' appear in Daniel's *Rural Sports.* They have lost the heavy shoulders and short muzzle of the original Spanish pointer.

ROCKINGHAM

The Rockingham factory produced a Spanish pointer (No 93), figure 82. It is clearly based on the engraving of George Stubbs' painting. Only one example has so far been recorded and this is the reverse of the engraving. It is a bitch, while the engraving is of a dog. Manifestly, Spanish pointers must have been made at Swinton in pairs.

A Rockingham model of what appears to be an English pointer is shown in figure 81. It is white and gilt and is incised 'No 101'. It has an identical Derby counterpart (figure 121b). This model was produced both as a dog and as a bitch. A considerably larger model of an English pointer was made at Swinton (No 85). One example only is recorded. It is a bitch, white with painted facial markings, standing, with a tree support, on a rocky base flecked with green and gold. It is 4½in. (11.4cm) high and 4⅝in. (11.7cm) long. It has a Cl 1 mark and is incised 'No 85'. Presumably, it was made to go with a companion dog in reverse.

DERBY

The Derby factory manufactured a pointer 4⅛in. (10.5cm) high by 6½in. (16.5cm) long (figure 77) as a companion in reverse to the setter

Figure 81. Rockingham white and gilt pointer, looking upwards, seated on an oval base, 3in. (7.6cm) high. Incised 'No 101'. Impressed mark. 1826-30. Cf. the Derby equivalent, figure 121b. (*Mr and Mrs Dunnington*)

Figure 82. Rockingham Spanish pointer bitch, white and gilt, trotting, after George Stubbs, 4½ in. (11.4cm) long. Incised 'No 93'. Impressed mark. 1826-30. Presumably there was a companion dog. *(T.A. Lockett Esq.)*

mentioned above. However, as explained earlier, although nineteenth century examples are known, the model originated in the eighteenth century. An interesting description of a marked pointer appears in Sotheby's sale catalogue of 25 April 1978 (lot 133):

'A Derby Figure of a Pointer, with dark-brown patched fur and gilt collar, standing against a treestump on an oval plinth enamelled to simulate grass, *2½ in. crown, crossed batons and D mark in iron-red, early 19th century'*.

Presumably, this was a smaller version of the pointer model mentioned above.

The Derby factory also produced an English pointer identical to the Rockingham model, No 101. An example 2½ in. (6.4cm) high overall is shown in figure 121b. It sits on a green mound base, which in accordance with the usual Derby practice is flat underneath and is closed-in save for a small centrally located hole. It would seem that this dog is to be identified with

	Enamelled and gilt	
	s	d
Dogs from the Dresden Shepherd, each	1	0

included by Haslem in his list of Bow and Chelsea models. The dog that accompanies the Dresden shepherd (model no. 55 in Haslem's general list) was produced as an independent model in the eighteenth century (see

Figure 83. Two Derby pointers, one with black, the other with liver markings, each lying recumbent on a shaped scroll base painted with forget-me-nots and pink roses, 5in. (12.7cm) long, c.1830-40. *(Ron Beech)*

for example, Sotheby's 'English Pottery and Porcelain Sale', 18 May 1982, lot 177). The dog of figure 121b is a nineteenth century example.

Of the two nineteenth century dogs illustrated in figure 83, one is white and black whilst the other has liver markings. Each lies on a scrolled rococo base, 5in. (12.7cm) long. In a way typical of Derby, the underside of the base is flat and closed-in save for a small, centrally located hole. An unusual feature is the fine painting of pink roses and blue forget-me-nots on the top of the base. The possibility suggests itself that these dogs might be examples of

	Enamelled and gilt	
	s	d
London Pointer...each	1	6

referred to by Haslem immediately after 'Dogs from the Dresden Shepherd'. However, the rococo base indicates that the model was executed either before 1770 (after which time the rococo style gave way to the classical) or, on the revival of the rococo forms, after about 1830. The absence of any eighteenth century examples suggests that the model was created by an unknown Derby modeller some time after 1830. Support for this view can be found in the fact that the same model, this time with the underside of the base deeply recessed, was produced in Staffordshire porcelain during the period 1830 to 1840. Perhaps the modeller of the original Derby version moved on to some Staffordshire factory and reproduced his work there.[1] The reverse model was also made, as is apparent from the example illustrated in *The Connoisseur*, September 1922, p.37 (no. 6). The dog was black and white and the base was 'embellished with dainty roses upon its top'. One wonders whether it had forget-me-nots as well, which were simply not mentioned in the description. The gilding was identical to that of the dogs of figure 83.

---

1. Just to complicate the matter, the same model was produced by the Samuel Alcock factory, see overleaf.

CHAMBERLAIN

A pointer with the impressed mark 'CHAMBERLAIN' in capitals was sold at Sotheby's on 25 February 1986, lot 345. White with brown patches and supported by a tree stump, it stood on a green and gilt mound base 2in. (5.1cm) high overall. It is clear from the mark that it was not made before 1847.

GRAINGER LEE & CO., WORCESTER

It is apparent from the Grainger Lee pattern book that the factory produced a trotting pointer (see chapter 6, page 236). Seemingly, it was made in reverse, though one of the animals appearing in the pattern book has an uncharacteristic fluffy tail. No porcelain examples are recorded.

MINTON

The finely modelled pointer shown in colour plate 18, from the Minton factory, is illustration no. 31 in the drawing book (see chapter 6, page 245). It is trotting beside a supporting tree on a green mound base, 3½in. (8.9cm) in length. A seated dog, which seems to be a pointer, is included in the Minton group from 'Tom Jones', design number 87, an example of which is illustrated in plate 144 of G.A. Godden's *Minton Pottery and Porcelain*.

SAMUEL ALCOCK

A Samuel Alcock pointer is known, numbered 108. Like the Minton pointer, the dog is modelled trotting beside a tree support on an oval base, 6in. (15.2cm) long. An example appeared at the Olympia Fine Art and Antiques Fair 1986. The dog was white with black patches and the base was light yellow.

Another version of a pointer, numbered '13', similar to the Derby pointer of figure 83, was also produced by the Samuel Alcock factory. It is illustrated in plate 47 of *Staffordshire Porcelain*. It is 5in. (12.7cm) long.

MINOR STAFFORDSHIRE FACTORIES

Pointers were produced by various Staffordshire factories operating during the period 1830-50. The two illustrated in figure 84 are white with liver markings, each animal standing on a rocky mound base edged with a gilt line, 1¾in. (4.4cm) long. Larger versions were also made. A reverse model appears in plate 134 of Bernard and Therle Hughes' *Collecting Miniature Antiques*. A particularly attractive group is recorded consisting of two pointers standing side by side, one slightly behind the other. The numeral '33' was written in red under the base.

Figure 84. Two Staffordshire pointers, white with liver markings, each standing on a rocky mound base edged with a gilt line, 1¾in. (4.4cm) long, c.1830-45.

GREAT DANES (OR DANISH DOGS)

As was stated earlier, the identification of a particular porcelain model with a particular contemporary breed of dog is not always easy, due to the genetic changes the breed has undergone. This is especially true of the Great Dane or, as it was sometimes called, the Danish dog. For a long time, the smooth coated Rockingham dog with pointed ears (No 87)

Figure 85. Two Rockingham white and gilt Great Danes, each lying recumbent on a rectangular base, 3¾in. (9.5cm) long, incised 'No 87'. Impressed mark. 1826-30.

Figure 86. Grainger Lee white and gilt Great Dane lying recumbent on a base edged with a continuous rope moulding, 3¼in. (8.3cm) long. Impressed 'GRAINGER LEE & CO WORCESTER', 1820-37.

shown in colour plate 19 and figure 85 left me wholly mystified as to its identity. Certainly it looks little like the modern Great Dane. However, an illustration in J.G. Woods' *The Illustrated Natural History* [1] resolved the matter, revealing the model to be in fact that of the Great Dane, as it then existed.

As its name suggests, the Great Dane was originally imported into this country from Denmark. It was used to accompany carriages and, during the master's absence to pay a call on an acquaintance, would guard the contents while the groom was fully occupied holding the horse's head. By the end of the eighteenth century the breed appeared in three different colours, fawn (colour plate 19), harlequin, and a bluish grey marbled with black. William Taplin in the *Sportsman's Cabinet* speaks of the dog in the following terms:

'The majestic and commanding aspect, bold muscular action, and elegant carriage of this dog would recommend him to notice, had he no other useful properties or points of attraction. Those he has already in possession we observe honoured in adding to the splendid pomp and magnificent retinues of the noble, wealthy and independent, before whose emblazoned vehicles he trots or gallops with a degree of dignity denoting no small consciousness of the patronage he is under and the state of grandeur he is selected to precede and support.'

Of the three Rockingham examples illustrated here (No 87) two are white and gilt (figure 85), the other fawn and gilt (colour plate 19). The rectangular base measures 3¾in. (9.5cm) in length. No other Rockingham model of a Great Dane is recorded. The other model shown here (figure 86) comes from the Grainger Lee factory. It is white and gilt, lying recumbent on a base 3¼ in. (8.3cm) in length, impressed faintly with the mark in capitals 'GRAINGER LEE & CO WORCESTER'. The dog from the factory's pattern book shown at page 235 looking at a rat in cage would also appear to be a Great Dane. However, no porcelain example is recorded.

Doubtless, however, one or more of the Staffordshire concerns operating during the period from 1830 to 1850 would have produced a certain number of Great Danes.

Figure 87. Pair of Staffordshire Dalmatians, each with a support standing on a mound base, their curled-over tails raised in the air, 3½ in. (8.9cm) high, c.1830-40. *(Grosvenor Antiques Ltd. and Mary Wise Antiques)*

1. *Mammalia*, p.257.

DALMATIANS

Certainly Staffordshire factories turned out Dalmatians, often lying recumbent on a cobalt-blue base. The Dalmatian, albeit smaller than the Great Dane, performed essentially the same function as the latter, that is to say, it ran with and protected carriages and their contents. An interesting pair of Staffordshire Dalmatians standing with erect tails are illustrated in figure 87.

Seemingly, one model is to be attributed to Samuel Alcock. For there is a reference in Sotheby's sale catalogue of 3 October, 1972, lot 35, to: 'A Rockingham [on no footing could it be Rockingham] Figure of a Dalmatian, sleepily emerging from his kennel surrounded by a border of green moss, gilt line-edged base, 2¼ in *impressed numeral 142.*'

MASTIFFS

The mastiff, if not native to this country, has certainly been here since at least the middle ages. Initially it was used as a guard dog, and very effective it was in this capacity. In 1586 William Harrison said of it in *The Description of England:* 'The mastiff is a huge, stubborn, ugly and impetuous hound, with a large frame that renders it slow of movement. Its natural savagery is increased by the course of training to which it is submitted, being pitted against bears, bulls, or lions, if the latter could be found.'

Apart from being a guard dog the mastiff was used for bull and bear baiting, but eventually it was replaced for this purpose by the bull-dog.

Being by virtue of its size an expensive dog to maintain, and having acquired an unsavoury reputation for sheep worrying, the mastiff fell out of favour. However, it was never forsaken altogether, and a model, lying recumbent with its tongue hanging out, was produced at Swinton (No 90). The only recorded example is shown in colour plate 20. It is interesting to note that virtually the same model, albeit in reverse (presumably after some unidentified engraving), was produced by Samuel Alcock (colour plate 21) with the impressed numeral 305. The latter model, which is 5 ½ in. (14cm) long, has a companion (colour plate 21), and accordingly it is reasonable to suppose that there is a Rockingham counterpart. However, so far no example has been discovered.

It is interesting to note that the King Street factory at Derby also produced a mastiff. An example in biscuit in a recumbent position 4 ¾ in. (12.1cm) long was sold at Sotheby's on 24 February 1987, lot 250. The Sampson Hancock mark shows it to have been manufactured after 1862. A mastiff in a recumbent position was also produced at the Royal Worcester factory at the commencement of its life (see item 37 in the factory list).[1]

---

1. Henry Sandon, *Royal Worcester Porcelain,* Appendix I.

FOXHOUNDS

By the end of the eighteenth century, the foxhound, which had started off very much a mongrel, had become the purest breed then existing. A fine pair were painted by George Stubbs (a reproduction of which is to be seen in Carson I. A. Ritchie's *The British Dog*). Another pair, by Reinagle, feature in *The Sportsman's Cabinet.* The qualities sought of a foxhound were a wide chest, a broad back, straight legs, a small head, a thin neck and a bushy tail.

Two toy dogs produced at Swinton's (Nos 71 and 74) (figure 88) appear to be foxhounds. They are extremely small, being only 1⅛ in. (2.8cm) and 1⅜ in. (3.5cm) high respectively. No others, apart from those shown here, are recorded as emanating from the Rockingham factory. Hounds of various sorts were, however, produced in Staffordshire during the period 1830-50. Two, each seemingly on a cobalt-blue base, are illustrated in figure 155 of Margaret Vivian's *Antique Collecting,* though they are erroneously attributed to Rockingham. Margaret Vivian points out in her book that the scarcity of hounds in porcelain is remarkable, in view of the large numbers of the actual hounds and their importance to the hunting community. However a particularly outstanding hound was produced by the Chamberlain factory. An example is illustrated in figure 89. It sits on a green stepped rectangular base with canted corners, 2⅝ in. (6.7cm) high in all. It is finely modelled, so much so that even the feathering of the animal's fur down its back can be seen clearly delineated in porcelain. The ears are beautifully formed, and the eyes are yellow. Presumably there was originally a companion bitch.

Figure 88. Two toy Rockingham foxhounds, white and gilt; one (left) 1⅛ in. (2.8cm) high, incised 'No 71'. Cl 1, the other (right), 1⅜ in. (3.5cm) high, incised 'No 74'. Cl 1. 1826-30.

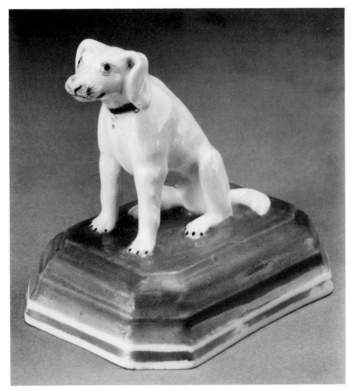

Figure 89. Chamberlain Worcester hound seated on a green stepped rectangular base with canted corners, 2⅝ in. (6.7cm) high, c.1820-40.

Figure 90. Rockingham shepherd with dog and sheep in biscuit, 7¾ in. (19.7cm) high. Incised 'No 58'. Impressed mark 1826-30. The dog would appear to be identical to that accompanying the shepherd in colour plate 24b and the sheep, with some adaptation, would appear to be the same as that shown in figures 100b and 101. *(John Gallagher Esq.)*

SHEEPDOGS

J.G. Wood, in his *The Illustrated Natural History*, depicts the sheepdog (described more aptly as 'the shepherd's dog') and says of it:[1] 'As the Sheep-dog is constantly exposed to the weather, it needs the protection of very thick and closely-set fur, which, in this Dog, is rather woolly in its character, and is especially heavy about the neck and breast... The

Figure 91. Rockingham shepherd with a white and black Continental dog at his feet, 7¼ in. (18.4cm) high. Incised 'No.4'. 1826-30. This is a copy of the Bow figure, which is in turn a copy of the Meissen figure.

muzzle of this Dog is sharp, its head is of moderate size, its eyes are very bright and intelligent, as might be expected in an animal of so much sagacity and ready resource in time of need. Its feet are strongly made, and sufficiently well protected to ensure severe work among the harsh stems of the heather on the hills, or the sharply-cutting stones of the high road. Probably on account of its constant exercise in the open air, and the hardy manner in which it is brought up, the Sheep-dog is perhaps the most untiring of our domesticated animals... As a general rule, the Sheep-dog cares very little for any one but his master, and so far from courting the notice or caresses of a stranger will coldly withdraw from them, and keep his distance. Even with other Dogs he rarely makes companionship, contenting himself with the society of his master alone.'

The dog which accompanies the shepherd of Rockingham model No 4 (second version) illustrated in colour plate 24b and the shepherd of model No 58 shown in figure 90 is, as we would expect, an excellent model of a sheepdog. Surprisingly, it seems never to appear separately from the group. The same is true of the Continental sheepdog that accompanies the first version of the Rockingham model No 4 (figure 91).

It is interesting to note that in the case of certain eighteenth century shepherd and dog groups (see, for example, colour plate J of my *Derby Porcelain 1750-70*) the dog wears a spiked collar. This is because the model is taken from a Meissen original. On the Continent, in those countries where the flock was still exposed to the attack of wolves, the dog was protected in this way, and was in fact used to guard the flock, not to drive it. The shepherd would control the direction of the flock by the use of 'a tame wether accustomed to feed from his hands. The favourite, however distant, obeys his call, and the rest follow'.[2] An alternative throat protection is worn by the dog in the Rockingham group of figure 91.

Although a sheepdog regularly accompanies the shepherd models produced by various porcelain factories during the nineteenth century, it seems rarely to appear as an individual model. An exception is the sheepdog lying on a rectangular base with rounded corners, illustrated in figure 92. It is white and gilt, is 4⅝in. (11.7cm) in length, and comes from the Grainger Lee factory. It bears under the base the impressed mark 'GRAINGER LEE & CO, WORCESTER'.

1. *Mammalia,* pp. 295, 297.
2. William Youatt's *The Dog* p.61.

NEWFOUNDLANDS

As the name suggests, this breed of dog came to this country from Newfoundland. There it was used as a draught animal. Teams consisting of three, four or five dogs were employed to drag sledges across the ice, often with loads of several hundredweight. They would travel without a driver, and on arrival at their destination they were unloaded, whereupon they would return home with the empty sledge. It was only then that they were fed, and often inadequately at that. The Newfoundland was docile

Figure 92. Grainger Lee white and gilt shepherd's dog lying recumbent, 4⅝ in. (11.7cm) long. Impressed 'GRAINGER LEE & CO WORCESTER', 1820-37.

Figure 93. Minton Newfoundland in biscuit standing with support on a rocky mound base, 4in. (10.2cm) high, c.1830-40. *(Grosvenor Antiques Ltd. and Mary Wise Antiques)*

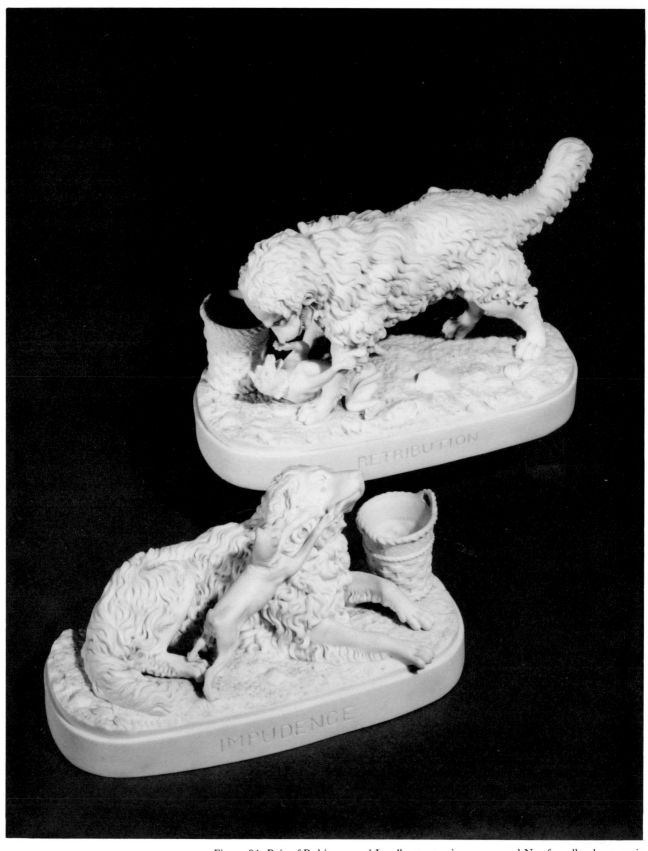

Figure 94. Pair of Robinson and Leadbeater terrier puppy and Newfoundland groups in Parian entitled 'Impudence' and 'Retribution' respectively, 11in. (27.9cm) long. Design registered 2 July 1872. (*Godden of Worthing Ltd.*)

and intelligent. In due course, its qualities became known to the English cod fishers who called at Newfoundland, and through their agency these dogs were introduced into their home ports and even into Scotland. The Newfoundland acquired a great reputation for saving sailors — sometimes the whole ship's company — and others from drowning. It was often employed on board both naval and merchant vessels, where it proved an ardent retriever of property and personnel. It frequently became the ship's mascot.

It was a short step from employment as a ship's dog to use as a working dog or pet.[1] As the Newfoundland had a great aptitude for retrieving it could be trained to perform all the duties of a gun-dog, and by the beginning of the nineteenth century, it was the second most popular dog. In 1803, in a musical afterpiece at the Drury Lane Theatre entitled *The Caravan,* a Newfoundland called Carlo created a sensation by plunging each night into water with an audible splash to rescue a child, a feat which was received by the audience with rapturous applause.[2]

Byron had a pet Newfoundland called 'Boatswain', on whose death he erected a monument, inscribing on the tomb an epitaph which concluded with the words: 'The poor dog! in life the firmest friend, The first to welcome, foremost to defend; Whose honest heart is still his master's own; Who labours, fights, lives, breathes for him alone.'

On 6 April 1803, as a result of a fight in Hyde Park between their respective Newfoundland dogs, Lt. Col. Montgomery and Capt. MacNamara R.N. fought a duel resulting in fatal consequences to the former and injury to the latter.

In view of the immense popularity of the Newfoundland at the beginning of the nineteenth century, it is surprising not to find it prolifically represented in porcelain during the period with which we are concerned. However, a model was produced by the Grainger Lee factory. It is in a standing position on a mound base, with its tongue hanging out, 4¾ in. (12.1cm) high. An example was sold by Sotheby's on 25 March

1. See the reference by Mrs Sherwood to 'our great Newfoundland house-dog' at p.47.
2. In *Memoirs of a Highland Lady* (ed. by Lady Strachey, published by John Murray, 1911) Elizabeth Grant of Rothiemurchus (afterwards Mrs Smith of Baltiboys) writes (at page 14) of the Spring of 1803: 'Amongst other indulgences this spring I was taken twice to the play, and once to Sadler's Wells with William. The first play was 'The Caravan'. John Kemble acted in it; the lover, and a very lugubrious one he seemed to be. The actor that delighted me was a dog, a real Newfoundland trained to leap into a cataract and bring dripping out of the water, *real* water, a doll representing a child which had spoken in the scene a few minutes before, and had then appeared to be dropped by a lady in distress while flying across a plank up at the top of the stage, the only bridge across the torrent. They could not persuade me [she was then six years old] the doll was not the real child: I thought it dead, drowned, and cried and sobbed so violently I was hardly to be pacified — not till all the audience had been attracted by the noise.'

1974, lot 152, and is illustrated in the sale catalogue. It bore the script mark in red 'Grainger, Lee & Co'. Another version, 6in. (15.2cm) long and also standing, was turned out at Derby. Sometimes this version can be found with a small boy or small girl riding on the dog in which event it is presumably identifiable with the John Whitaker models 'Boy and dog' and 'Girl and dog'. An example of the dog by itself, standing on an oval base, with the Bloor Derby mark, appears in *The Connoisseur,* September 1922, p.34 (illustration no. 11). Interestingly, it would seem to be the reverse of a dog depicted in a sand painting by B. Zobel illustrated in *The Connoisseur,* April 1927, (pl.III). That particular sand painting had a note on the back: 'A curious whole-length figure, "Nelson", the favourite dog of the Duke of York'.

What seems to be a Newfoundland appears in each of the two Parian groups illustrated in figure 94. In the first the Newfoundland, which is lying recumbent either asleep or resting, is being provoked by a terrier puppy ('Impudence') whilst the other Newfoundland, now thoroughly roused, is taking counter measures against its tormentor ('Retribution'). Each group was made by Robinson and Leadbeater and is 11in. (27.9cm) long, the design having been registered on 2 July 1872.

A Newfoundland appears in the Minton factory drawing book as illustration 21 (see chapter 6, page 244). Somewhat surprisingly, it is free-standing, i.e. without a base. Moreover, it has no support. No example is recorded, and one wonders whether in actual production the factory attached a base, for the biscuit Newfoundland shown in figure 93 would seem to be a Minton porcelain representation of the dog as drawn except that it stands on a base and has a support. The same model, ridden by a small boy with a sword in his hand to symbolise war or by a girl with a crook to symbolise peace, appears in illustrations 25 and 26 respectively of the drawing book. This time the dog does stand on a base. A porcelain example in biscuit of illustration no. 25 can be seen in G.A. Godden's *Minton Pottery and Porcelain,* plate 137. The base is oval with some raised mouldings around the edges, features which occur on the rectangular base of the setter of colour plate 17. Newfoundland dogs were also produced by some of the minor Staffordshire factories.

SALUKI OR PERSIAN GREYHOUND

The saluki is an Arab dog, the origin of which goes back thousands of years, first appearing in Egyptian carvings of about 6000 to 5000 BC. Throughout the nineteenth century it was used for hunting gazelles, often in conjunction with hawks. Salukis can gallop for miles over the sands of Arabia and over rough ground that would break every bone in an English

Figure 95. Samuel Alcock saluki or Persian greyhound, white with grey markings, seated on a yellow rocky base, 3½in. (8.9cm) high. Impressed '311', c.1830-45.

Figure 96. Minton Persian greyhound in Parian seated on a high rocky base, 7in. (17.8cm) high, no. 119 in the factory drawing book, c.1850-70.

greyhound. Whereas gazelles are credited with speeds of between 45 and 52 mph, salukis reach between 37 and 40 mph. Nevertheless, although slower than the gazelle, this handicap was compensated for in the following manner. The dogs would separate a gazelle from the bewildered herd and would then, by their various manoeuvres, so terrorise the animal that it eventually tired. They would then draw level with it and strike. Sometimes they would chase a gazelle in a circle, eventually killing it at the point where the race began. When used in conjunction with a hawk, the saluki was slipped from its leash when the bird was released, and pursued the game by following its flight. When the hawk 'stooped' on the gazelle, the saluki was expected to come up and hold the creature until the riders arrived for the kill.

In Persia the saluki was known as the 'Persian greyhound'. An interesting print exists of a Persian greyhound bitch, 'Zillah' after the painting by C. Hamilton. A note on the back states that the animal was 'the property of Mr George Lock, Kentish Town, bred in the Zoological Gardens, Regent's Park, 1835. She is the only thoroughbred bitch at present in this country'. It was not until 1897 that the saluki was properly introduced into this country and it was not registered as a breed by the Kennel Club until 1922. Salukis rarely feature in porcelain.

SAMUEL ALCOCK

However, an interesting porcelain saluki is recorded from the Samuel Alcock factory. Impressed with the number 311, it is illustrated in figure 95. White with grey markings, it sits on a yellow rocky base, 3½ in. (8.9cm) high in all.

MINTON

The same model, but on a larger scale and on a deep rocky base, was executed by the Minton factory in Parian. It is number 119 in the factory drawing book and replaced a setter in biscuit, which previously appeared in the list under that number. An example, 7in. (17.8cm) high, is illustrated in figure 96. The model is often paired with no. 120 (figure 29), an Italian greyhound, although the real dogs they represent are quite dissimilar in size.

MISCELLANEOUS DOGS

Henry Sandon has in his *Royal Worcester Porcelain* shown from examination of the factory records that in 1873 the factory modelled a Skye terrier (in two sizes) (item 374 in the factory list), in 1874 a spitz dog (item 443) and a St. Bernard (item 444), and in 1876 a dachshund (item 550). Examples of a Skye terrier and a St. Bernard are illustrated in figure 35b and c. It

Figure 97. Rockingham dog looking at a rat, in biscuit, 5in. (12.7cm) long. Incised 'No 89'. Impressed mark. 1826-30.

should also be mentioned that in 1862 the factory modelled a group of 'dogs and rat' (item 25) and a group of 'dog and pheasant'. The Minton factory produced a 'wolf dog' as item 227 in its drawing book (see chapter 6, page 247). Seemingly, several dogs of this breed were in 1830 in the Regent's Park Zoo, for in *The Gardens and Menagerie of the Zoological Society Delineated,* published in 1831, the following comment is to be found:[1] 'Although regarded by Buffon, in common with the Shepherd's Dog, as an example of the species in the very lowest stage of cultivation, but one degree removed from a state of nature, the present variety is in fact one of the most intellectual of all the races of Dogs... By continued intercourse with man these valuable dogs have become more highly improved in all that constitutes moral superiority, than almost any other breed; the Newfoundland Dog, the Esquimaux, and the Spaniel, alone evincing an equal share of docility, fidelity, and intelligence. According to Buffon, the breed in question are denominated Wolf-Dogs: ''because they resemble the Wolf in ears and length of hair''. Their ears, it is true, are of small size, and frequently erect; but they have a strong tendency to become pendulous, as is actually the case in the Society's specimens,

Figure 98. Rockingham white and gilt dog looking at a rat, 5in. (12.7cm) long. (Model No 89 but unnumbered). Cl 1. 1826-30.

and thereby approach more closely to the Spaniels. Their hair too is long and straight, but by no means like that of the Wolf; and we can hardly conceive a greater contrast in physiognomy and general appearance than is presented by the two animals. Others again have derived their name from the services which they render to the shepherd in protecting his flock from the nightly marauder; but although strong-built and muscular both in body and limb, they seem too gentle in their disposition to be peculiarly adapted for pulling down so powerful and so ferocious an animal as the Wolf...' Presumably the Minton wolf-dog was only executed in Parian and no example has so far come to light.

---

1. At pp.257, 258.

UNIDENTIFIED DOGS

Reference has been made earlier to the difficulty sometimes encountered of identifying a particular porcelain model with the breed it was intended to represent. I confess myself defeated where the Rockingham dog (No 89) is concerned. It is really part, albeit the major part, of a group, for it stands looking at a rat. Possibly it was intended to represent an Esquimaux dog, but lacks the correct tail. Only two examples of this

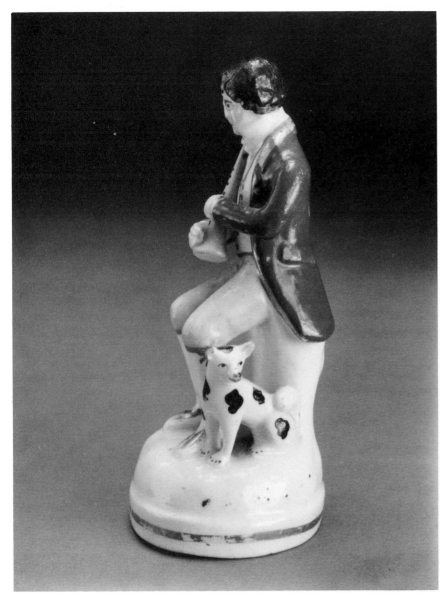

Figure 99. Staffordshire seated musician, with a green coat, white waistcoat and pink breeches, accompanied by his black and white dog seated at his feet, 4½ in. (11.4cm) high, c.1840-50.

group are recorded, one in biscuit (figure 97), the other white, on a white and gilt base (figure 98).

The Minton factory modelled as item 46 in its list what it calls a 'Russian Dog on cushion' (see page 246). It is difficult to say what breed of dog this is. It looks like an English greyhound with a somewhat burly tail. Seemingly a short-coated animal, it cannot be identified with a Russian greyhound or borzoi and no example is recorded. The dog from the Grainger Lee pattern book shown at page 234 together with what appears to be the same dog in reverse illustrated at page 235 is not easy to identify. Possibly it is an Esquimaux dog.

Figure 99 shows a dog accompanying a musician. Here again it is difficult to identify the breed in question.

Colour Plate 22. Pair of Rockingham sheep (left and right), the ram 2½ in. (6.4cm) long, marked 'Cl 2', the ewe 2¼ in. (5.7cm) long, marked 'Cl 1', each incised 'No 108', together with a white ewe, decorated with a gilt garland, on a green base (centre), 2¼ in. (5.7cm) long also incised 'No 108'. 1826-30.

2. Animals of the Farm

Not surprisingly, the English porcelain factories of the nineteenth century turned out replicas of animals found on the farm, particularly sheep, and to a lesser extent cows, bulls, horses and goats.

Sheep

During the period 1800-1850 Great Britain was still essentially agricultural and sheep were an important element in her economy. Different parts of the country tended to produce different breeds, but the numerous porcelain replicas do not seem to be easily, if at all, identifiable with any particular contemporary breed. They were usually made in pairs; the ram with horns, the ewe without. However, it is interesting to note that by about 1830 horned sheep had largely disappeared from the countryside, so that from this time the porcelain replicas of rams with horns were really recalling an earlier period.

Thus, W. Youatt writing in 1837 says: 'It has already been stated that the primitive sheep were probably horned. Those which the Israelites possessed during their wanderings in the desert undoubtedly were so. The polled breed springs from some accidental variety, and was cherished on account of the superior quietness of the animal and his aptitude to fatten.

Of these points in modern sheep there can be no doubt. Half a century has scarcely passed since the rams of the Romney-marsh breed were all of them horned. At a little greater distance of time, the Midland long-woolled sheep were horned. At the present day almost all the long-woolled sheep, and the best of the short-woolled are polled, and he would be a bad farmer who would endeavour to recall this useless appendage.'[1]

A distinctive feature of sheep is their wool and this was represented in porcelain in four different ways. The first was by moulding the body of the animal to delineate the contours of the fleece. According to B. and T. Hughes in their *Collecting Miniature Antiques*[2] this was achieved by the use of 'a quill notched at the point like the teeth of a saw'. This method of representing wool was the original technique and went back to the middle of the eighteenth century when porcelain production in this country first began to be established (see for example, the Planché ram and ewe in plate 31 of my *Derby Porcelain 1750-70*). This technique virtually ceased around 1830 and thereafter one of the other three methods was used. This is clear from a comparison between the techniques employed on models which are known to have been produced prior to 1831, e.g. those of the Rockingham,[3] Derby and Charles Bourne factories, and the techniques used on models known, whether from marked examples or otherwise, to have been made after 1830. Further information on the dateline which divides the original from the later techniques is obtainable by comparing the different methods of representing wool on poodles. The Minton drawing book which depicts models around 1831 clearly shows poodles where the new practices have been adopted.

Of the three post-1830 techniques, the first, used in the finest work, consisted of applying extremely thin threads of porcelain to the body of the animal (figure 109. See also the same technique applied to the mane of the lion of figure 144). The second technique involved adding small granules of porcelain and glazing them together to present a fuzzy or rough texture (figure 111), and the third involved applying a thin coating of particularly small granules to give a somewhat 'pebble-dash' effect (see figure 55).

Porcelain sheep were turned out in profusion by the many minor Staffordshire factories operating during the period 1830-50, but they were also manufactured at varying dates by the great concerns listed below.

---

1. *Sheep, their Breeds, Management and Diseases,* p.363.
2. At p.99.
3. Except seemingly for model No 98 (see page 127).

Figure 100a (left). Rockingham lamb, with brown patches, on a green round base edged with a gilt line, 1⅝in. (4.1cm) long. Incised 'No 109'. Cl 2. 1826-30. b (right). Rockingham ewe, with brown patches, lying on a green oval base edged at the top with a gilt line, 3in. (7.6cm) long. Incised 'No 100'. Cl 2. 1826-30.

ROCKINGHAM

The Rockingham factory produced a variety of different sheep and lambs. Some accompany human figures, e.g. the shepherdess (No 4) of colour plate 24, the girl (No 44) of colour plate 23 and the biscuit girls (Nos 26 and 35) of figures 103 and 104, but sheep and lambs were also modelled independently. Thus, an individual ewe (No 100), figures 100b and 101, and an individual lamb (No 109), figure 100a, are recorded, the

Figure 101. Rockingham white and gilt ewe recumbent on an oval base, 3in. (7.6cm) long, incised 'No 100'. Cl 1. 1826-30.

former lying recumbent on an oval base, 3in. (7.6cm) in length, the latter on a round base 1⅝in. (4.1cm) in diameter. Further, a pair comprising a ram and a ewe (No 108), 2½in. (6.4cm) and 2¼in. (5.7cm) long respectively, are also known. Examples exist in white and gold (figure 105 — note the gilt garlands around the neck), in enamel colours and gold (colour plate 22), and unusually in a combination of decoration where the sheep is white and gold, whilst the base is coloured and edged with a gilt line (colour plate 22). The wool is normally represented by the moulding of the animal's body. However an exception seems to be model No 98. An example appeared at the Boothman Smallwood sale (conducted by Christie's South Kensington on 26 and 27 April 1989) lot 1031: 'A ROCKINGHAM BISCUIT STANDING SHEEP with encrusted fleece and supported by a tree-stump on an oval rockwork base...impressed Rockingham Works Brameld and incised No 98...3⅛in. (8cm) high'.

DERBY

There is a reference in Haslem's list of 'Bow and Chelsea models' to:

	Enamelled and gilt		Biscuit	
	s	d	s	d
Fleecy Sheep, each	-	-	5	0

Figure 102. Derby ewe in biscuit lying on an oval base, 3½in. (8.9cm) long, c.1810-30. Compare this model with the Rockingham ewe in figures 100b and 101.

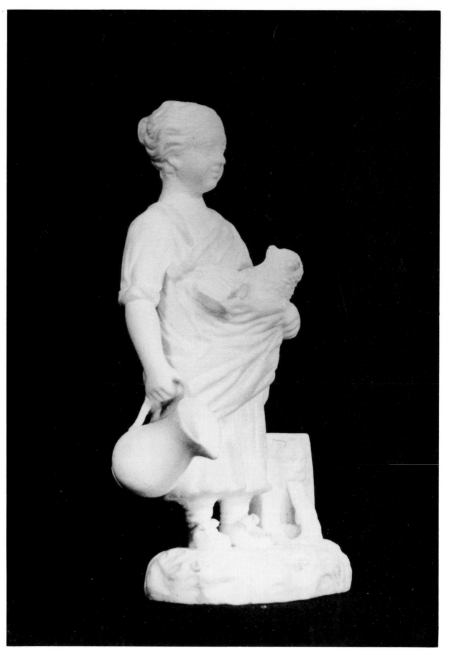

Figure 103. Rockingham girl with a lamb in biscuit, 5½in. (14cm) high. Incised 'No 26'. 1826-30.

Although it is impossible to be certain, the sheep of figure 102 would appear to be an example of the above 'fleecy sheep'. It lies recumbent on an oval base similar to the Rockingham model of figures 100b and 101 (No 100). The example shown is in biscuit and is slightly larger than its Rockingham counterpart, being 3½in. (8.9cm) in length.

Figure 104. Rockingham boy with dog (left) and girl with lamb (right) in biscuit, each on a pierced scroll base, 5¾ in. (14.6cm) high. Incised 'No 35'. Impressed mark. 1826-30. These models, probably the work of George Cocker, are more frequently found in Derby porcelain.

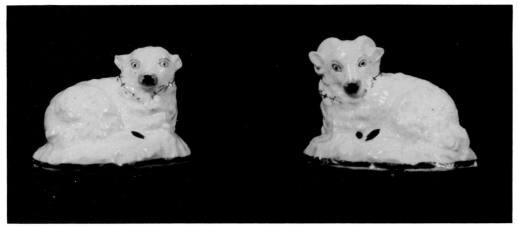

Figure 105. Pair of Rockingham white and gilt sheep lying recumbent on an oval rocky base. The ram is 2½ in. (6.4cm) long, the ewe is 2¼ in. (5.7cm). Incised 'No 108'. Impressed mark. 1826-30.

Figure 106. Pair of Derby white and gilt sheep with bocage lying recumbent on an oval rocky base, the ram 2½in. (6.4cm) long, the ewe 2¼in. (5.7cm), c.1810-30. These Derby models sometimes appear without bocage and are then easily confused with Rockingham sheep.

In the list of unnumbered models referred to by Haslem there are to be found:

	Enamelled and gilt	
	s	d
Large Sheep and Lambs, per pair, Holmes	7	0
Sheep lying down, ditto, ditto	4	0
Standing sheep, ditto, ditto	4	0
Ditto, ditto, two smaller sizes, ditto		
Lambs with Sprigs, per pair, Chelsea	2	0
Ditto without ditto, each, ditto	0	10

Charles Holmes is known to have been working as a modeller in the early part of the nineteenth century. The difficulty lies in identifying his work. Presumably the 'Large Sheep and Lambs' are the pair of groups from time to time encountered consisting of a ram with a recumbent lamb and a ewe suckling a lamb. The other sheep have not so far been identified.

The so-called Chelsea lamb is seen often enough in the eighteenth century and was carried over into the nineteenth. Sometimes it is, in the latter century, accompanied by a ram in reverse, the lamb being treated in the context as a ewe. They appear sometimes in biscuit, sometimes in white and gold, and sometimes decorated in enamel colours and gold. They are identical to the Rockingham ewe and ram (No 108). Unlike the Rockingham version the Derby ewe and ram sometimes have a tree behind them as in figure 106.

Figure 107. Two toy Derby biscuit sheep lying recumbent, each 1¼ in. (3.2cm) long, c.1830-45. These may be the work of George Cocker or Robert Blore.

In the list of models attributed by Haslem to Edward Keys there appears the following:

	Biscuit	
	s	d
Small Standing Sheep	7	0

Unfortunately, this particlar model has not been identified, but judging by the price it is, notwithstanding the adjective 'small', still reasonably large, though perhaps 'sheep' is to be interpreted in the plural, embracing a pair.

The two miniature sheep in biscuit (each with a typical Derby base, i.e. flat and completely closed in save for a round hole in the centre), which are illustrated in figure 107, almost certainly come from the town of Derby, but it is problematical whether they were products of the great Derby factory then being run by Robert Bloor. The representation of the wool by means of the moulding of the animal's body indicates that the sheep were probably made before about 1831. The paste is chalky, and the animals may well have been turned out by George Cocker after he left the Derby factory in 1825, for in 1826 in partnership with John Whitaker senior, also from the Derby factory, he set up a small china works in Friar Gate, Derby and produced, among other things, small animals. The partnership only lasted a year, but thereafter George Cocker continued on his own with the aid of his wife, his two sons, his three daughters and a nephew, until his move in 1840 to London. Alternatively the sheep may be the products of Robert Blore. Examples of his work have been recorded with 'Blore' incised in script under the base. Finally, an interesting ewe lying recumbent on a mound base with distinctive scroll edges from the Sampson Hancock factory at King St, Derby (1849-1935) is illustrated in figure 23 of Gilhespy and Budd's *Royal Crown Derby China.*

131

SWANSEA

During the period 1817 to 1822 when the porcelain factory at Swansea was under the control of Timothy Bevington and his son, John, an interesting recumbent ram, 4¼ in. (10.8cm) long (figure 109) was modelled by Isaac Woods, who after accompanying Billingsley and Walker from Nantgarw stayed on with the Bevingtons.

Some twelve examples of this model, all in biscuit, are recorded, two of which (marked 'BEVINGTON AND CO, SWANSEA 1.W' impressed) are illustrated in W.D. John's *Swansea Porcelain,* plate 57A. Another example can be seen in the Victoria and Albert Museum. An interesting feature of this model is that, contrary to the general rule that prior to about 1831 the wool on a sheep is represented by the moulding of the porcelain, in this case the wool is represented by the application of separate threads of china, a technique normally associated with the later period (see page 125).

One would have expected a companion ewe, but as some twelve examples of the ram have been recorded, but none of any corresponding ewe, it may be that the latter was simply never modelled.

W.D. John also illustrates (*Swansea Porcelain,* plates 57A and 58C) a standing ewe and a standing ram, each in biscuit, which he attributes to Swansea. However, they are unmarked and the attribution should be treated with caution.

CHAMBERLAIN

In figure 108a is a ewe from the Chamberlain factory. It lies recumbent on a green high-mound oval base, 2¼ in. (5.7cm) long. The wool is delineated by means of the moulding of the porcelain, and the mark 'Chamberlains Worcester' appears in script under the base. Presumably there is a reverse in the form of a ram. Another sheep model of the factory is recorded in which the animal, 1⅝ in. (4.1cm) high, lies on a flat oval base.

GRAINGER LEE & CO., WORCESTER

Although no Grainger Lee sheep has been identified, it is difficult to believe that the factory never made one. It is far more likely that as yet an example has simply not come to light.

MINTON

No independent model of a Minton sheep is recorded. However, included in the factory drawing book as designs 34-36 are: '34 Sheep Fold; 35 Large Sheep Fold; 36 Small Sheep Fold'. Unfortunately illustrations do not accompany any of those items, so that we do not know what form they took, and so far no porcelain examples have come to light. Presumably

Figure 108a. (left). Chamberlain Worcester white sheep, recumbent on a green oval base, 2¼ in. (5.7cm) long, marked 'Chamberlains Worcester' in script, c.1820-30. b (right). Staffordshire toy white sheep standing on a mound base with a hollow tree stump behind, 1⅜ in. (4.1cm) long, c.1830-45.

Figure 109. Swansea ram in biscuit lying recumbent on an oval base, 4¼ in. (10.8cm) long. Modelled by Isaac Wood. 1817-22. (*Sotheby's*)

sheep were included in each variety of fold, but were not made as independent models.

The Rockingham girl holding a lamb shown in figure 103 was reproduced at Minton as item no. 39 in the drawing book (see chapter 6, page 243). The shepherdess appearing as model no. 80 has a sheep by her side and model no. 82 shows a seated man shearing a sheep.

CHARLES BOURNE

The Charles Bourne factory produced a distinctive pair of sheep, both the ram and the ewe lying recumbent on an oval base. They were made in two sizes, either 3½ in. (8.9cm) or 2¼ in. (5.7cm) in length. A pair of the larger version are illustrated in figure 110. They rest on a green base edged with a gilt band. Each has a black muzzle and orange/red lips and eyes, the ram with gilt horns. A pair of the smaller version, where the ram and ewe lie on a matt-blue base, is illustrated in plate 378 of G.A. Godden's *Staffordshire Porcelain*. These animals, together with those of figure 110, were made somewhere between 1817 and 1830 and the wool is represented by the moulding of the porcelain. Under the base of each is the painted mark 'CB'.

SAMUEL ALCOCK

The ram lying on a yellow rocky mound base shown in figure 111 is one of a pair. The other, a ewe, is the exact reverse of the example illustrated. Each measures 2¾ in. (7cm) in length. The model is usually impressed with the number 86 (or if viewed the other way up, 98). That this model comes from the Samuel Alcock factory is proved beyond any doubt by the survival of an example from under the foundation stone of the new factory erected in 1839. Sometimes the ram appears as the reverse of the example shown here, in which event the positioning of the companion ewe is adjusted accordingly.

The pair of sheep illustrated in figure 112 are similar in form to model 86, but considerably larger, measuring 3½ in. (8.9cm) in length. The ram is impressed with the numeral 8. The ewe does not have a number, but is impressed with a triangle. Both are white except for the coloured markings on the muzzle and feet and the naturally coloured horns. Another example of the ram is recorded where mistakenly the numeral 13 has been impressed, a number which properly belongs to a model of a recumbent pointer illustrated in plate 47 of G.A. Godden's *Staffordshire Porcelain*. The ram and ewe of figure 113 are substantially the same models as the pair of figure 112 — they are, however, reversed — but they lie on a somewhat higher mound base, 3¾ in. (9.5cm) long,

Figure 110. Pair of Charles Bourne sheep, each on green oval base, 3½in. (8.9cm) long, CB mark, 1817-30. *(Messrs Graham & Oxley)*

decorated in yellow. Both are impressed with the number 6 (or possibly 9). The ram also has an impressed cross. They are interesting for their unusual grey painted faces and grey legs and, in the case of the ram, for the horns that curl right round the animal's face.

The Samuel Alcock factory also produced a charming, albeit small, group comprising a sheep and lamb, the latter lying in front of the

Figure 111. Samuel Alcock ram lying recumbent on a yellow mound base edged with a gilt line, 2¾in. (7cm) long. Impressed '86' or '98', c.1830-45.

Figure 112. Pair of Samuel Alcock white and gilt sheep, with naturally coloured horns and black markings on the muzzle, lying recumbent on mound bases, 3½in. (8.9cm) long. Impressed '8', c.1830-45.

former, on a mound base backed by a flowering tree. The group bears the impressed number 168.

The white and gilt sheep with two hollow trunks (used as a flowerholder) on a base 5in. (12.7cm) long, illustrated in figure 114, may also have come from the Samuel Alcock factory. The hollow tree trunks and the base are similar to those of a Samuel Alcock group impressed with the number 135 and consisting of a naturalistic scene of rabbits playing

Figure 113. Pair of Samuel Alcock sheep with grey painted faces, on yellow rocky bases edged with a gilt line, 3¾in. (9.5cm) long. Impressed '6' or '9', c.1830-45.

Figure 114. Staffordshire white sheep lying between flower-holders which are in the form of tree-trunks, on a base edged with gold, 5in. (12.7cm) long, c.1830-40. (Possibly from the Samuel Alcock factory.)

on a grassy mound (figure 44b). Although the porcelain of the group of figure 114 is of a higher order than that of the general run of Alcock models, it would seem that the factory turned out a wide range of qualities, presumably reflected in different selling prices.

However, there can be no uncertainty as to the origin of the well-modelled sheep that accompanies the shepherdess of figure 115. For the group, which stands 7⅞in. (20cm) high, carries under the base the Samuel Alcock factory mark. The group is made of Parian, and as such belongs to the second half of the century.

LLOYD SHELTON

No independent model of a sheep from this factory is recorded. However, a sheep appears in a group of a shepherd and sheep and another of a shepherdess and sheep illustrated in plate 151 of Anthony Oliver's *Staffordshire Pottery*. In the case of the former group, sometimes a dog is substituted for the sheep (see the example in the City Museum and Art Gallery, Stoke-on-Trent illustrated in G.A. Godden's *An Illustrated Encyclopaedia of British Pottery and Porcelain,* plate 352).

Figure 115. Samuel Alcock girl and lamb group in Parian, on an oval base, 7 ⅞ in. (20cm) high. Factory mark, c.1850-70.

Figure 116. Staffordshire white sheep with black eyes and toes, a flower-holder behind in the form of a hollow tree trunk, 3⅜ in. (8.6cm) long, c.1830-40.

MINOR STAFFORDSHIRE FACTORIES

Although sheep seem always to have been a popular subject for representation in porcelain right from the commencement of porcelain manufacture in this country, they appear to have attracted particular public attention during the period 1830-50, and were produced in profusion by the numerous minor Staffordshire concerns then operative. As in the case of poodles, which were likewise turned out during this period in vast quantities, their fleece was represented by the application of threads or granules of porcelain in the way described at page 125. Why this unprecedented popularity should have prevailed at the time is unknown. As the industrial revolution began to make itself felt over an ever-increasing area of the country, was there a growing yearning for the countryside conveniently symbolised by the image of the sheep? Or was it that the new technique of representing wool on sheep (and, for that matter, on poodles as well) was particularly easy to execute and therefore an encouragement to the production of animals having such wool? Or was it a combination of these reasons that made sheep so fashionable during the period 1830-50? Whatever the cause, the fact is that the

Figure 117. Pair of Staffordshire sheep, the ram with yellow horns, each standing on a base supported by four paw feet, 3⅝ in. (9.2cm) high, 2¾ in. (7cm) long, c.1830-45.

Figure 118. Staffordshire ram of the kind shown in the preceding plate together with a Staffordshire ewe supported by a tree trunk, 3⅛ in. (7.9cm) long, c.1830-45.

Colour Plate 23. Two Rockingham girl and lamb groups, each 3¾ in. (9.5cm) high and
incised 'No.44', one with a Cl 2, the other with an impressed mark. 1826-30.

Figure 119. Staffordshire sheep with tree support standing on a mound base edged at the front with a gilt line, 5in. (12.7cm) high, c.1830-45.

Figure 120. Staffordshire girl and sheep on a square green tiered base, 4in. (10.2cm) high, c.1840-50.

numerous minor Staffordshire factories turned out sheep of varying quality in considerable profusion. They were generally produced as pairs, a ram and ewe, though generally today not more than one has survived. Sometimes the sheep are standing, sometimes sitting, sometimes without a supporting tree, sometimes with. A selection is shown in figures 116-119. The animal that the girl of figure 120 is fondling looks more like a sheep than a lamb.

Horses

The importance of the horse to the contemporary economy, both as an animal on which to travel from point to point and as a beast of burden, cannot be overstressed. It is all the more remarkable, then, that horses in porcelain, whether in the eighteenth or nineteenth century, feature very rarely in this country. Why this should be so is something of a mystery. Bronze horses are frequent enough. Perhaps some of the explanation lies in the difficulty of producing porcelain horses in a standing position without some support such as a tree, and a support of this nature detracts from the line of the model. However, this cannot be a complete explanation. Perhaps for some reason or other there was not a strong contemporary demand, and without such a demand the supply was not forthcoming, or perhaps they were played with by nineteenth century children and in due course broken. Be that as it may, three nineteenth century factories are known to have produced horses — Derby, Royal Worcester and Minton.

DERBY

Included among the models attributed by Haslem to Edward Keys are:

	Enamelled and gilt	
	s	d
Large Horses	2	0
Pony	1	6

The animal illustrated in figure 121a, which has under its base a crown over crossed batons, dots and a 'D' written in red script indicating a Derby origin, is presumably an example of either the large horses or the pony referred to above. It is white, standing 3⅞ in. (9.8cm) high, on a base decorated with a shade of green distinctive of Derby animals (the same green appears on the base of the Derby dog shown next to it and on the base of the Derby cow of colour plate 25). Examples of this model are very rare indeed.

Margaret Vivian illustrates a similar or possibly the same example in figure 148 of her *Antique Collecting*. Writing in 1937 she says, at p.181: 'Fig. 148 shows a white horse without saddle or bridle, standing on a green base and bearing the late Duesbury Derby mark. This model is so scarce that during the many years that I have been collecting animal figures, I have been unable to acquire it. The one illustrated belongs to a friend who refuses to part with it, another was sent to America the day before the owner received my letter asking for it, and a third was recently sold by one dealer to another and cannot now be traced'.

Figure 121a (left). Derby white horse standing on a light green base, 3⅞in. (9.8cm) high. Crown over crossed batons, dots and 'D' mark in red, c.1810-25. b (right). Derby pointer, grey and white, looking upwards, seated on a light green base, 2½in. (6.4cm) high. 'Dog from the Dresden Shepherd', c.1830. (Cf. the Rockingham equivalent 'No 101' shown in figure 81.)

Apart from the example shown in figure 121a I have seen pass through the salerooms two further specimens, one white, the other black.[1] Moreover, an identical horse to that illustrated here is to be seen in the Victoria and Albert Museum, and a superlative example with a dappled brown coat standing on a green base appeared in the Loan Exhibition arranged by the Derby Porcelain International Society at the Burlington House Fair, September 1985 (item 82).[2] The latter had the 'crossed swords in blue' mark in imitation of Meissen.

Edward Keys made some thirteen models of Doctor Syntax after illustrations appearing in William Combe's publications on the adventures of Doctor Syntax. One such model portrays Doctor Syntax mounted on a horse with its front legs raised in the air. In view of its stance the horse had to have a support. The group, which is 6in. (15.2cm) high, rests on an oval base. An example with the Bloor mark is in the Derby Museum and is illustrated in Gilhespy's *Crown Derby Porcelain*, figure 169.

Also in the Derby Museum is a biscuit group, 5½in. (14cm) high, consisting of a galloping horse without saddle or bridle, carrying a naked

---

1. Sotheby's sale, 9 November 1976 lot 89. This black horse was marked in red with a crown, crossed batons, dots and a 'D'.
2. It passed through Sotheby's auction room on 25 March 1974 and is illustrated in the catalogue (lot 194a).

youth tied to its back whilst three fierce dogs or wolves are attacking it. The horse receives support from a tree. The group, which is of Derby origin and stands on an oval moss-encrusted base, is illustrated in Barrett and Thorpe's *Derby Porcelain,* plate 176. Presumably, the scene is of 'Mazeppa on Wild Horse', afte the story immortalised by Byron in his poem 'Mazeppa' published in 1819. According to that story Mazeppa, a page to Casimer V, King of Poland, having been detected in an intrigue with the wife of a local magnate, was bound naked to a wild horse which, loosed and lashed into fury, carried its unwilling burden through rivers and forests all the way to the Ukraine. There the animal collapsed and died, whilst Mazeppa himself only just survived. Among the models attributed by Haslem to John Whitaker is a model of 'Mazeppa on Wild Horse' and presumably the group described above is that model.

However, at the Chelsea Antiques Fair of March 1986, there appeared another Derby model in biscuit, seemingly dealing with the same theme, but representing the final stage of Mazeppa's horrendous journey. The group consisted of two horses, without saddles or bridles; one had collapsed with a naked youth still tied to its back, whilst the other (with tree support) was standing upright, its head turned back to look at its fallen companion. Quite what the relevance was of the standing horse to the story is not clear. Again the group was on an oval moss-encrusted base. Presumably, this model was also the work of John Whitaker, although it is not included in Haslem's list of models attributed to his hand. It is difficult to see how this model rather than the one mentioned earlier can be the group 'Mazeppa on Wild Horse' because there are two horses, not one.

ROYAL WORCESTER

Henry Sandon's researches have revealed that, in 1875, the Royal Worcester factory modelled a horse and panniers as item 483 in its list. No porcelain example is recorded.

MINTON

Illustration no. 23 of the Minton drawing book shows a 'Horse Rampant' (see page 244). Whilst the two back legs are firmly on the oval mound base, the two front legs are raised in the air. The animal is supported by what appears to be a tree stump. It stands 4¼ in. (10.8cm) high. How many examples the factory made is, of course, unknown. But so far no specimen has been recorded. Having regard to the dearth of horses generally, it may be that the model is now extinct.

There are, however, various other Minton models to which reference should be made. Two are silhouette or flat-back figures — one of Don

Quixote on his horse, the other of his servant, Sancho Panza on a donkey, the latter supported by a tree. These two models appear as illustration nos. 8 and 7 respectively of the factory drawing book. Examples of Don Quixote on his horse are recorded. The Rotherham Museum has a coloured example, 4¾ in. (12.1cm) high, of Sancho Panza on his donkey (see G.A.. Godden's *Minton Pottery and Porcelain,* plate 129). The third model to which the reader's attention should be drawn is the group appearing as illustration no. 24 of the drawing book with the description 'Tom O'Shanter'. A man is seen riding a horse whilst a woman gives chase. So far no porcelain example has come to light. Finally, a French horse, presumably executed in Parian only, appears in the drawing as no. 286 (see page 250). Note also the two models of a horse being attacked by a lion illustrated in the drawing book as items 238 and 239.

Cows

Although cows are very much a feature of the English countryside, somewhat surprisingly they were only rarely represented in porcelain. Perhaps to the eyes of prospective purchasers cows did not have the same appeal as woolly sheep, and no manufacturer produces what he can not readily sell. During the nineteenth century the number of cow models seems to have been even less than was produced in the eighteenth century. Some are in the form of creamers, others in the form of animals pure and simple.

Most cow-creamers are of Staffordshire origin, although Derby examples are known. A reference to one of the latter is to be found in lot 293 of Christie's sale catalogue of 28 June 1971: 'A Bloor Derby Cow Creamer and Cover, the animal naturalistically modelled in lowing attitude, its body mottled in russet and with its tail curled over its back to form the handle, on a fluted gilt-edge base, 4¼ in. [in height] *mark printed in red.'* It measured 5¾ in. (14.6cm) in length. This model was continued at the King St. factory and is illustrated in its 1934/35 catalogue.

The Copeland factory also produced cow-creamers. An example was sold at Sotheby's sale on 25 March 1974 lot 157: 'A Copeland white-glazed Cow-Creamer and Cover standing four-square, its tail curled over to form the handle and standing on a fluted base 5½ in. *impressed COPELAND LO* 86...'

Apart from an unknown manufacturer's[1] particularly fine cow, lying recumbent on an oval mound base edged with a gilt line (about 6in. (15.2cm) in length) which appears in figure 123 — there was an example at the Olympia Fine Art and Antiques Fair 1986 — I can only bring to

Figure 122. Derby white and gilt cow and calf group with bocage, 5¾ in. (14.6cm) high, c.1810-30.

Figure 123. Staffordshire cow with gilt horns lying recumbent on a green oval mound base, 6in. (15.2cm) long, c.1830-40. Possibly Davenport. *(Grosvenor Antiques Ltd. and Mary Wise Antiques)*

mind cow models, other than creamers, from two identifiable factories, although doubtless other well-known concerns also turned them out, and in the fullness of time examples will come to light. These two factories are Derby and Chamberlain.

---

1. Possibly it was made by the Davenport factory.

DERBY

Among the models attributed by Haslem to Edward Keys are:

	Enamelled and gilt	
	s	d
Lean Cows, per pair	3	6

The lean-looking cow illustrated in colour plate 25 is presumably an example of this particular model. It stands 2¼in. (5.7cm) high without support, on a rectangular base with rounded corners, 3in. (7.6cm) long. The distinctive green of the base appears on the bases of the Derby horse and dog shown in figure 121. Marked examples are known.

A pair of cow and calf groups originally produced at Derby in the eighteenth century were referred to by Haslem in his list of 'Bow and Chelsea models'. The pair were priced 6s.6d. when enamelled and gilt and 9s.0d. when in biscuit and were continued into the nineteenth century. One such group, white and gilt, with bocage, is illustrated in figure 122. The group measures 5¾in. (14.6cm) high by 3½in. (8.9cm) long. Another example is illustrated in Sotheby's sale catalogue of 25 March 1974 (lot 194). Both the cow and calf were coloured in a shade of magenta, on a green mound base, but the really interesting feature was

Figure 124. Staffordshire bull, white with reddy-brown patches and black spots and with horns of grey, standing on a hollow oblong base with rounded corners, 4in. (10.2cm) long, c.1830-40.

the crown, crossed batons, dots and 'D' mark in red. Derby animals are so rarely found marked.

It is clear from the 1934/35 catalogue that the King St. factory produced a cow seemingly without a base. It may be that examples of this model were also turned out in the nineteenth century.

CHAMBERLAIN

The Chamberlain factory produced a model of a cow lying down on a mound base, rectangular in form, with canted corners. An example, with the animal in natural colours recumbent on a green base, edged with a gilt pattern, is to be seen in the Hove Museum. It is marked 'Chamberlain's Worcester' in red script and measures 2¾ in. (7.1cm) in length.

In addition, of course, cows were produced by unidentified factories throughout Staffordshire.

Bulls

Bulls are even rarer than cows. One in white standing on an oval base impressed with the Lloyd Shelton mark appeared as part of lot 220 of Sotheby's sale on 27 May 1986. The model shown in figure 124 which comes from one of the better, albeit unidentified, Staffordshire factories, has a white body with reddy-brown patches and small black spots and horns of grey. 4in. (10.2cm) long by 2⅝ in. (6.7cm) high, it stands, unsupported, on a hollow oblong base, with rounded ends, edged with a continuous gilt line.

Colour Plate 25. Derby 'lean cow', 2¼in. (5.7cm) high, 3in. (7.6cm) long, c.1810-30.

Colour Plate 26. Derby fox seated on a rectangular base, 4½in. (11.4cm) high, c.1810-30.

Figure 125. Pair of Derby goats ridden by the Welsh tailor and his wife, 10in. (25.4cm) high. Originally 18th century models (after the Meissen) continued into the 19th century. *(Sotheby's)*

Goats

Unlike sheep, goats did not commend themselves to English porcelain manufacturers of the nineteenth century, and are rarely found. However, a fine pair of early nineteenth century standing goats in biscuit, seemingly from the Derby factory — the base of each approximately 4in. (10.2cm) long and of the traditional Derby 'flat and closed-in save for a small hole' variety — were to be seen in 1984 at the well-known dealer Delomosne & Son Ltd. Perhaps they were modelled by Holmes.

An interesting pair of Derby goats, seemingly of the early nineteenth century, are illustrated and described in Sotheby's sale catalogue of 25 March 1984 (lot 192): 'A PAIR OF DERBY GOATS, each lying on a rococo base, the scroll edges picked out in puce and green, the animals' coats marked in brown and their hooves in black, 3¾in. and 4¼in.'

The Derby Welsh tailor and wife, each riding on a goat, originally eighteenth century models (after the Meissen), were also continued into the nineteenth century (figure 125).

It is interesting to note that the King Street factory at Derby also produced a goat. An example in biscuit in a standing position, 3½ in. (8.9cm) high, was sold at Sotheby's on 24 February 1987 lot 250.

Apart from the two Derby factories there is a reference[1] in the Chamberlain Worcester documents to 'Stag and goat at 4s.0d.' (February 1812), albeit no example has so far come to light.

A distinctive Staffordshire goat on a mound base, sometimes ridden by a boy, sometimes by a girl, is also recorded. A pair, 4¾ in. (12.1cm) high, were sold at Christie's on 13 April 1970 (lot 140). A rare group, 5½ in. (14cm) high, shown in colour plate 14, consists of a seated girl, with purple dress and yellow scarf, feeding a goat with gilt horns and orange and grey body markings suckling a kid. Interestingly, in 1896 the Royal Worcester factory modelled a group of a boy and goat (item 1886 in the factory list) and a group of a girl and goat (item 1887).[2]

---

1. G.A. Godden's *Chamberlain Worcester Porcelain*, p.213.
2. Henry Sandon's *Royal Worcester Porcelain*, Appendix 1.

Pigs

The public appeal of porcelain pigs in the eighteenth and nineteenth centuries seems to have been virtually non-existent. The only pig I can actually recall seeing is the one held by the farmer in the famous 'tithe group' (see plates 84 and 85 of *Derby Porcelain 1750-70*). Although this model was essentially eighteenth century it was carried over into the nineteenth century. The pig was included as a necessary part of the joke to which the group gives rise. The farmer's wife refused to allow the tenth pig to be handed over to the rector in payment of the tithe due, unless the rector would take also her tenth child, which she was holding in her arms.

Although no example has so far come to light, the Chamberlain factory would appear to have produced a model of a pig. For at p.104 of his *Chamberlain Worcester Porcelain*, G.A. Godden, drawing on the factory records, refers to a variety of animals having in 1816 been sent to the factory's Bond St. premises, and these animals included pigs.

It is interesting to note that the Minton factory illustrated as item 228 in its list of models a 'Wild Boar, from the Vatican' (see page 247) and as item 235 a group consisting of a 'Sow and Pigs, from the Vatican' (see page 250), both items being presumably only produced in Parian.

Further pigs are mentioned in the 1934/35 catalogue of the King St. factory, Derby, and they may have been made in the nineteenth century.

Colour Plate 27a (left). Rockingham rabbit, 2¾ in. (7cm) long. Incised 'No 110'. Cl 3. Impressed mark. 1826-30. b (right). Rockingham squirrel, 2⅜ in. (6cm) high. Incised 'No 111'. Cl 2. 1826-30.

Colour Plate 28a (left). Samuel Alcock mouse on a green mound base nibbling cheese, 2¼ in. (5.7cm) long. Impressed '91' or '16', c.1830-45. b (right). Derby Mouse on a green rectangular base with rounded corners, 2½ in. (6.4cm) long. Bloor Derby circular mark in red, c.1825-35.

Colour Plate 29. Two Royal Worcester animals. a (left). A mouse, 2in. (5.1cm) long. Registered Design no 1563?? — design registered 1890. b (right). Rabbit, 2in. (5.1cm) long. Registered design no 556159 — design registered 1910.

3. Animals of the Countryside

Certain animals of the English countryside came, naturally enough, to be represented in porcelain during the nineteenth century. They include deer (although they were also domesticated, being kept in parks attached to country houses), squirrels, foxes, rabbits, hares, mice, rats and hedgehogs. For purposes of classification, squirrels, foxes and rabbits present something of a difficulty. They regularly appear with collars, usually gilt, suggesting that they enjoyed the status of pets, and that the porcelain models derived their inspiration from a domestic rather than a wild animal.

There can be no doubt that squirrels and rabbits were kept as pets. To the modern reader (provided, of course, he or she is not concerned with silviculture), the squirrel is a charming creature of the woods which can, with a plentiful supply of nuts, be induced to frequent domestic gardens and become remarkably tame. But our forebears went further and to them it was often a pet and as such kept captive. Although usually given the run of a portion of the house, sometimes it was confined in a special cage with a revolving treadmill. In the words of Matthew Arnold:

'Did you ever see a squirrel vent his tiny rage
In turning round his tiny cage.'

The contemporary attachment to pet squirrels is illustrated by Lady Sarah Lennox's alleged reaction to George III's marriage to another, after earlier hints that he had chosen her. Her son, Henry Napier, observed: 'My mother would probably have been vexed, but her favourite squirrel happened to die at the same time, and his loss was felt more than that of a crown.' An interesting account of a squirrel as a pet is given by Elizabeth Moulton-Barrett (who later in such dramatic circumstances married the poet Robert Browning) in her diary of 1821. (The relevent extracts are set out in Appendix D.)

Rabbits have always been kept as pets, being found in a variety of different colours. They have the added advantage of being readily edible if they become too prolific. Accordingly, porcelain rabbits with collars can be associated with the domestic rather than the wild animal. However, what is more difficult to understand is why collars are given to porcelain foxes. Although attempts have been made, with varying degrees of success, to bring up a fox as a pet, on no footing could this be said to be common practice. The prevalence of collars on foxes (colour plate 26, figures 25b and 134) must be a concession to artistic licence on the part of the decorator. The practice of embellishing some sheep with gilt garlands of vine-leaves (figure 106) or with similar forms of adornment (figure 105) is a further instance of such artistic licence.

Figure 126. Pair of Rockingham deer in natural colours at lodge, the stag 2¾ in. (7cm) long, the hind 3¼ in. (8.3cm). Incised 'No 80'. 1826-30.

Deer

Deer, which lived in the wild providing sport for the hunt, and also roamed the parks attached to the great houses, were frequently represented in porcelain.

Figure 127. Pair of Derby white and gilt deer at lodge, with bocage, the stag 3¼ in. (8.3cm) long, the hind 3½ in. (8.9cm) long, c.1800-1830.

ROCKINGHAM

The stag and hind, each incised 'No 80' shown in figure 126, come from the Rockingham factory. The animals measure 2¾in. (7cm) and 3¼in. (8.3cm) in length respectively, lie on mound bases that are somewhat triangular in shape, and are decorated in natural colours. They are extremely rare.

DERBY

The Derby factory produced a variety of different models of deer during the eighteenth century, but they seem to have been discontinued in the succeeding century and replaced by a new version. The stag and hind of the new design are illustrated in figure 127. They measure 3¼in. (8.3cm) and 3½in. (8.9cm) in length respectively, and are white and gilt. Sometimes these models have bocage, sometimes not. Presumably, they are to be identified with the 'Bucks and Does' appearing in the list given by Haslem of the models by Edward Keys.

Haslem also gives a list of models for which he states John Whitaker was responsible during the period 1830 to 1847, and this list includes: 'Group of Stags' and 'Leaping Stag'. An example of the former is to be seen in the Victoria and Albert Museum (see page 218). It consists of two stags in biscuit linked together with chains. So far no example of the 'Leaping Stag' has been recorded.

KING ST. FACTORY, DERBY

A recumbent doe 3¼in. (8.3cm) from the King St. factory is recorded. An example in biscuit was sold at Sotheby's on 24 February, 1987, lot 250.

CHAMBERLAIN

The Chamberlain factory produced models of a stag and hind in at least two different sizes. A toy pair, each on a matt-blue oval base, 1⅞in. (4.7cm) long, are shown in figure 128. They are each marked under the base 'Chamberlain, Worcester' in red script. A stag on a rare pink base was sold by Christie's on 15 October 1973, lot 194. A larger version of the hind, white and gilt on an oval base 2⅞in. (7.3cm) long, is illustrated in figure 129. Under the base is the mark 'Chamberlains Worcester' in script and '155 New Bond St. London'.

There are a considerable number of references to stags in the factory documents.[1] The markedly different prices suggest a considerable variation in the size of the animals.

---

1. G.A. Godden's *Chamberlain Worcester Porcelain*, pp.213, 214, 138.

Figure 128. Pair of Chamberlain Worcester deer, each animal at lodge on a dry-blue base, 1⅞ in. (4.7cm) long. Marked 'Chamberlain Worcester' written in script, c.1820-40.

	£	s	d	
Stag and goat		4	0	(Feb. 1812)
2 Stags with ornamental trees	1	0	0	(Apr. 1819)
1 Pair plain stags		7	6	(May 1820)
2 Pairs stags, dry blue cushions		15	0	(Apr. 1821)
New small stags		(unpriced)		(Dec. 1821)
A pair stags, large		7	6	(June 1823)
A pair stags, small		6	6	(June 1823)
6 large stags, gilt horns at		4	6	(Jan. 1824)
A pair of stags with green cushions		7	6	(Apr. 1826)

Figure 129. Chamberlain Worcester white and gilt hind lying on an oval base, 2⅞ in. (7.3cm) long. Marked 'Chamberlains Worcester' and '155 New Bond St. London' written in script, c.1820-40.

Surprisingly, hinds or does are not mentioned above. However, amongst the animals recorded as having been sent from the factory to the London shop in December 1816 are '2 Does'. Moreover, there is a reference in the Bond St. sales journal of the 1821-22 period[1] to

	s	d
1 Buck and Doe	7	6

It is interesting to note that sometimes stags were represented on cushions. On no footing is a stag an indoor animal akin to a lap-dog or cat, and accordingly a cushion seems a wholly inappropriate form of base. Presumably, the attractiveness of this composition was thought sufficient to justify a deviation from reality.

1. G.A. Godden's *Chamberlain Worcester Porcelain,* p.137.

COPELAND AND GARRETT

A rare pair of deer from the Copeland and Garrett factory (each bearing the factory mark) were in the possession of Mercury Antiques Ltd. in November 1984. The stag and hind were dappled and in natural colours on a green rectangular base some 4in. (10.2cm) long with rounded and shaped ends.

GRAINGER LEE & CO., WORCESTER

A stag bearing the impressed mark Grainger Lee & Co. is recorded. It assumes a recumbent position on a deep rocky base, and measures 3½in. (8.9cm) high overall. A white and gilt example is illustrated in an advertisement of D.M. & P. Manheim appearing the *Antique Collector,* June 1961, p.XLIX. Another is in the possession of the Dyson Perrins Museum, Worcester. Presumably, there was a companion hind (or even a stag) in reverse. In the factory pattern book there appear a standing stag and a standing hind (see chapter 6, page 237). However, no porcelain examples are known.

CHARLES BOURNE

The Charles Bourne factory is known to have produced a stag and hind. The former is described in lot 98 of Christie's sale of *English Pottery and Porcelain* held on 24 July 1972: 'A Charles Bourne figure of a stag at lodge with gilt antlers, on blue base with gilt band — *3½in. (9cm) wide, red CB mark'*. The factory also made a companion hind, as is apparent from the description of lot 206 of Sotheby's sale of 27 May 1986: 'Three Rare

Charles Bourne Figures of Two Stags and a Doe, 1820-25, the larger of a recumbent stag, the pair smaller and in similar pose, each wearing a gilt collar and resting on a matt-blue oval mound base... *painted CB mark in red, 5cm and 8.8cm (2in. x 3¼ in.)'* It is to be noted that the Charles Bourne deer were made in two different sizes.

SAMUEL ALCOCK

A Samuel Alcock deer is recorded. It lies recumbent on a yellow rocky base, impressed with the numeral '38'; behind are trees in white and gold. Doubtless it once had a companion in reverse. It was produced in two different sizes.

It is interesting to note lot 75 of Christie's sale of *Fine English Porcelain* which took place on 28 June 1971: 'A pair of English porcelain figures of a recumbent stag and hind, before leafy trees, on yellow bases — 5in. (12.5cm) high — *impressed numbers* 34.' In all probability these animals were of Samuel Alcock origin.

MINOR STAFFORDSHIRE FACTORIES

Deer were also produced by the various minor Staffordshire factories operating during the period 1830-50, though they varied considerably in quality.

Squirrels

During the nineteenth century squirrels were, of course, red. Grey squirrels, which nowadays have almost entirely displaced the red in this country, had not as yet been imported from America.

ROCKINGHAM

The Rockingham factory is known to have produced at least two different models, each animal holding a nut in its paws. One is a toy seated on a tree stump, measuring only 2in. (5.1cm) high overall. A white and gilt example with the 'Cl' mark in gold and incised 'No 73' is illustrated in figure 130. Another is in the possession of the British Museum, and a third example belongs to the Yorkshire Museum.[1] The other model (No 111) which is considerably larger, standing on an oval base, 2⅜ in. (6cm) high overall, is shown in colour plate 27b. It is naturally coloured and marked with a 'Cl 2' in gold. The model number with which it is incised is indecipherable, but it is known from another example to be 'No 111'.

Figure 130. Rockingham toy white and gilt squirrel, 2in. (5.1cm) high. Incised 'No 73'. Cl 1. 1826-30.

1. This model would seem to have been made only in one size, not in two sizes as has been stated by A. and A. Cox.

Figure 131. Derby white and gilt squirrel eating a nut, 3½ in. (8.9cm) high, c.1800-30. (Cf. the coloured example illustrated in figure 25a.)

DERBY

During the eighteenth century the Derby factory turned out two different models of squirrels. One seems to have originated around 1760 and to have been discontinued shortly thereafter, but the other, which first appeared around 1770, was carried on into the nineteenth century. The latter was produced in different sizes, seemingly three in all. An example of the largest version, 3½ in. (8.9cm) high, in white and gold, clasping a nut between its paws, is illustrated in figure 131. A coloured version incised '3' appears in figure 25a.[1] This would appear to be the model referred to by Haslem in his list of Bow and Chelsea models:

Enamelled and gilt

ṡ   d

'Large Squirrel   1   3
'Two smaller sizes of same, 1/- and 10d. each.'

Moreover, mention is made of these squirrels in Bemrose's list of moulds and models existing in 1795.

'Squirrels, 3 sizes
'Eighteen squirrels, 3 sizes'

---

1. This animal, which appeared in Sotheby's sale of 15 June 1970, lot 172, was described by the cataloguer as being both 3¼ in. (8.3cm) high and incised '3'. However, size 3 must be significantly less than size 1 and since the latter is 3½ in. (8.9cm) high, some error would seem to have occurred. Perhaps the factory should have incised '2' instead of '3'.

Figure 132. Chamberlain Worcester white and gilt squirrel eating a nut seated on a stepped rectangular base with canted corners, 3in. (7.6cm) high, c.1820-30. (*Grosvenor Antiques Ltd. and Mary Wise Antiques*)

An eighteenth century example, large size in natural colours can be seen in the Schreiber Collection in the Victoria and Albert Museum.

CHAMBERLAIN

Seemingly, very early on in the nineteenth century squirrels were made at the Chamberlain factory. In a document of March 1802[1] there is a reference to the sale of four squirrels for 12s. 0d. How long they continued in production is unknown. The Chamberlain squirrel of figure 132 is presumably an example.

---

1. G.A. Godden's *Chamberlain Worcester Porcelain,* p.213.

GRAINGER LEE & CO., WORCESTER

A naturally coloured squirrel from the Grainger Lee factory is currently in the possession of the Dyson Perrins Museum, Worcester. It is a loan item.

Figure 133. Rockingham toy white and gilt fox. 1½in. (3.8cm) high. Incised 'No 81'. Cl 1. 1826-30.

Foxes

Although foxes were a conspicuous feature of the countryside in the nineteenth century and the raison d'être for the all-important hunt, they are only rarely represented in porcelain. Models were produced at the Rockingham, Derby, Chamberlain, Royal Worcester and certain Staffordshire factories. It may be that they were made by other concerns, but that examples have simply failed to come to light.

ROCKINGHAM

A Rockingham toy fox is recorded. A white and gilt example, a mere 1½in. (3.8cm) high, marked 'Cl 1' and incised 'No 81' is illustrated in figure 133. It is the only one so far known.

DERBY

The Derby factory produced two different fox models, both in a sitting position. One is quite small, measuring 2¾in. (7cm) high, and was produced in reverse. An example in white and gold is shown in figure

Colour Plate 30. Rockingham boy feeding a rabbit, 5½ in. (14cm) high. Incised 'No 44'.
Impressed mark. 1826-30.

Figure 134. Derby white and gilt fox, 2¾ in. (7cm) high. Incised '3', c.1810-30.

134. It is incised with the number '3' indicating that the model was made in three sizes and that this was the smallest. Another example, this time in natural colours, appears in figure 83 of Vivian's *Antique Collecting*. Doubtless this particular model is to be identified with the:

	Enamelled and gilt	
	s	d
Small Sitting Foxes	1	6

attributed by Haslem to the hand of Edward Keys.

The other model made at Derby is larger, measuring 4½ in. (11.4cm) in height and has a companion in reverse. An example in natural colours is illustrated in colour plate 26. The reverse appears in figure 25b. The pair are shown in figure 83 of Margaret Vivian's *Antique Collecting*, immediately beneath two identical models in bronze (figure 82). Presumably, the porcelain models — the same models also appear in pottery, presumably from somewhere in Staffordshire — were either copies of the bronze models or copies of some other originals which came to be represented in bronze, porcelain and pottery. Included among the Bow and Chelsea models[1] listed by Haslem are

	Enamelled and gilt	
	s	d
Sitting Foxes, per pair	7	0
Foxes, per pair	10	6

One or other of these entries would seem to refer to the Derby models of colour plate 26 and figure 25b.

CHAMBERLAIN

No example of a Chamberlain fox has so far come to light, but that the factory undoubtedly produced a model of this animal is demonstrated by a reference to a fox in the factory papers of July 1829.[1]

1. *Chamberlain Worcester Porcelain,* p.214.

ROYAL WORCESTER

The Royal Worcester factory modelled in 1862 a fox and rushes (item 27 in the list) and a fox and goose (item 29) and in 1877 an individual fox (item 597).[1]

1. See Henry Sandon's *Royal Worcester Porcelain* Appendix I.

STAFFORDSHIRE

Porcelain foxes of varying quality were also produced by some of the minor Staffordshire factories. They are, however, rare.

Rabbits

The natural prey of the fox is the rabbit, and in the nineteenth century, long before the arrival of myxomatosis, rabbits were plentiful, so not surprisingly, they are found in porcelain.

ROCKINGHAM

Five rabbit models are recorded as emanating from the Rockingham factory. One is part of a group (No 44) and is obviously a pet. It sits upright whilst a kneeling boy feeds it with a lettuce. An example is shown in colour plate 30. An independent model of a rabbit — far and away the finest independent rabbit model the factory produced — is shown in colour plate 27a. It lies couchant on an oval base, 2¾ in. (7cm) long, nibbling some form of vegetation. It has a gilt collar and grey markings. A further example, cream in colour and also with a gilt collar, is illustrated in figure 135. Both examples have the impressed mark and are incised 'No 110'. The model was also made in reverse.[1] The only known example of the third rabbit model to be made by the Rockingham factory appeared in lot 94 of Sotheby's sale of English Pottery and Porcelain on 21 November 1972 incised 'No 78'. Unfortunately its ears were entirely missing, so that it might conceivably have been a hare. It would appear

Figure 135. Rockingham crouching rabbit, cream and gilt, 2¾ in. (7cm) long. Incised 'No 110'. Cl 2. Impressed mark. 1826-30. (Cf. the example in colour plate 27a.)

to have been identical to the Derby biscuit animal in figure 137. The fourth model is a toy in the form of an adult lying with its two young on a rocky base, 1⅞ in. (4.7cm) long. The group is incised under the base 'No 70', figure 136a. One of the young was produced independently of the group and is the fifth model. It lies on a base, a mere ⅞ in. (2.2cm) long. A white and gilt example is illustrated in figure 136b incised 'No 72'.

---

1. When I illustrated the model in my *Rockingham Ornamental Porcelain* and *Illustrated Guide to Rockingham Pottery and Porcelain* I inadvertently referred to it as a hare.

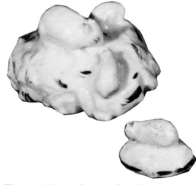

Figure 136a. (above). Rockingham toy group of rabbit and young, white and gilt, 1⅞ in. (4.7cm) long. Incised 'No 70'. 1826-30. b (below). Rockingham toy baby rabbit, white and gilt, ⅞ in. (2.2cm) long. Incised 'No 72'. 1826-30.

DERBY

Included in the list of Edward Keys' models compiled by Haslem are:

	Enamelled and gilt	
	s	d
Rabbits on Plinths	2	0
Ditto without Plinths	1	6

However, so far no examples have been recorded, unless the animal of figure 137 is an example of a rabbit without a plinth[1] from the above list.

An interesting biscuit group, formerly in the possession of Klaber and Klaber, may have come from the Derby factory. It consisted of a centrally positioned doe with three young. It had a typical Derby base — flat and

Figure 137. Derby rabbit in biscuit couchant, 2⅜ in. (6.7cm) long, c.1810-30.

closed-in save for a small central hole — and unlike the somewhat larger Rockingham model of figure 136a, to which it was in some ways similar, it had no incised number. It could conceivably have been made by Cocker.

The biscuit animal illustrated in figure 137 would seem to be a rabbit rather than a hare, albeit the tips of the ears are missing, and it would appear to have been made at the Derby factory around 1830. The construction of the underside of the base is typical of the factory, and although such construction would be equally consonant with a Rockingham origin — the animal is also of the same form as model No 78 — the absence of both a Rockingham mark and also an incised number suggests, on the balance of probability, a Derby provenance. The absence of the model from the Minton drawing book would seem to dissociate the animal altogether from any connection with that particular factory.

---

1. Or possibly with a plinth, depending on whether a base alone constitutes a plinth.

CHAMBERLAIN

The Chamberlain factory produced a small rabbit couchant on an oval base 1¾ in. (4.4cm) long. Two examples are shown in figure 138; in each case the rabbit is white and the base green. One of them is marked 'Chamberlains', the other 'Chamberlains Worcester', in script.

The animal illustrated in figure 139 would seem more likely to be a rabbit than a hare. It lies on a matt-blue oval base, 2¾ in. (7cm) long, in front of a bush, and is marked under the base with the words 'Chamberlain Worcester' in script. This model is also recorded on a pink base.

Figure 138. Two Chamberlain Worcester toy white rabbits, each on a green oval base, 1¾in. (4.4cm) long. One marked 'Chamberlains', the other 'Chamberlains Worcester' in red script, c.1820-40.

There are certain interesting references[1] to rabbits in the factory documents, namely:

		s	d	
4 Rabbits and 3 with young	at	4	0	(Mid-
2 do young, single	at	2	0	1820s)
2 single rabbits	at	2	0	
4 rabbits with trees	at	4	0	
4 rabbits with young	at	4	0	
4 do common	at	3	0	
A pair of Rabbits with small trees	at			(July 1825)
2 Rabbits with bush	at	5	0	(August 1825)

Presumably, the animal of figure 139 is an example of a 'rabbit with bush' and the small rabbit couchant of figure 138 is an example of a 'rabbit young single' or of a 'single rabbit'.

---

1. See G.A. Godden's *Chamberlain Worcester Porcelain* pp.142, 214.

GRAINGER LEE & CO., WORCESTER
In the Grainger Lee drawing book (see chapter 6, page 233) is an illustration of a crouching rabbit on a deep rocky base, rectangular in shape with rounded corners. Unfortunately, so far no porcelain representation has been discovered.

ROYAL WORCESTER
A rare yellow rabbit from the Royal Worcester factory is shown in colour plate 29b. It measures only 2in (5.1cm) in length and like the mouse appearing with it is clearly based on a Japanese netsuke.

Figure 139. Chamberlain Worcester white rabbit with bocage on a dry-blue base, 2 ¾ in. (7cm) long. Marked 'Chamberlain Worcester' written in script, c.1820-40.

COPELAND

An interesting Parian group impressed 'COPELAND' 7 ½ in. (19.1cm) long is shown in figure 140. It consists of a doe rabbit with three young, amid carrots and other vegetables, on a stepped elliptical base. It belongs to the second half of the nineteenth century.

Figure 140. Copeland group of rabbit and young with carrots, lying on an oval stepped base, in Parian, 7 ½ in. (19.1cm) long. Impressed 'COPELAND', c.1850-70. *(Godden of Worthing Ltd.)*

Figure 141. Staffordshire group of rabbit and young, white with black spots, on a green mound base, 3⅝in. long, c.1830-40.

SAMUEL ALCOCK

The rabbit group illustrated in figure 44b would appear to be from the Samuel Alcock factory. This group 4½in. (11.4cm) high is, strictly speaking, a spill-holder — the holders are in the form of hollow tree trunks — but the really interesting feature consists of the rabbits sitting on a rocky mound base. The group is impressed '135'.

Figure 142. Rockingham recumbent hare, light to middle brown shaded, on a maroon oval base edged white with a gilt band, 2⅜in. (6cm) long. Incised 'No 106'. Cl 2. Impressed mark. 1826-30. (Yorkshire Museum)

STAFFORDSHIRE

Where exactly in Staffordshire the rabbit and young illustrated in figure 141 emanate from is unknown. The group is, however, of good quality on a green mound base, 3⅝ in. (8.9cm) long. The doe is suckling one of her young and washing the ear of the other, and all the animals are white with black spots.

A recumbent rabbit lying on a high rectangular base, with rounded corners, which likewise originated somewhere in Staffordshire, is illustrated in figure 134 of Bernard and Therle Hughes' *Collecting Miniature Antiques* (from the moulding of the base, it is conceivable that the animal may be a product of the Lloyd Shelton factory). An interesting group, 5in. (12.7cm) high, consisting of a boy kneeling beside a rabbit-hutch out of which several rabbits are seen to be running — an example in white and gold is recorded — would also seem to have a Staffordshire origin.

Hares

Hares were occasionally represented in porcelain, but far less frequently than the coursing greyhounds with which they were naturally linked in the minds of the sportsmen of the nineteenth century. The Rockingham factory produced a fine example (No 106) in a crouching position on an oval base, 2⅜ in. (6cm) long. An example, light to middle brown shaded, on a maroon base, belongs to the Yorkshire Museum and is shown in figure 142. An interesting group comprising a pair of greyhounds, and also a dead hare, has already been referred to (see page 57).

Mice (or Rats)

Mice were only too well known in the nineteenth century and are occasionally found represented in porcelain. It is not always easy to distinguish between a porcelain mouse and a porcelain rat. Moreover, the problem is aggravated by the fact that there is more than one type of mouse. However, it is difficult to see how rats could have appealed to prospective purchasers and accordingly it is to be presumed that normally the porcelain animals in question represented mice, not rats. Also mice were often kept as pets, but this was not usually the case with rats. Mice as independent models were produced at a variety of different concerns including the Derby, Chamberlain, Grainger Lee, Royal Worcester, and Samuel Alcock factories.

171

DERBY

There are two references to mice appearing in Haslem's lists. The first occurs under the heading 'Bow and Chelsea Models':

	Enamelled and Gilt		Biscuit	
	s	d	s	d
Mice, each	1	6	1	6

The second reference is to be found among the models attributed to Edward Keys.

	Enamelled and Gilt	
	s	d
Worcester Mice, each	2	0

The mouse which is shown in colour plate 28b undoubtedly comes from the Derby factory, it has under the typical Derby base the Bloor mark printed in red. The animal is white and lies on a green rectantular base with rounded corners, 2½ in. (6.4cm) in length. Presumably, it is an example of one of the two models referred to by Haslem. In view of its size, it is more likely to have commanded a price of 2s.0d. than 1s.6d., in which event it is an example of a Worcester mouse.

CHAMBERLAIN

The grey mouse on a matt-blue oval base 1⅝ in. (4.1cm) long, which is illustrated in figure 42b, emanates from the Chamberlain factory. It has under the base the mark 'Chamberlains' written in script. Another example, this time on a green base, appears in G.A. Godden's *Chamberlain Worcester Porcelain,* plate 249.

GRAINGER LEE & CO., WORCESTER

The Grainger Lee drawing book illustrates two different models of a mouse. One would appear to be the long-tailed harvest mouse, the other the common house mouse (see chapter 6, page 233). Each lies on a rectangular base with rounded corners. Unfortunately so far no examples have been discovered.

ROYAL WORCESTER

An interesting mouse (colour plate 29a) was produced late in the nineteenth century at the Royal Worcester factory. Somewhat earlier, in 1873, the factory modelled as item 313 in its list 'Mice and egg, pair'.[1]

---

1. See Henry Sandon's *Royal Worcester Porcelain,* Appendix 1.

SAMUEL ALCOCK

The mouse of colour plate 28a, which lies on a green oval mound base, 2¼ in. (5.7cm) long nibbling a piece of cheese, comes from the Samuel Alcock factory. It is impressed with the number '91' or '16' depending on which way up the item is viewed.

ROCKINGHAM

The Rockingham factory does not appear to have included in its output of animals any independent model of a mouse, though it is always possible that such an animal will in due course come to light. The animal which the dog of figure 97 and 98 is carefully scrutinising would seem to be a rat.

Hedgehogs

Hedgehogs in porcelain are very rare. A small pair on matt-blue bases, unmarked but seemingly from the Chamberlain factory appeared at the Grosvenor House Antiques Fair in the early 1960s, then in the possession of D.M. and P. Manheim. More recently, a large hedgehog on a mound base from the Samuel Alcock factory has been recorded. It had an impressed number under the base and a printed asterisk in red. Appearing in figure 143 is a pair of hedgehogs from an unknown early nineteenth century factory. They were sold by Sotheby's on 6 December 1977 lot 48 and are described in the catalogue in the following terms: 'AN AMUSING PAIR OF HEDGEHOGS with sharp snouts and applied sherds to simulate spines, on rocky bases picked out in gilding, *3in., about* 1825'.

Figure 143. Pair of Staffordshire hedgehogs, with applied sherds to simulate spines, on rocky bases flecked with gold, 3in. (7.6cm) long, c.1830-40. *(Sotheby's)*

Colour Plate 31. Staffordshire lioness and cub group, the animals lying recumbent on a circular rocky base, 4¼in. (10.8cm) long, c.1830-45.

4. Animals from Abroad

A strictly limited range of animals from abroad was represented in porcelain in this country during the nineteenth century. Sometimes the models seem to have derived their inspiration from illustrated books on natural history, but more often from the theatre or from travelling menageries or circuses, possibly based on posters advertising the coming of such shows. They included lions, tigers, leopards, wolves, monkeys, giraffes, bears, camels, zebras, kangeroos and elephants.

Figure 144. Lion lying down with a lamb, both white on a gros bleu base, rectangular with shaped ends, 4¾ in. (12.1cm) in length, c.1840. Under the base is inscribed the following misquotation: 'The young Lion shall lie down with the Lamb, Isaiah XI 6.' Possibly from the Lloyd Shelton factory.

Lions (and Lionesses)

Lions and lionesses were produced during the first half of the nineteenth century at Derby. For in Haslem's list of animals modelled by Edward Keys there is a reference to

	Enamelled and Gilt	
	s	d
Lion and Lioness, each	2	0

Unfortunately, so far no examples have been identified. A lion from the King St. factory is however recorded. It is illustrated in figure 166 of Gilhespy's *Crown Derby Porcelain*. An interesting feature is that the animal with its bottom upraised is free-standing, i.e., it has no base.

The Minton factory, as is clear from its drawing book, was responsible for a variety of different lion models. These all belong to the second half

Figure 145a. (left). Van Amburgh, the lion-tamer, in theatrical Roman costume with a lion, a lioness, a lamb and a leopard, 5¾ in. (14.6cm) high, c.1840. (The inclusion of a lamb made to lie down with a lion was a theme of Van Amburgh's act.) b (right). As above, but this time a lamb is not substituted for the more usual lion cub, c.1840. (These groups would seem to come from the Lloyd Shelton Factory.) *(Sotheby's)*

of the nineteenth century. They include 'Lion on Shield', Lion Asleep', 'Lion Enraged', 'Lion Reposing', and 'Lion attacking Horse' (see pages 249-250).

An extremely rare, not to say unique, lion is recorded as having come from the little-known Madeley factory in Shropshire (c.1828-40). It reclines on a stepped rectangular base with rounded ends and is marked

TMR

Madeley

S

The initials are of the owner of the works, Thomas Martin Randall. The animal is illustrated in Geoffrey A. Godden's *An Illustrated Encyclopaedia of British Pottery and Porcelain,* plate 368.

The Copeland factory is known to have produced lions in Parian. For a pair dated c.1880, 4¾in. (12.1cm) in length, recumbent on a shaped rectangular base and impressed with the Copeland mark, were sold at Sotheby's sale of 21 October 1986, lot 525.

A variety of different lion and lioness models were produced in Staffordshire. A particularly fine lion accompanied by a lamb is illustrated in figure 144. It lies on a gros bleu base, essentially oblong in shape but with shaped ends, 4¾in. (12.1cm) long. The mane of the lion and the wool of the lamb are represented by thin threads of applied porcelain (see page 125). It may be that the group comes from the Lloyd Shelton factory. Underneath the hollow base there is printed what purports to be a quotation from Isaiah: 'The young Lion shall lie down with the Lamb', Isaiah XI 6. It is interesting to note that the quotation is wrong. It should read: 'The wolf also shall dwell with the lamb, and the leopard shall lie down with the kid; and the calf and the young lion and the fatling together; and a little child shall lead them'.

The reason for this inaccuracy is puzzling. Perhaps the model was based, without further enquiry, on a poster advertising Van Amburgh's celebrated act with a lion and lamb. For almost certainly the group derives its inspiration from the theatre. In 1838 the then manager of the Drury Lane Theatre, in order to off-set the losses from his production of Rossini's opera *La Gazza Ladra,* running at the rate of almost £100 a night, added to the programme the famous lion-tamer, Van Amburgh 'The Brute Tamer of Pompeii' and his 'celebrated felines'. The introduction of this hippodromatic spectacular, which went under the name 'Charlemagne, or the Moors of Spain', was a conspicuous success, and one of the 'turns' was Van Amburgh making his fiercest lion lie down with a lamb. A Staffordshire pottery group of the same scene, though quite different in composition from the porcelain group shown here, is illustrated in Anthony Oliver's *The Victorian Staffordshire Figure* plate 202.

The lion and lamb group of figure 144 was also made in reverse, and a pair, 4¾in. (12.1cm) high (seemingly by this time in pottery) are illustrated in the catalogue of Christie's sale of 30 September 1974 lot 124 (plate 4). Between this pair there is a further illustration of the same lion and lamb group (lot 123), similarly decorated, but slightly smaller, 4in. (10.2cm) high. Around the front edge of the base appears the erroneous inscription recited above.

A spectacular porcelain group consisting of the same Van Amburgh, this time with a lion and lioness standing each side of him, with a recumbent cub lying in front of the latter and with a leopard hanging on his back, is illustrated in figure 145b. The group is almost certainly attributable to Lloyd Shelton. An interesting variant is shown next to it.

177

Here a lamb replaces the lion cub, and presumably the theme was 'the making of the lion to lie down with the lamb'.

The lioness and cub group on a rocky mound base, 4¼ in. (10.8cm) long shown in colour plate 31, is Staffordshire in origin. (It comes from a distinctive but unidentified Staffordshire factory responsible for a variety of different animals, including the pair of coursing greyhounds in the Schreiber Collection referred to at page 57). The animals are beige, the base dark green. Doubtless there was a companion in reverse in the form of a lion. However, no example has so far been recorded.

An interesting pair of white and gold animals modelled as a lion and a unicorn, each with a gilt crown and lying on a rectangular mound base with shaped ends, appeared (duly illustrated in the catalogue) as lot 264 of Sotheby's sale of 'British and Irish Ceramics' 24 July 1984. Another pair, 4in. (10.2cm) wide, with gilt chains round their bodies, lying on pale yellow mounds and shaped rectangular bases, were sold at Christie's on 25 October 1971 (lot 154).

Tigers

Tigers are extremely rare in porcelain. The tiger and leopard illustrated in colour plate 32 are, as far as modelling is concerned, smaller versions (albeit with rococo, instead of simple pad bases) of the eighteenth century leopards (c.1760) appearing in plate 76 of my *Derby Porcelain 1750-70*. However, although one of the animals continues as a leopard, the other has been decorated as a tiger. Both assume an aggressive pose and stand on a green rococo base 2¾ in. (7cm) and 2in. (5.1cm) high overall respectively.

It is interesting to note that in the various lists of models recorded by Haslem there is no mention of a tiger or, for that matter, of a leopard, albeit there is a reference to a panther. However, the animals illustrated manifestly come from the Derby factory, because, apart from having all the requisite Derby characteristics, including the typical construction of the underside of the base, they are printed with the Crown over 'D' mark in red. The elaborate rococo base suggests that each model was first produced in the eighteenth century. It is interesting to note that there is a reference in Bemrose's list to 'Pair large tygers, 2 sizes'.

Leopards

The Derby model of the leopard of colour plate 32 has already been mentioned. There is an interesting reference in Haslem's list of 'Bow and

Colour Plate 32. Derby tiger (left), 2¾ in. (7cm) high and leopard (right), 2in. (5.1cm) high, each in a menacing pose on a scrolled base. Both marked with a crown over 'D' mark printed in red, c.1820-30.

Colour Plate 33. Rockingham monkey eating fruit, 2¾ in. (7cm) high. Incised '2' to indicate size and 'No 142'. 1826-30.

179

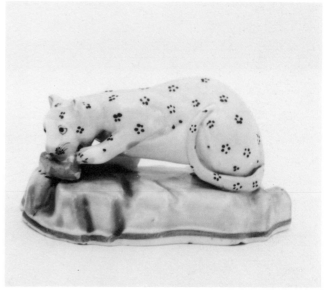

Figure 146. Pair of Samuel Alcock leopards, yellow with black spots, recumbent on rocky green bases edged with a gilt line, one eating a piece of meat, both 3½in. (8.9cm) long. Impressed '236', c.1840. *(Sotheby's)*

Chelsea Models' to

	s	d
Large Panthers		
Small ditto per pair	3	0

The low price of the small panthers suggests that the reference was to animals of the size of those illustrated in colour plate 32. It may be that the leopard shown there was listed as a panther and that sometimes it was made with a companion panther instead of a tiger. A panther or leopard would be distinguished from a tiger, not by the modelling, but by the subsequent decoration.

A particularly fine pair of Derby leopards on rocky bases are recorded, each 5in. (12.7cm) long. The male is modelled by himself, but the leopardess has three cubs — one she is licking whilst the other two are climbing over her back. In 1986, such a pair in biscuit were in the possession of Mercury Antiques Ltd. They were incised with the numbers 10 and 11, which are not associated with leopards (or panthers) in either Haslem's or Bemrose's lists. On the contrary, they are assigned to completely different models. However, as is clear from Bemrose's list the same number was sometimes allotted to more than one figure. Thus, in his list, nos. 8 and 9 are assigned to a pair of goats as well as to two other models. Manifestly, nos. 10 and 11 were used twice over, once for the above pair of leopards, and again for two other models. As there is no reference in Bemrose's list to any leopard (or panther) presumably they were modelled after 1795. Certainly the biscuit pair in the possession of Mercury Antiques Ltd. belonged to the nineteenth century, as was apparent from the absence of any patch marks and the dry chalky appearance of the biscuit. These two groups of animals were also produced in pottery. (See the illustration of the coloured pair c.1830 in

Figure 147a. (left). Staffordshire leopard, decorated with shaded yellow and black spots, standing unsupported on an oval base decorated with a gilt pattern in the front, 3in. (7.6cm) long. c.1840-50. b (right). Staffordshire leopard cub, decorated with shaded yellow and black spots, lying recumbent on a rectangular base with canted corners, 1⅝in. (4.1cm) long, c.1835-50.

Figure 148. Pair of Staffordshire leopard and cub groups in natural colours, the leopard standing unsupported, on shaped bases, 4¼in. (10.8cm) long, c.1835-50. *(Christie's)*

181

Colour Plate 34. Staffordshire camelopard or giraffe, 4½ in. (11.4cm) high, c.1828.

Colour Plate 35 a (left). Rockingham elephant on a rocky base, 1⅝ in. (4.1cm) high. Incised 'No 69'. Cl 2. 1826-30. b (right). Elephant on a rectangular base, 2in. (5.1cm) high, possibly from the Davenport factory, c.1830.

Figure 149a. (left). Staffordshire standing leopard, without support, on a white and gilt base, 4½in. (11.4cm) long, c.1830-40. (*Grosvenor Antiques Ltd.*) b (right). The same model leopard standing with supporting hollow tree trunk, on a white and gilt mound base, 5in. (12.7cm) long, c.1830-40. (*Mary Wise Antiques*).

Sotheby's catalogue 23 July 1985, lot 88.) The porcelain leopardess group appeared in colour as lot 162 of Sotheby's sale of 17 March 1970, although this time there is mention of only two cubs — was this an original variation or had one cub subsequently been broken off? 'A Derby group of a Leopard [ess] with two cubs, the mother crouched over one of her young licking it with her tongue, on a rocky base coloured in browns, yellows and green edged in gilding, *5in'*.

The fine pair of leopards illustrated in figure 146 was produced by the Samuel Alcock factory. They assume a relaxed pose on a mound base impressed with the numeral '236'. Their coats are enamelled in bright yellow and spotted in black, one recumbent, the other eating a piece of meat, on green mound bases with gilt-line borders, 3½in. (8.9cm) long.

An interesting leopard from one of the minor Staffordshire factories is illustrated in figure 147a. It is decorated with black spots on a shaded yellow coat, and stands on an oval base, 3in. (7.6cm) long with a gilt pattern in front. It has no support and was probably made somewhere between 1840 and 1850. The cub (figure 147b), similarly decorated lying on a rectangular base with canted corner, 1⅝in. (4.1cm) long, shown beside it, may have come from the same factory, but perhaps was made a few years earlier.

A distinctive Staffordshire leopardess and cub group, 5in. (12.7cm) long, is illustrated in Sotheby's sale catalogue of 21 October 1986, lot 377. The leopardess and cub, decorated in natural colours, lie recumbent on an oval base moulded with gilt foliate scrolls, the latter under a mossy arbour encrusted with flowers. The bases — each with shaped ends,

183

4¼ in. (10.8cm) long — of the pair of leopardess and cub groups shown in figure 148 are similar to the base of the lion and lamb group illustrated in figure 144, suggesting that they come from the same factory, possibly Lloyd Shelton. The leopardess is standing, whilst the cub lies recumbent under her. The two leopards appearing in figure 149, in the one case with a hollow tree trunk support, in the other without any support at all, are particularly striking. They may well be based on a print from a book on Natural History.

It is interesting to note that leopards in porcelain (whether of the eighteenth or nineteenth century) are far more common than tigers. Why this should be so is puzzling. Perhaps their coats were easier to depict, or perhaps the explanation lies in the more frequent appearance of leopards as against tigers, if such was the case, in the various travelling menageries (the inspirational source for many porcelain animal models). Leopards are smaller than tigers, and therefore more easily transported and less costly to feed. Conceivably for these reasons, they were more popular than tigers with owners of itinerant zoos and circuses.

Wolves

Wolves, which were once prevalent in this country, had been hunted to extinction long before our period, the last survivor being killed in 1682. Wolves, however, survived on the Continent. Not being a popular animal with the general public, it is not surprising to find it only infrequently represented in porcelain. However, a fine model, originating somewhere in Staffordshire, is shown in figure 150. Its long-haired coat is shaded in brown and it is seated on a high rocky base edged with a gilt line, 8¼ in. (21cm) high in all. The date appears to be around 1830. Its teeth are noteworthy, and J.G. Wood in his *The Illustrated Natural History* writes: 'There is something remarkable about the bite of a Wolf. Instead of making its teeth meet in the flesh of its antagonist, and then maintaining its hold, as is done by most of the carnivora, the Wolf snaps sharply, fiercely, and repeatedly at its opponent or its quarry; delivering these attacks with such furious energy that when it misses its mark its jaws clash together with a sound that has been likened to the sudden closing of a steel-trap. These sharply snapping bites, so rapidly delivered, are of terrible efficacy in destroying an enemy, or bringing down the prey.'[1]

1. J.G. Wood, *The Illustrated Natural History, Mammalia*, p.327.

Figure 150. Staffordshire wolf seated on a deep rocky mound base, edged with a gilt line border, 8¼ in. (21cm) high, c.1830. *(Sotheby's)*

Figure 151. Derby monkey and bear band, 4in. (8.2cm) and 4¾in. (12.1cm) high. Marked with crossed swords in blue enamel and printed Bloor Derby marks in iron red, c.1825-30. *(Sotheby's)*

Monkeys

Monkeys are associated with English porcelain more as caricatures of human beings than as natural animals in their own right. Although the famous Meissen factory produced in the eighteenth century a variety of perfectly natural monkeys in different poses, Kändler also modelled his celebrated 'monkey band', each animal playing an instrument, singing or conducting. Some say that the band was intended to satirise the Dresden orchestra, but there is no firm evidence of this. In any event the 'monkey band' is manifestly a caricature of human beings. At least some of the members of this band were copied by the Chelsea and Derby factories during the eighteenth century, and the latter factory continued to produce its monkey musicians in the nineteenth century.

Included in Haslem's list of models attributed to Edward Keys are:

	Enamelled and gilt	
	s	d
Large Monkey Musicians, each	7	6
Small ditto ditto	5	0

Examples of the above models appear from time to time, but, of course, these are not natural animals in their own right either; they are merely caricatures of human beings. A set was offered for sale at Sotheby's on 21 July 1970 (lot 307): 'A DERBY MONKEY BAND, comprising ten Musicians, each shown seated on a flat shaped green base, and wearing white ruffs over a flowered jacket picked out in colours, including a cellist, a violinist, a drummer and a monkey playing the cymbals, *4 ¼ in. to 5 ¼ in, simulated cross sword marks in blue*'.

A band where the membership was mixed, consisting of bears as well as monkeys (figure 151), appeared in Sotheby's auction rooms on 27 April 1976 (lot 188). It was described in the catalogue as follows: 'A RARE AND AMUSING DERBY MONKEY OR BEAR BAND, each seated with gaily-coloured coat and white ruff on flat green bases edged in gilding, their fur naturalistically coloured in varying tones of brown and greenish grey, in two sizes comprising

Two large 'Cellists
Two large Violinists
One Drummer
One Triangle Player
One Cymbal Player
One Harpist
Three Trumpeters
Three Singers

4 ¾ in. and 4 in., *marks include crossed swords in blue enamel and printed Bloor Derby marks in iron-red about* 1825, repaired. Sold in these rooms 6 December 1966 lot 150.'

Three similar musicians are in the Derby Museum.

The Copeland and Garrett factory also produced monkey musicians. Marked examples of a monkey organ-grinder and a monkey beating a drum are shown opposite page 180 of Arthur Hayden's *Spode and his Successors*. A rare group of grotesque monkeys, eating and drinking, which appears immediately beneath the previously mentioned illustrations, also came from the Copeland and Garrett factory — the group carries the factory mark — but like the Derby musicians, the members of the group

187

are simply caricatures of human beings. As also are the 'Burlesque Sculptor', 7in. (17.8cm) high, design no. 117, and the 'Burlesque Painter', 7¼in. (18.4cm) high, design no. 118, from the Minton factory. The former consists of a monkey sculpting a bust, the latter of a monkey wearing a hat seated before an easel. The former is illustrated as item B19 in the catalogue to the *Exhibition of Minton 1798-1910,* held at the Victoria and Albert Museum in 1976. Interestingly the Minton factory produced two later models of monkeys in caricature, both presumably executed in parian. One monkey is kneeling by an open barrel playing an instrument (no. 291 in the list), whilst the other monkey, seemingly the reverse, is singing, seated by the same barrel (no. 292) (see page 251).

Interestingly, the Samuel Alcock factory produced a monkey band based on the Derby models, again as caricatures. Three members of the band have been recorded, each seated in costume on a yellow rectangular base with canted corners, one blowing a trumpet 2¾in. (7cm) high, one playing a cello, 2½in. (6.4cm) high and one holding cymbals, 2½in. (6.4cm) high. Each is impressed '117'. Another Samuel Alcock monkey, likewise seated, but this time reading at a desk, is also known to exist. It too is a caricature. It is 2⅝in. (6.7cm) high in all and is impressed '120'. The desk has a practical use as an inkwell.

Presumably, the three monkey models produced by the Royal Worcester factory in 1862 were also caricatures. For the factory modelled a 'Monkey cobbler' (item 14 in the list), a 'Monkey cobbler, smaller' (item 15) and 'The monkey host' (item 23).[1] Towards the end of the century in 1886, the factory modelled as item 1171 'Pair monkey and lotus'. Presumably, this was a natural monkey.

However, be that as it may, the Rockingham factory did turn out natural monkeys, albeit they are now very rare. An example — incised under the base 'No 142' — is shown in colour plate 33. It is beige in colour and sits on a pink base eating fruit. It measures 2¾in. (7cm) in height, being the second size. An example of the same model (first size), white on a gilt-edged claret base, and measuring 3⅛in. (7.9cm) in height, is illustrated in Sotheby's catalogue of 21 October 1986, lot 375. It is to be noted that a similar model of a monkey, normally gilded[2] but on occasion in colour[3], sometimes surmounts the cover of the factory's hexagonal vases.

---

1. See Henry Sandon's *Royal Worcester Porcelain* Appendix 1.
2. See D.G. Rice, *Rockingham Ornamental Porcelain* Pls. 27 and 28.
3. See D.G. Rice, *Illustrated Guide to Rockingham Pottery and Porcelain* Pl. 118.

Figure 152. Grainger Lee white and gilt giraffe, kneeling down, 4in. (10.2cm) long. Impressed 'GRAINGER LEE & CO WORCESTER' in capitals, c.1820-37.

Giraffes

In August 1827 a giraffe, accompanied by two Nubian attendants, was presented by the Pasha of Egypt to George IV. Probably it was intended that the animal would in due course be housed in the zoo in Regent's Park, which was opened to the public on 27 April 1828. Unfortunately, notwithstanding careful nursing at Windsor Castle, the giraffe died in August 1829. The attempt to restore the animal to health formed the subject matter of a cartoon — so great was the public interest in the matter — by William Heath, under the pseudonym Paul Pry. George IV and the unpopular Lady Conyngham, at that time his constant companion, were portrayed trying with the aid of a windlass, clothing and medicine to nurse the giraffe back to health. In 1836 a small herd of giraffes was purchased for the Zoo. Fortunately, these particular animals settled down well, and were induced to breed. The latin name for giraffe was *camelopardalis,* which gave rise to the English word camelopard, and this name recalled the mythological origin of the animal as a hybrid from a camel and a leopard. Doubtless, the giraffe or camelopard of colour plate 34 was produced to celebrate the arrival of the giraffe given to

George IV. It was presumably based on an unidentified illustration appearing in some book on Natural History, which was not entirely accurate anatomically. A white and gilt example from the Grainger Lee factory (one of a pair) is shown in figure 152 in a kneeling position. It is impressed with the factory mark and measures 4⅛ in. (10.5cm) high. A pair are in the possession of the Dyson Perrins Museum, Worcester. This particular model is illustrated in the factory pattern book (chapter 6, page 236).

Staffordshire models are also known, appearing both in white and gold and also in enamel colours and gold. An interesting example[1] in white and gold, 4¾ in. (12.1cm) high, is illustrated in an advertisement appearing in *The Antique Collector* June 1961, p.XLIX, where it accompanies a marked Grainger Lee specimen on a somewhat different base to that of figure 152.

1. Conceivably, this too could be a Grainger Lee example.

Bears

Bears in the form of musicians have already been referred to (see page 187). The only other bear model that I have seen belonging to the period with which we are concerned was a small, naturally coloured animal with a collar and muzzle. It was manufactured somewhere in Staffordshire and was presumably inspired by the bears of Wombwell's and other travelling circuses. Interestingly, the Royal Worcester factory modelled in 1862 a 'bear and drum' (item 35 in the factory list).[1]

1. See Henry Sandon's *Royal Worcester Porcelain* Appendix 1.

Camels

English porcelain camels of the nineteenth century are very rare. However, a Staffordshire or more likely a Derby pair, standing with supports, are illustrated in figure 153. One is a dromedary, the other a bactrian. An interesting reference occurs in Sotheby's sale catalogue of 28 February 1978 lot 137 to 'a miniature white recumbent Dromedary, 1⅞ in. *19th century'*. A pair of grey-coated bactrian camels on shaped oval bases edged with a gilt line, 3½ in. (8.9cm) high overall, appeared in the Boothman Smallwood sale conducted by Christie's South Kensington on 26 and 27 April, 1989 (lot 1078).

A large camel from the Royal Worcester factory is illustrated in figure 154. It is in a lying down position with an elaborate cloth and seat, and measures 6¾ in. (17.1cm) high. The design (not recorded by Henry Sandon) was registered on 22 June 1870.

Figure 153. Pair of camels of Derby or Staffordshire origin. The top camel is a dromedary, and the other a bactrian, and each stands with a support on a shaped oval base edged with a gilt line, 3¼ in. (8.3cm) high, c.1830-40. *(Grosvenor Antiques Ltd. and Mary Wise Antiques)*

Figure 154. Royal Worcester camel, with elaborate seat and cloth in a recumbent position, glazed and tinted Parian, 6¾ in. (17.1cm) high, signed 'Hadley Sc'. Design registered 22 June 1870. *(Godden of Worthing Ltd.)*

Figure 155. Staffordshire zebra with black stripes standing on a mound base edged with a gilt line, 3⅛ in. (7.9cm) long, c.1840.

Figure 156. Staffordshire white and gilt kangaroo, 2½in. (6.4cm) high, c.1830-40. *(Grosvenor Antiques Ltd. and Mary Wise Antiques)*

Zebras

Zebras in nineteenth century porcelain are extremely rare. Doubtless they were inspired by travelling menageries. The zebra illustrated in figure 155 is of Staffordshire origin. It measures 3in. (7.6cm) high in all by 3⅛in. (7.9cm) in length and stands with a support on a mound base edged with gilt line. It looks exactly like a donkey painted with zebra stripes. Presumably, the factory responsible also produced donkeys, and when it decided to issue a zebra it preferred to adopt the simple expedient of decorating a donkey with stripes rather than model a fresh animal of correct shape and form.

Kangaroos

A white and gilt kangaroo with its head turned backwards has been recorded. It was made by one of the Staffordshire factories and is illustrated in figure 156.

Elephants

Elephants of the nineteenth century appear very rarely in porcelain. Those that do may well have owed their inspiration to the travelling circus, but it is impossible to be sure. A small, but very charming model was produced at Swinton. An example is illustrated in colour plate 35. Naturally coloured, it stands a mere 1⅝in. (4.1cm) high on a shaped base, 1⅞in. (4.4cm) long. It has the 'Cl 2' mark and is incised 'No 69'. The elephant appearing in the same colour plate is equally charming. It is cream coloured with gilt ears and eyes and with a trunk splashed with gold. It stands 2in. (5.1cm) high overall on a green rectangular base, 3³/₁₆in. (8.1cm) long, edged with a thick gilt line. It shares with the King Charles Spaniel of figure 62 the characteristics of the Davenport factory, and notwithstanding that it is unmarked, it may well have its origins in that quarter.

The Derby factory turned out a small elephant model, albeit no example has so far been recorded. It is referred to by Haslem among the models attributed to the hand of Edward Keys.

	Enamelled and gilt	
	s	d
Small elephant	1	6

In the same list are also included the following

	Enamelled and gilt	
	s	d
Large Elephant, with Driver	10	6
Ditto with cloths, no Driver	9	0

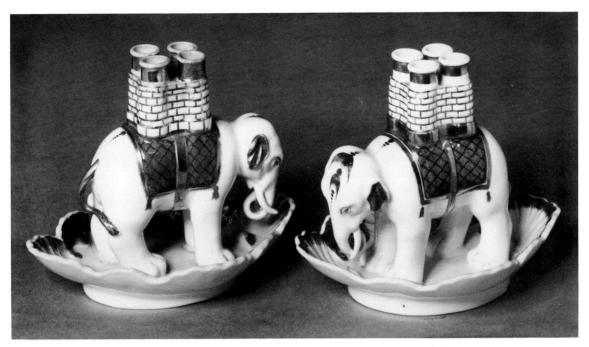

Figure 157. Pair of elephant and castle inkstands, each animal with puce ceremonial cover, 4¾in. (12.1cm) long, Cl 3, red griffin mark, c.1826-30.

Figure 158. Royal Worcester elephant (with howdah and elaborate cloth), glazed Parian with enamelled and gilt enrichments, 7¾in. (19.7cm) high. Incised 'Hadley Sc'. Design registered 19 November 1869. *(Godden of Worthing Ltd.)*

Figure 159a and c. (left and right). Pair of Derby peacocks, naturally coloured, each on a tree stump with curved flower-encrusted branches, all on an elaborate scroll base, 6½ in. (16.5cm) high. Crown over 'D' mark, c.1830. Modelled by John Whitaker. b (centre). Bloor Derby elephant with driver, the animal coloured in dark greyish-brown and covered wth a brightly decorated cloth, a turbanned boy seated on his neck, 5½ in. (14cm) high. Crown over 'Derby' mark, c.1830. *(Sotheby's)*

An example of the former model appears in figure 159b. The animal is coloured dark greyish-brown and stands on an oval grassy mound. It has a colourful cloth with gilt edging and a turbanned boy sits on its neck. It carries the Crown over Derby mark and stands 5½ in (14cm) high. An example without a rider is in the Derby Museum.

A more elaborate model altogether appears in figure 88 of Margaret Vivian's *Antique Collecting*.[1] The elephant has a black turbanned rider, and the richly decorated cloth that covers the elephant's back is surmounted by a howdah in the form of a castle, on top of which sits another black turbanned figure. Dr Vivian describes the piece in the following terms: 'The elephant (Fig. 88) bears the Derby mark and has an apple-green [rectangular] base. It was probably copied from a similar Meissen figure that was sold recently [c.1937] for nearly £100. The howdah is in the form of a castle made of scarlet and gold bricks, and has a small landscape on each side...'

There is also a Rockingham elephant and castle, which measures 3⅝ in. (9.2cm) in height. This particular model is really a toy inkstand — the howdah, in the form of a four-turreted castle, taking a pen in each turret — and is not actually one of the Rockingham figure series. Thus,

---

1. The same or a similar example, 8½ in. (21.6cm) high, is illustrated in figure 115 of Gilhespy's *Crown Derby Porcelain*.

it bears no incised number. (Of course, it may be that the model was used again, this time without the inkstand accessories, as an independent animal within that series, and an example has simply not come to light.) The elephant stands on a shell-edged oval tray, 4¾in. (12.1cm) long, and was produced in both the red (1826-30) and the puce (1831-42) periods. These elephant inkstands were made in pairs, one looking to the left, the other to the right (figure 157). The model was occasionally produced in a smaller size.

It is known that an elephant was also produced by the Chamberlain factory, for in a factory document of around January 1829 there is a reference to an elephant priced at 2s.6d.[1] No example has so far been recorded.

A late elephant (with howdah and elaborate cloth) from the Royal Worcester factory is illustrated in figure 158. The design (not recorded by Henry Sandon) was first registered on 19 November 1869. It stands 7¾in. (19.7cm) high by 8¾in. (22.2cm) in length. These elephants were produced in pairs in reverse.[2]

The factory modelled two further elephants in 1875 (items 473 and 496 respectively in the list) and an elephant on pedestal in 1877 (item 626).[3]

---

1. See G.A. Godden's *Chamberlain Worcester Porcelain*, p.214.
2. See Sotheby's sale of 15 March 1988 lot 298.
3. Henry Sandon's *Royal Worcester Porcelain*, Appendix 1.

---

5. Birds

Birds feature very much in the eighteenth century as subjects for modelling in porcelain. However, by the beginning of the nineteenth century they appear to have gone out of fashion with only swans and pea fowl being produced in any quantity thereafter.

Swans

Swans mate for life, and if one of the pair dies, normally the other will pine away and perish. Not surprisingly, in paintings, drawings and prints, swans are generally represented in pairs, and it would seem that when they were produced in porcelain, they were likewise issued in pairs, albeit often only one has survived. Swans were manufactured at Swinton, at Derby, at Worcester and in Staffordshire.

ROCKINGHAM

An example of a Rockingham swan appears in figure 162. It is finely decorated with gilt markings outlining the feathers, the beak and legs being painted in natural colours. It measures 2¼ in. (5.7cm) in height and is incised 'No 99'.

DERBY

The Derby swan, which is occasionally encountered, is very similar to the Rockingham version and was made in three different sizes, often indicated by an incised '1', '2' or '3', as appropriate. The swan appears in the list of items stated by Haslem to be from the Bow and Chelsea models.

	s	d
Large Swan	1	3

Two smaller sizes of same, 1s and 10d each

CHAMBERLAIN

Although I have not as yet seen a Chamberlain swan, the evidence for one having been made by this particular factory is overwhelming, for there are references to this bird in various of the factory documents:[1]

	s	d	
1 Swan	2	6	[Aug. 1805]
2 large Swanns, white and gold	14	0	[June 1806]
4 Swanns and 4 Pelicans, large at	4	0	[Oct. 1811]
1 small swan	2	6	[1821/22]
2 swans	4	0	[June 1823]

The price for four swans together with four pelicans mentioned above seems so remarkably low, particlarly as they are described as being large, that presumably the 4s 0d was meant to indicate the price of each bird.

1. See G.A. Godden's *Chamberlain Worcester Porcelain* at pp.213, 137-9.

ROYAL WORCESTER

The Royal Worcester factory also produced swans. In 1875 it modelled a Swan (item 471 in its list] and a 'Swan and Cupid or swan without cupid' (item 532] and in 1877 a 'Swan and Stump' (item 593).[1]

1. See Henry Sandon's *Royal Worcester Porcelain*, Appendix 1.

Figure 160. Pair of Rockingham white and gilt peacocks, with open fantails, each standing on a rocky base picked out in green and gold, 3⅞ in. (9.8cm) high. Incised 'No 136'. Impressed mark. 1826-30. *(Sotheby's)*

STAFFORDSHIRE

Swans were also produced in Staffordshire. They vary considerably in quality, reflecting the different standards of the manufacturers concerned.

Peacocks and Peahens

ROCKINGHAM

The white and gilt peacocks on a rocky base picked out in green and gold which are illustrated in figure 160 come from the Rockingham factory. Each measures 3⅞ in. (9.8cm) in height and is incised 'No 136'.

DERBY

A similar bird, likewise with open fan-tail, was turned out at Derby. It was modelled by Edward Keys and was originally priced at 2s when enamelled and gilt and 3s when in biscuit. A coloured example is illustrated in Sotheby's sale catalogue of 25 March 1974 (lot 186): 'A DERBY MODEL OF A PEACOCK with tail fully displayed, its plumage picked out in coloured enamels and standing on a green-washed mound base with a tree-stump support, 3¾ in.' A larger and far more elaborate

197

Figure 161. Chamberlain Worcester white and gilt peacock, with open fantail, standing on a dry-blue circular base ringed with gold, 3in. (7.6cm) high. Marked 'Chamberlains Worcester', written in script, c.1820-40.

version was modelled by John Whitaker. A pair 6½ in. (16.5cm) high are illustrated in figure 159a and c. Each bird (with the Crown over 'D' mark) has a long tail naturally coloured with 'eyes' and richly gilded, and stands on a tree stump with flower encrusted branches resting on an elaborate scrolled base.

CHAMBERLAIN

In the factory documents there are frequent references[1] to Chamberlain peacocks and peahens, including the following:

	£	s	d	
1 Peacock (glass shade 2s)		10	0	[1821/22]
1 Peacock white and gold		8	0	[1821/22]
17 Pea hens	10	10	0	[early 1822]
9 Peacocks	3	6	6	[Feb 1822]
1 Peacock white and gold		8	0	[April 1822]
A pair pea birds		10	0	[June 1823]

1. See G.A. Godden's *Chamberlain Worcester Porcelain*, pp. 137, 214, 138.

Figure 162. Rockingham white and gilt swan, with naturally coloured beak and legs and with a gilt bell and chain around its neck, 2⅞ in. (7.3cm) long. Incised 'No 99'. Cl 2. 1826-30.

It is to be noted that, if the surviving factory documentation is an accurate guide, pea fowl would seem to have largely replaced swans from the early 1820s onwards, and to have started off at least as more expensive items. Perhaps they were initially much larger. An example of a Chamberlain peacock, white and gilt, with open fan-tail standing 3in. (7.6cm) high overall on a stepped matt-blue round base, is shown in figure 161. It is marked under the base 'Chamberlains Worcester' in red script.

STAFFORDSHIRE
Peacocks and peahens, similiar to the Rockingham examples of figure 160 but not so well modelled, also appear in Staffordshire porcelain. A pair which recently came to my attention were white and gilt standing with open fan-tail on a round base decorated with a gros bleu ground.

Miscellaneous Birds
A Rockingham figure of a dove with open wings on a rocky base (No 112) is recorded. It measures 3in. (7.6cm) in height (figure 163). In the case of another Rockingham figure a somewhat nondescript bird rests on the wrist of a standing boy (No 30).

Included in Haslem's list of unnumbered Derby models are:

Figure 163. Rockingham white and gilt dove with open wings, 3in. (7.6cm) high. Incised 'No 112'. Cl 1. 1826-30. *(Yorkshire Museum)*

		Enamelled and gilt	
		s	d
Canary Birds, each Chelsea		1	0
Tomtit	ditto ditto	1	0
Linnet	ditto ditto	1	0

As the price of 1s each indicates, these birds were very small. Interestingly, Haslem's list of models attributed to John Whitaker includes a parrot. No example has so far been recorded.

Although Chamberlain birds other than swans and pea fowl are rare in the extreme (the only example I have seen is of a small white and gilt finch sitting on a tree stump marked underneath 'Chamberlain Worcester' in red script, some 2in. (5.1cm) high in all), the factory documentation indicates that birds such as geese and parrots were made from time to time. The following references are to be noted.[1]

---

1. See G.A. Godden's *Chamberlain Worcester Porcelain* p.213.

	s	d	
2 Geese	5	0	[July 1802]
2 Parrots	8	0	[Oct. 1802]
3 Small birds, with their bills to the left, gilt	6	0	[around 1803]
1 Kingfisher	4	0	[December 1803]

In addition, the reader is reminded of the reference to pelicans in conjunction with swans:

	s	d	
4 Swanns and 4 Pelicans, large at	4	0	[Oct. 1811]

Moreover, '2 Canarys' and '6 Canary birds coloured' were sent to the factory's London shop (together with two does, two stags, six cats, two pugs and four lambs) in December 1816.[1] No examples of any of the above species of bird are recorded. It is to be remarked that most of these miscellaneous birds seem to belong to the first years of the nineteenth century and may well have been discontinued early on.

For completeness, it should be mentioned that a goose is included in the 'Mother Goose' group appearing as item 4 in the Minton drawing book. For an illustration see plate 128 of G.A. Godden's *Minton Pottery and Porcelain*. The 'Mother Goose' group stands 3⅝ in. (9.2cm) high.

In addition to birds from the Derby and Chamberlain factories, others of various species were undoubtedly produced in Staffordshire. They differ in quality. They are not frequently encountered. Particularly worthy of mention is a Phoenix-like bird resting on a high mounded base and bearing the Lloyd Shelton mark. It belongs to the Victoria and Albert Museum, and is illustrated in G.A. Godden's *An Illustrated Encyclopaedia of British Pottery and Porcelain*, figure 354.

As regards the second half of the nineteenth century, the Royal Worcester factory is known to have modelled a variety of different birds (in addition to swans). In 1872 it modelled a Hawk (item 295 in its list) and a Dove (item 296), in 1874 an Owl (item 376), a Parrot (item 377), a 'Cock and hen group and single' (item 378), a Cockatoo (item 411), a Hanging dove (item 416) and a Stork (item 467). In 1877 it modelled a Cockatoo and frame (item 610) and a Magpie and frame (item 611), and in 1880 a Fowl (item 790).[2] See also the Dog and pheasant and Fox and goose referred to at pp.121 and 165 respectively.

---

1. Ibid., p.214.
2. Henry Sandon's *Royal Worcester Porcelain* Appendix 1.

6. The History of the Factories

The Rockingham Factory

HISTORY

The finest porcelain animals to be produced in this country in the nineteenth century were made at the Rockingham factory, which was located at Swinton, near Rotherham, Yorkshire. During its short life as a porcelain producer, the factory was under the patronage of Earl Fitzwilliam and dependent upon him for financial support, taking its name from the Earl's relative, the Marquis of Rockingham. In 1806 the factory, which had produced earthenware from about the middle of the eighteenth century, came under the ownership of the Brameld family. However, by 1826 the business had become insolvent and it was only saved from extinction by the timely financial assistance of Earl Fitzwilliam. The Brameld brothers — Thomas, George and John Wager — had persuaded him that they were capable of manufacturing porcelain and that, given the requisite financial backing, they could equal, not to say surpass, in quality the products of all contemporary factories. In the event, they were largely successful in this ambition, turning out, *inter alia,* the famous Royal Service for William IV. However, their financial management was not on a par with their artistic attainments, and in 1842 the Earl's successor, despairing of the Bramelds ever getting the factory to pay its way, withdrew all further support and the production of this outstanding nineteenth century factory came to an end for ever.

GENERAL CHARACTERISTICS

The output of the Rockingham factory was varied in the extreme, and, for a short period at least, included figures and more particularly porcelain animals. It is perhaps surprising that a factory, which undertook such ambitious projects as the Royal Service and turned out ornamental pieces of truly outstanding quality, should have bothered to produce such modest items as small porcelain animals, but luckily for us it did. In quality Rockingham animals surpass all others from English factories of the nineteenth century. Although the modelling is no better than that of contemporary Derby animals, generally speaking, the paste and glaze are superior and the palette used significantly more tasteful.

Rockingham animals appear sometimes in the biscuit state (figures 73, 75 and 97), but more frequently glazed. If glazed, they are either white and gilt or enamelled and gilt. Like the contemporary Derby models Rockingham animals usually have bases with flat undersides that are unglazed and closed in, save for a small round hole centrally located[1], although in the case of the rare white and gilt cat illustrated in figure 5

---

1. This form of base construction would appear to have been introduced from Derby, probably by Thomas Griffin, who may well have been the modeller of many, if not most, of the Rockingham animals.

these characteristics are strangely missing. Instead the underside of the base assumes a slightly recessed form, is glazed, and is without any hole (figure 4).

Nearly all Rockingham animals have under the base an incised model number preceded by the incised letters 'No' in script. This feature, incidentally, is not found on contemporary Derby models. The only numbers appearing on the latter are 1, 2 or 3 without the prefix 'No', and these were intended to indicate size, a practice likewise, but less frequently, adopted at Swinton, where occasionally the explanatory word 'size' in script is also incised against the relevant number (see colour plate 1 and figure 1b and c). It is an interesting characteristic of Rockingham animals that, unlike their Derby counterparts, the facial markings of non-enamelled examples are not normally represented by gilding (an exception is the squirrel of figure 130).

MARKS

Most Rockingham animals are marked, sometimes with the impressed words 'Rockingham Works Brameld' (with or without an impressed griffin[1]), at other times simply with the letters 'Cl'[2] written (normally in script) in red, gold, mauve or black followed by a similarly written '1' in the case of white and gilt examples,[3] and '2' in the case of enamelled and gilt specimens.[4] Not infrequently both forms of mark appear together. Very rarely variations of the impressed mark are found, e.g. the words 'ROCKINGHAM WORKS' appear alone (figure 1b) or the single word 'BRAMELD' (colour plate 1a) and in three recorded instances (almost certainly early models), the cat of figure 5, the pug bitch of colour plate 11 and the black cat (model 77) sold at Sotheby's on 22 May 1984 (lot 585 of their 'British and Irish Ceramics' sale), in the place of the impressed mark there is to be seen the printed red griffin mark consisting of the griffin and the words in two rows underneath 'Rockingham Works, Brameld', all printed in red.

---

1. The griffin was the heraldic emblem of Earl Fitzwilliam, who allowed the factory to use it as part of its mark.
2. 'Cl' almost certainly stands for 'Class'. See A. and A. Cox's *The Rockingham Works,* p.61.
3. However, one of the ewes in colour plate 22 and a matching ram belonging to the Yorkshire Museum, which are enamelled, but without any gilding, have in each instance a 'Cl 1' notation. Such was the case also with the two white monkeys seated on claret bases sold at Sotheby's on 21 October 1986, lots 375 and 376. These would seem to be exceptions to the general rule.
4. However the setter shown in figure 72 and a ram sold by Christie's on 27 November 1978 (lot 164), though in both cases gilt and enamelled, have the 'Cl 1' mark.

INCISED NUMBERS

The presence, under the base of a porcelain animal, of both a

Rockingham mark and an incised number (prefaced by 'No' in incised script) enables us to identify that model with the Swinton factory, and the effect of this is that where an *unmarked* example bears the same incised number (preceded by the letters 'No') it can confidently be attributed to the Rockingham factory. In other words, notwithstanding the absence of a mark, an incised number is enough to link the relevant animal with the factory, provided that the number has at least on one occasion been found in company with a Rockingham mark and is preceded by the letters 'No'. All the Rockingham models identified to date are contained in the list set out at the end of this section.

Rockingham animals are very rare — indeed not infrequently there is only one recorded example of a particular model — and this gives rise to special difficulties in identification. For a perfectly genuine Rockingham animal may come to light which bears a number after the letters 'No' in incised script, but its provenance cannot be confirmed by comparison with a marked specimen, similarly numbered, for the simple reason that no such specimen is known to exist. However, as the presence of an incised number (preceded by 'No' in script) would seem, in the case of nineteenth century models, to be unique to Rockingham, if that number corresponds with a vacancy in the series of numbers known to have been used on Rockingham models, an attribution to the Rockingham factory is fairly safe, provided at least that there is nothing in the paste, glaze, gilding or palette used to put the issue in doubt.

Before leaving the matter of incised numbers, a further difficulty should be briefly mentioned. The numbers were manually incised by the factory workmen, and sometimes they made a mistake, putting the wrong number on a particular model. Thus, the dog illustrated in figure 72 bears the incised number 90 when it should be 94. If there are at least three examples of a particular model still extant, an isolated error will be shown up by the conflicting number on the other two examples. However, where two examples only of a particular model are recorded, although the existence of an error will be clear from the difference in numbering, it will not always be possible to say which number is correct. Sometimes, of course, the difficulty is resolved by other evidence, e.g. one of the two conflicting numbers may be known as belonging to a totally different model, so that it is obvious that this is the number that has been misused. Needless to say, where there is only one recorded example of a model, and that has been misnumbered, the difficulties will be aggravated still further. Indeed, it will not necessarily be known that there is any error in the first place. However, most examples are correctly numbered, so that the problems mentioned above should not be exaggerated.

At the end of this section is a list of numbers which have been identified with particular Rockingham models. The first part consists of animals or groups of animals. The second part contains groups where one or more animals are combined with a human figure. The third part sets out the numbers belonging to human figures *simpliciter*. Although human figures unaccompanied by any animal do not fall within the compass of this book, the model numbers assigned to them are relevant, in that they serve to eliminate numbers which might otherwise be thought available for animal models. A careful study of the list suggests that separate individual animal models were not among the first figures to be produced at the factory, if, of course, the numbers indicate the order in which the various models were produced. (The lowest number so far recorded is 69, and in the light of the information contained in Parts 2 and 3 of the list at the end of this section it is unlikely that any individual animal model ever bore a number lower than 67). However, this view as to the chronology of the factory's figures may be an over-simplification. For on the three animals where the red printed griffin mark was used (see the paragraph on marks), there is no incised number, presumably because, at the time they were produced, the numbering system had not yet started. The black cat which was sold at Sotheby's on 22 May 1984 was actually the model now known as No 77, but the fact that that model was in due course given so high a number does not necessarily mean that it was the seventy-seventh model to be produced, and therefore issued some significant time after the factory's opening; it could well have been an early model, subsequently brought into the numbering system.

It is interesting to note that certain Rockingham models, e.g. No 76 (a pug[1]), No 77 (a cat seated on a tasselled cushion, not the alternative version on an oval base[2]), No 101 (a seated pointer looking upwards[3]) No 104 (a recumbent cat[4]) and No 108 (a ram and a ewe[5]), are almost identical with items found at the Derby factory. The Rockingham models would seem to be copies of Derby models (see pages 220 and 223).

Although it is impossible to be certain, in all probability the following numbers (so far unassigned to any Rockingham figure) relate to animals: 75, 79, 86, 88, 95, 97, 103 and 105. (The basis for this assertion is that all the assigned numbers from 69 to 112 belong to animals with one solitary exception, viz 102. However, this very exception, assuming that

---

1. Cf. colour plate 12 with colour plate 5a.
2. Cf. colour plate 1b with colour plate 5b.
3. Cf. figures 81 and 121b.
4. Cf. figures 9 and 10.
5. Cf. figures 105 and 106.

the sole surviving example was not erroneously numbered, prevents dogmatism.) Although animal models initially stopped at 112, they resumed later, for the peacocks of figure 160 are incised 'No 136' and the monkey of colour plate 33, 'No 142'. However, there may not be many animals in this high number range. Numbers 138, 139, 146 and 148 are, for a start, known to belong to Continental peasant figures, and not to animals.

Although most Rockingham animals are in the form of independent individual models,[1] occasionally composite models are encountered comprising both a human figure and an animal. Thus the pair of figures, each incised with 'No 4', shown in colour plate 24, consist of a shepherd and dog, and shepherdess and sheep. These models were produced at an early stage in the factory's life in that some examples have the red-printed mark, and not the more frequent impressed mark. Neither the dog nor the sheep has so far been found as an individual model, though it would be surprising if the factory lost an opportunity of producing them separately.

Strangely 'No 4' also appears under the base of the shepherd and dog group illustrated in figure 91. The model is quite different from that shown in colour plate 24, and is in fact a copy of the Bow model, itself a copy of the Meissen model. It too bears the printed red mark. The device tied to the dog's throat was probably something worn by Continental sheep dogs to protect their throats from the attacks of wolves. Once again the dog has not been recorded as an individual model. Notwithstanding that we have here two completely different 'shepherd and dog' models incised with the same number, it is unlikely that there is any misnumbering. For the version shown in colour plate 24 appears with reasonable frequency (insofar as any Rockingham figure can be said to appear frequently) and it invariably has 'No 4' incised under the base. The other shepherd and dog model (the 'eighteenth century version') was the first to be produced, but was subsequently replaced by the other more modern version. However, the later more common model was nevertheless of early origin, in that it is sometimes found with the printed red mark, and if the 'eighteenth century version' predates that, then the latter was probably one of the first figures ever to have been produced at Swinton. It follows as a necessary corollary that the dog appearing with the shepherd can be regarded as having been modelled at the very commencement of the factory's life as a porcelain producer.

There is no known alternative version of the shepherdess and sheep

---

1. See Part I of the list at the end of this section. There are also a few animal groups, e.g. nos. 70, 89 and 107.

group, but in a case where this model appeared in company with an 'eighteenth century version' of the shepherd and dog group, it is recorded that the former was incised, not as it normally is with 'No 4', but instead with 'No 5'. This could, of course, be an example of an error on the part of one of the factory hands, but another possible explanation is that originally the shepherd and dog and shepherdess and sheep groups were not produced as a pair with the same incised number, but were individual groups separately numbered. It was only when the 'eighteenth century version' of the shepherd and dog was 'modernised' that the shepherdess and sheep group came to be paired with it. Further support for this view can be found in the discovery by A. and A. Cox of the base (intended to support a standing figure) of a master model (excavated from the factory site) inscribed 'June 10th 1830 No 5'.[1] The size of the base (only 1 ½ in. (3.8cm) in diameter) shows that it did not belong to the shepherdess and sheep group and the late date of the inscription surely indicates that the model was a replacement for the original shepherdess and sheep group which had been renumbered 'No 4'. In any event, the sheep is clearly a very early animal model, and it was probably one of the first items of porcelain the factory produced.

Other examples of composite groups where a human figure appears with an animal are a girl playing with a kitten (No 40, colour plate 4a), a boy feeding a rabbit (No 44, colour plate 30), a companion model of a girl about to give the lamb she is holding a drink of milk (also No 44, colour plate 23), a girl clutching a lamb (No 26, figure 103), a girl standing on a pierced scroll base holding a lamb (No 35, figure 104) and the companion model of a boy with a dog (also No 35, figure 104). None of the animals appearing in these composite groups has so far been recorded as existing as an independent model. However, in the case of a group consisting of a Continental shepherd with a dog and sheep (No 58, figure 90), the sheep would appear to be an adaptation of the individual sheep shown in figures 100b and 101 (No 100), and the dog seems to be the same model (in reverse) as accompanies the shepherd of colour plate 24b (No 4).

There is some evidence for the view that Thomas Griffin was the modeller of at least some of the animals produced at Rockingham (see page 223). Moreover, there may be some connection with William Coffee (see page 220). Interesting examples of all-animal groups are a dog looking at a rat (No 89, figures 97 and 98), a rabbit with young (No 70, figure 136a) and a cat with three kittens (No 107, colour plate 3 and figures 6 to 8).

---

1. See *Trans E.C.C.*, Vol. 12, Part 3, p.243.

Dating

A particular feature of Rockingham animals (and for that matter Rockingham figures generally) is that they can be dated to within a comparatively short period, namely from 1826 to about 1830. This is extremely important in the study of nineteenth century porcelain animals, which are notoriously difficult to date with any precision, for by being able to attribute the Rockingham models to a brief period of some four or five years we have a comparative yardstick by which to date other porcelain animals produced by other factories.

The reason for supposing that Rockingham animals were only made during the opening four or five years of the factory's life as a porcelain producer is based on the form of the mark used (where the mark is the full version and not merely a 'Cl' with the numeral 1 or 2). As explained, earlier, that mark consists of the impressed words 'Rockingham Works Brameld' with or without an impressed griffin, or very rarely the printed mark in red. Not all examples were so marked, but where they were, the use of the early form of mark which makes no reference to the factory's being 'Royal' or to its being 'Manufacturer to the King', descriptions assumed as part of the mark after the order for the Royal Service had been received in 1830, would indicate that all the animals are to be assigned to the period from 1826 to 1830 or slightly later. A contrary view has been expressed by A. and A. Cox, but in my judgment, this view simply cannot stand in the face of the evidence as a whole. For a discussion of this issue see Appendix C.

Models

PART I

Individual models or groups consisting of animals alone

Model Nos	Description	Height in./cm	Length in./cm	Width in./cm	Colour Plate	Figure
69	An Elephant	1½ in./3.8	1⅞ in./4.7	1¼ in./3.2	35a	
70	A toy group of rabbit and young	⅞ in./2.2	1⅞ in./4.7	1⅜ in./3.5		136a
71	A toy foxhound sitting	1⅛ in./2.8				88b
72	A toy rabbit	½ in./1.2	⅞ in./2.2	⁹/₁₆ in./1.4		136b
73	A toy squirrel	2 in./5.1				130
74	A toy foxhound sitting	1⅜ in./3.5				88a
76	A pug dog (also modelled in reverse to form a pair)					
	First size	2⅝ in./6.7			12	
	Second size	2⅛ in./5.2			12	
76	A pug bitch	2⅝ in./6.7				
77	A cat sitting on a tasselled cushion					
	First size	2½ in./6.4 or 2⅜ in./6			1b	1a
	Second size	2⅛ in./5.2				1b
	Third size	1¾ in./4.4				1c
	Toy	1⅜ in./3.5			2	2
77	A cat sitting on an oval scroll base					
	First size	2¼ in./5.7			1a	
	Second size	1⅞ in./4.7				3
78	A rabbit on an oval base, with a tree stump behind		2½ in./6.4			Cf.137
80	A stag at lodge		2¾ in./7	1⅞ in./4.7		126
80	A doe at lodge		3¼ in./8.3	1⅞ in./4.7		126
81	A toy fox	1½ in./3.8				133
82	A seated poodle	3 in./7.6				37
83	A springer spaniel running	2⅞ in./7.3	3¼ in./8.3			57
84	A standing setter drinking from a bowl	3¼ in./8.3	3¾ in./9.5			75
85	A standing English pointer bitch	4½ in./11.4	4⅝ in./14.3	1⅝ in./4.2		
87	A great Dane lying recumbent with head raised	2⅝ in./6.7	3¾ in./9.5	2⅜ in./6.1	19	85
89	A dog standing watching a rat	3¼ in./8.3	5 in./12.7	2¼ in./5.7		97 & 98
90	A recumbent mastiff with tongue hanging out	1⅝ in./4.2	4⅝ in./11.7	1¾ in./4.4	20	

Model Nos	Description	Height in./cm	Length in./cm	Width in./cm	Colour Plate	Figure
91	A small setter lying curled up (Presumably there was also a companion dog or bitch in reverse — pp.96, 97).	1⅛ in./2.8	2⅝ in./6.7	1⅝ in./4.2	16b	73a
92	A dog lying down with raised head	2¼ in./5.7	3¾ in./9.5	2½ in./6.4		
93	A Spanish pointer bitch walking (Presumably there was also a companion dog in reverse)	2¼ in./5.7	4½ in./11.4			82
94	A setter lying recumbent with head raised. Also in reverse	2in./5.1	4¼ in./10.8	2¼ in./5.7	16a	72, 73b
96	A toy seated setter		1¾ in./4.4			60
98	A standing sheep	3⅛ in./8				
99	A swan	2¼ in./5.7	2⅞ in./7.3			162
100	A sheep lying on a circular base	2⅜ in./6	3in./7.6			100b & 101
101	A seated pointer looking upwards Also a bitch in reverse	3in./7.6				81
104	A cat lying down	1¾ in./4.4	2¾ in./7	1¼ in./3.2	4b	9b
106	A crouching hare on an oval base	1⅝ in./4.2	2⅜ in./6	1½ in./3.8		142
106	The above model in reverse					
107	A group comprising a cat and three kittens					
	First size	2in./5.1	4¼ in./10.8	2in./5.1	3	6-8
	Second size	1¾ in./4.4	3⅞ in./9.8	1¾ in./4.4		
108	A recumbent ram	1¾ in./4.4	2½ in./6.4	1¾ in./4.4	22	105
108	A recumbent ewe	1¾ in./4.4	2¼ in./5.7	1¾ in./4.4	22	105
109	A small sheep or lamb recumbent on a round base	1⅜ in./3.5	1⅝ in./4.2			100a
110	A crouching rabbit	2in./5.1	2¾ in./7	1¾ in./4.4	27a	135
110	Also in reverse					
111	A squirrel	2⅜ in./6			27b	
112	A dove with open wings	3in./7.6				163
136	A peacock with fanned tail	3⅞ in./9.8				160
142	A seated monkey eating fruit					
	First size	3⅛ in./7.9				
	Second size	2¾ in./7			33	
Unnumbered	A pug dog sitting on an oval base	2⅝ in./6.7			11	
	A pug bitch sitting on an oval base	2½ in./6.4			11	
	A cat sitting on on oval base	2½ in./6.4				5
	Silhouette or flat-back models Group comprising a pair of greyhounds the bitch standing the dog lying recumbent		2¹³/₁₆in./7.2			24

PART 2

Groups where an animal or animals are combined with a human figure

Model Nos	Description	Height in./cm.	Colour plate	Figure
4	A shepherd and dog, '18th century' version	7¼ in./18.4		91
	Later version	8¼ in./21 or 8½ in./21.6	24b	
4	A shepherdess and sheep	6¾ in./17.1	24a	
5	A shepherdess and sheep (see p.207)	6¾ in./17.1	(As for No 4)	
26	A girl holding a lamb	5½ in./14		103
30	A boy with a bird on his left hand	4⅞ in./12.4		
35	A boy standing on a pierced scroll base clasping a lamb	5¾ in./14.6		104
35	A girl standing on a pierced scroll base clasping a lamb	5¾ in./14.6		104
40	A kneeling girl with a kitten playing with an apple in her hat	3¾ in./9.5	4a	
44	A kneeling boy feeding a rabbit	5½ in./14	30	
44	A seated girl with a lamb under her right arm	3¾ in./9.5	23	
58	A Continental shepherd with a sheep and dog	7¾ in./19.7		90

PART 3

Non-animal models

1, 2, 6-11, 13-15, 18, 19, 21-23, 25, 26 (boy with pitcher), 28, 29, 31, 32, 36-39, 42, 48-50, 53, 57-58, 63-66, 102, 113-115, 119, 120 and 139.

To these should be added the following models, namely 17, 125, 126, 138, 146 and 148. Although no examples of these six have so far been recorded, A. and A. Cox have unearthed from the factory's site, bases from master models incised with these numbers. These bases would appear to belong to 'Continental Peasants' (see *Trans. E.C.C* vol. 12, Part 3, p.247).

The Derby Factory
(at the Nottingham Road)

HISTORY

The Derby factory came into existence about 1750. Its early history[1] is not altogether clear. It appears originally to have been owned by Andrew Planché, a goldsmith by training. In January 1756, Planché was joined by William Duesbury, a china decorator and John Heath, a banker, but shortly thereafter Planché left the partnership and disappeared from the scene altogether. The management of the factory devolved on William Duesbury, albeit John Heath remained a partner until his bankruptcy in 1780. Thereafter William Duesbury remained sole owner until his death in 1786, when he was succeeded by his son, also called William. The latter died in 1796 or 1797, but prior to his demise, when his health was failing, he took into partnership Michael Kean, an artist of considerable merit in his own right. In 1798 Michael Kean married Duesbury's widow. Her eldest son, William Duesbury III, was then only about eleven years old and, of course, too young to assume control of the business. However, even when he reached maturity he never really took any interest in the concern and eventually left the town of Derby. In 1809 the business was advertised for sale and in 1810 or 1811 was sold to Robert Bloor, who agreed to pay, in addition to certain annuities to the family of the late proprietor, £5,000 in instalments. Robert Bloor had been employed as a clerk and salesman under Duesbury and Kean. In order to pay off the instalments he resorted to the highly dubious expedient of selling by auction various 'seconds' which had accumulated at the factory under his predecessors. He was also responsible for some debasement in the standard of decoration. In consequence the business suffered a decline in reputation during the Bloor period of control. In 1828 Bloor became insane and the management of the business fell to James Thomason, who discharged his duties both honestly and competently. In 1844 Thomas Clarke, malster and corn factor, married Bloor's granddaughter and sole surviving descendant, and 'took out a Statute of Lunacy'. He carried on the works until 1848 when they were finally closed down and the whole plant was sold to Samuel Boyle of Fenton.[2] Derby animals of the first half of the nineteenth century are of high quality, falling only marginally short of the standard set by the Rockingham factory.

PASTE AND GLAZE

The Derby paste and glaze are so similar to those employed at the Rockingham factory that differentiation is extremely difficult. However,

---

1. See D.G. Rice, *Derby Porcelain, The Golden Years, 1750-70* pp.9-22.
2. For a more detailed history see Haslem's *The Old Derby China Factory* pp. 15-31.

Rockingham animals usually appear slightly softer to the touch than their Derby counterparts.

BASES

The construction of the underside of Derby bases is the same as that employed at Swinton and on contemporary animals at the Minton works. The underside is flat, unglazed and closed-in save for a small hole to allow the escape of occluded gases, and this hole is usually located in an approximately central position. Derby (and Minton) animals, unlike those of the Rockingham factory, are never incised with a model number. However, sometimes 1, 2 and 3 appear under the bases of Derby animals, so as to indicate size, i.e. whether the item is the first (the largest), the second or the third size.

MARKS

Although Derby animals of the first half of the nineteenth century are rarely marked (those of the second half of the century are dealt with under the King Street factory), nevertheless when they are, they carry one or other of the following:

1. A crown over crossed batons, dots and a 'D' written in red script (as under the base of the horse of figure 121a and the cat of colour plate 6). This mark ceased about 1825.

2. A crown over 'D' in red (as under the bases of the dogs of figure 38, the tiger and leopard of colour plate 32 and the pair of peacocks of figure 159).

3. A crown over the name 'DERBY', the latter appearing within a ribbon band, all printed in red, as under the base of the elephant and driver of figure 159b.

4. A circular band encompassing a crown, the words 'Bloor Derby' appearing within the band, all in red (as under the base of the cat of figure 10a and the mouse of colour plate 28b). This mark was employed from about 1825 onwards.

5. Crossed Swords in blue, an imitation Meissen mark (as under the base of the horse appearing in the Loan Exhibition of the Burlington House Fair September 1985 (item 82) (see page 145) and on certain members of the monkey and bear band of figure 151).

MODELS

John Haslem in his *The Old Derby China Factory* sets out in numerical order the various models turned out by the factory in the eighteenth century. Each figure produced from about 1770 onwards was frequently incised with the appropriate model number. This numbered list (unlike that of

Bemrose[1]) does not contain any independent animal models. However, Haslem refers to a short list of unnumbered models, most of which appear to have been made in the eighteenth century, though some were continued into the succeeding century. The list, which consists exclusively of animals together with prices set against each model, is as follows:

	Enamelled and gilt		
	£.	s.	d.
Pointer and Setter, per pair, Coffee	0	7	0
Large Pug Dogs ditto ditto	0	4	0
Less ditto ditto ditto	0	3	0
Small ditto ditto ditto	0	2	0
Begging Pugs, ditto Chelsea	0	2	0
Ditto French Dogs[2] ditto ditto	0	2	0
Large Sheep and Lambs, per pair, Holmes	0	7	0
Sheep lying down, ditto ditto	0	4	0
Standing sheep, ditto ditto	0	4	0
Ditto ditto, two smaller sizes, ditto			
Lambs with Sprigs, per pair, Chelsea	0	2	0
Ditto without ditto, each, ditto	0	0	10
Canary Birds, each, ditto	0	1	0
Tomtit, ditto ditto	0	1	0
Linnet, ditto ditto	0	1	0
Birds on Branches, two sizes, ditto			

The above models have been discussed in earlier chapters under the appropriate animal headings. The next list given by Haslem is headed 'THE FOLLOWING ARE FROM BOW AND CHELSEA MODELS'. It includes the following animals (their price, where this is given by Haslem, being shown against the relevant item).

---

1. See William Bemrose: *Bow Chelsea and Derby Porcelain* pp 69-85.
2. Presumably poodles.

	Enamelled and gilt			Biscuit		
	£	s	d	£	s	d
Large Stags, per pair	0	15	0			
Ditto, two smaller sizes						
Large Sitting Cat						
Cat lying down	0	0	6			
Ditto with gold collar	0	1	0			
Cow and Calf, per pair	0	6	6	0	9	0
Ditto, ditto, lying down						
Large Swan	0	1	3			
Two smaller sizes of same, 1s. and 10d. each						
Large Squirrel	0	1	3			
Two smaller sizes of same, 1s. and 10d. each						
Mice, each	0	1	6	0	1	6
Poodle Dogs and Fleecy Sheep, each				0	5	0
Lowing Cow, each	0	5	0			
Sitting Foxes, per pair	0	7	0			
Large Panthers						
Small ditto per pair	0	3	0			
Foxes, per pair	0	10	6			
Dogs from the Dresden Shepherd, each	0	1	0			
London Pointer and Greyhound, each	0	1 ·	6			

(The list also includes certain animal heads and animal boats, but these cannot properly be regarded as animals within the ambit of this book and are therefore omitted.)

Now, although there is no evidence, apart from Haslem's statement, that the above animals ever came from the Bow and Chelsea models (it is not even absolutely certain that the Derby factory ever acquired the Bow concern), nevertheless, it is reasonable to assume that they were at least all eighteenth century in origin. Certainly some of them are referred to in Bemrose's list of moulds and models existing in 1795, e.g:

'Pair laying cats, 2 sizes'
'Pair large siting [sic] cats'

'Pair greyhounds with ground pedestal'
'Pair laying cows, small'
'Ditto, larger'
'Pair large stags'
'Squirrel, 3 sizes'
'Swans, 3 sizes'
'Laying cows' [the lowing cow is in a recumbent position]
'Small foxes'
'Two foxes'
There is also a reference to 'Pair large tygers [sic], 2 sizes'. These could be the same models as the panthers listed in Haslem's list, save for the difference in decoration.

Many of the models included by Haslem in the above list were carried over into the nineteenth century, the colouring, the gilding, the glaze and the paste serving to connect them with the later century. In fact some models are far more associated with the nineteenth than the eighteenth century. Although identification with a particular model included in Haslem's list is not always easy and there can never be any absolute certainty — the description is so brief — we can with reasonable confidence assert that the following examples from the list have been identified:

Large sitting cats (see pages 25 and 26)
Cats lying down (see page 25; figures 10 and 11)
Swans (see page 196)
Squirrels (see pages 161 and 162; figures 25a and 131)
Poodle dogs (see pages 66 and 67)
Fleecy sheep (see pages 127, 130; figure 102).
Sitting foxes (see pages 162, 164; colour plate 26 and figure 25b).
Small panthers (if they can be regarded as leopards) see page 180; colour plate 32).
Dogs from the Dresden Shepherd (see pages 104, 105; figure 121b).

Some of the most interesting Derby animal models are those attributed by Haslem to Edward Keys. The list includes:

	Enamelled and gilt			Biscuit			Figures
	£	s	d	£	s	d	
Large Elephant, with Driver		10	6				159b
Ditto, with cloths, no Driver		9	0				
Peacock		2	0		3	6	

	Enamelled and gilt			Biscuit			Figures
	£	s	d	£	s	d	
Lean Cows, per pair		3	6				(colour plate 25)
Small Elephant		1	6				
New Sitting Pugs, on Cushions		1	6				
Small Sitting Foxes		1	6				134
Large Monkey Musicians, each		7	6				
Small ditto ditto		5	0				
Doctor Syntax Mounted on Horseback		12	6				
Bucks and Does		4	0		7	0	127
Small Standing Sheep					7	0	
Rabbits on Plinths		2	0				
Ditto without Plinths		1	6				137
Large Horses		2	0				121a
Pony		1	6				
Cats on Cushions, large, each		2	0				
Ditto ditto small, ditto		1	6				(colour plate 5b)
Lion and lioness, ditto		2	0				
Worcester Mice, ditto		2	0				(colour plate 28b)
New Poodle Dogs, ditto		2	0				38
New Cats with prey, ditto		1	6				
Sheep in Fold, ditto		4	0				

Some of the above models have already been discussed in earlier chapters under the appropriate animal headings. As Edward Keys left Derby in 1826, all the models must have been executed before that date. Exactly how long the factory continued to produce them is not known.

The cats of colour plate 6 present something of a puzzle. They are undoubtedly from the Derby factory and one of them carries the crown over batons, dots and 'D' mark in red, a mark which it is generally accepted ceased around 1825. However, the model is rare, as is the group on a similar base comprising a recumbent cat and kitten (colour plate 7a), which likewise does not occur in Haslem's lists. Moreover, a pug dog (illustrated in Sotheby's sale catalogue of 9 February 1971 lot 104), marked in the same way as the cat, is also unrecorded by Haslem. There are also other animal models seemingly from the Derby factory which have likewise been omitted e.g. camels. All that can be said is that Haslem's lists are not complete.[1]

Certainly Haslem never claimed that the various lists included all the later models. According to him, 'A number of other Figures were published which were not entered in this list, the keeping of the list probably having ceased at the time they were modelled. Thus Louis Bradley modelled two Dancing Figures, and John Whitaker, between 1830 and 1847, among others modelled the following . . .' There then appears a list of models which as far as animals are concerned consists of:

Boy and Dog
Girl and Dog
Mazeppa on Wild Horse
Boy with Greyhound
Girl with Falcon
Group of Stags
Ditto of Dogs
Leaping Stag
Peacock among flowers
Parrot

A Derby group consisting of a small boy riding a Newfoundland dog, based on an engraving, is recorded, and this same dog bearing the Bloor mark was also produced as an independent model.[2] It may well be that the group was the 'Boy and Dog' referred to in Haslem's list.

An example of the 'Group of Stags' in biscuit is to be seen in the Victoria and Albert Museum, and an example of 'Mazeppa on Wild Horse', likewise in biscuit, 5½ in. (14cm) high, is in the possession of the Derby Museum. Interestingly, an example of the 'Group of Stags' appears as item 174 of *A Descriptive Catalogue of Porcelain and other Art Objects in the Collection of William Bemrose*, privately printed in 1898. The entry reads:

'Group, in biscuit, of two stags; modelled by J. Whittaker [sic]; h.6in'.

This group was included in the sale of the collection, which took place in March 1909, and realised £5.15s.6d.

Far and away the best known of John Whitaker's models is the 'Peacock among flowers'. These Peacocks, 6½ in. (16.5cm) high, were sometimes sold in pairs (figures 159a and c). It is to be noted that the 'Boy and Dog', the 'Mazeppa on Wild Horse', the 'Group of Stags' and the

1. This is certainly true as regards human figures. Thus, not included in the lists, are recorded marked examples from the Bloor period of such figures as George IV, Rev. George Selwyn, a milkman, a milkman, and a Swiss boy and Swiss girl.
2. See *The Connoisseur*, September 1922, p.34 (illustration no. 11).

'Peacock among flowers' are all comparatively large as against the general run of Derby animals of the immediately preceding period. Examples of the other models appearing in the list of John Whitaker's work are unrecorded.

It is clear from Haslem's remarks quoted above that, after Edward Keys left Derby, no new models were listed by the factory, and we have no means of knowing from its records (save to the extent that Haslem attributes certain models to John Whitaker) what new animals were produced after 1826. We are dependent on surviving examples. In this category would appear to fall the pair of goats referred to at page 152.

Modellers

WILLIAM COFFEE (d. 1848)

For our knowledge of William Coffee we are dependent on what Jewitt and, to a lesser extent, Haslem tell us of him. He was the son of a potter who worked at either Hempel's or Triquet's pottery, Chelsea. After first being employed at Coade's Lambeth Pottery he commenced employment at the Derby works in 1791, initially it would seem, merely as a kilnman. Shortly thereafter he must have been put onto modelling; for in 1794 his abilities as a modeller were criticised by the factory's London agent. A short while after that adverse comment a new agreement was made between Coffee and Duesbury regulating the method of payment for Coffee's models. On 30 January 1795, another contract of service was entered into, but in that same year Coffee left to work for Sir Nigel Gresley Bt. and Mr Adderley, at their china works at Burton-on-Trent. On 9 September 1795 his father wrote to Duesbury asking him to take back his son. Duesbury acquiesced and Coffee returned to his job. However, after a few years, he left (c.1798) to work on his own account at Friar Gate, Derby, taking with him as a partner a fellow-modeller, William Duesbury, known as 'Billy' to distinguish him from the proprietor of the Derby factory. The partnership only lasted a year, with Billy returning to his old employment. However, Coffee continued on his own account until at least 1810, albeit he ceased to model in porcelain, turning instead to terracotta and plaster-of-Paris. Some of his work he stamped with his name, occasionally with the relevant model number or date added. Jewitt says of his production that: 'a wolf, a lion, a dog and others are strikingly good'.[1]

An interesting example of his work as an independent operator is shown in plate 42 of the *Ceramics of Derbyshire* (ed. by H.G. Bradley). The

---

1. *Ceramic Art in Great Britain*, Vol. II, p.98.

material used would appear to have been, not terracotta, but a kind of unglazed creamware. The model which is signed 'W Coffee' on the upperside of the base is of a setter lying curled up on a rectangular plinth 3⅝ in. (9.3cm) long. After leaving Derby, Coffee is said by Haslem to have gone to London and at a later date to America. He died in 1848. Presumably the signed dog mentioned above was turned out sometime between (say) 1798 and 1810, but what is especially interesting is that the same model, albeit somewhat smaller (see colour plate 16b and figure 73a) was produced at the Rockingham factory during the period 1826-30, probably around 1827. Was there some connection between Coffee and the Rockingham factory?

An intriguing feature of this problem is the existence of another porcelain example of Coffee's setter (figure 74). It is the reverse model albeit not the same in size as the animal of colour plate 16b. Whether it was produced by the Rockingham factory is uncertain. It does not carry a Rockingham mark or even the incised 'No 91'. Although the absence of these distinguishing features is not necessarily fatal to a Rockingham attribution, it at least brings such a provenance into question. However, the only other factory which could conceivably have produced the animal of figure 74 is the Derby factory, but this model does not appear in any of Haslem's lists. The porcelain itself and the palette employed do not conclude the matter one way or the other. Unfortunately, the base is enamelled black and the dog itself is cream and brown, colours which do not suggest unequivocally either a Rockingham or Derby origin. There is no evidence that Coffee ever worked at Swinton, but did he supply the model or even the moulds from London, or if he was in America at the relevant time, did his son, who continued the business in London, do so? Moreover if the animal of figure 74 is Derby rather than Rockingham — and on balance this is more likely to be the case — did he or his son supply the model or moulds to that factory?

Whilst Coffee was working at the Derby factory he was responsible for modelling a pair of pugs in three different sizes, copied from earlier Derby pugs produced from c.1758 onwards. Although Coffee's models must have been produced before 1800 (see page 219), all the surviving examples seem to belong to the nineteenth century (see colour plate 5a and figures 25c and 31). It is interesting to note that the Rockingham factory during the period 1826-30 produced almost identical models (see colour plate 12). Again was Coffee in any way involved? Unfortunately the evidence is wholly insufficient to enable us to make any firm pronouncements in the case of either the pugs or the setter.

EDWARD KEYS (b.1798) and **SAMUEL KEYS** (b.c.1804)

We are indebted to Haslem for the following biographies of Edward and Samuel Keys:[1] 'Edward and Samuel, two sons of Samuel Keys, sen., served their apprenticeship at Derby, as modellers and ornamental repairers, and each was, for a time, foreman of that department. Edward Keys left Derby about 1826, and went into the Staffordshire Potteries, where he worked first for Messrs Daniell, and afterwards for Messrs Minton and other firms. He was the modeller of a number of figures which were issued at Derby; among them were twelve or fourteen different statuettes of Dr Syntax, which, as they were brought out shortly after the publication of Combe's graphic adventures of the Doctor, had a large sale. He also modelled portrait statuettes of George IV and Napoleon, ten or twelve inches in height, together with several smaller figures and animals, a set of grotesque monkey musicians, some of the characters from Pierce Egan's then popular work, *Life in London* etc.... [Isaac] Farnsworth died at a good age in 1821, and Edward Keys succeeded him as foreman in the figure department. Edward Keys left Derby in 1826, and Thomas Griffin, another of the modellers, was then appointed foreman, but only for a short time. Samuel Keys jun., succeeded Griffin, and filled the situation until 1830.'

The list of Derby animals attributed to Edward Keys is set out at pages 216 and 217, and some of them are illustrated. Like all Derby figures, whether of the eighteenth century or later, the underside of the base of each of his models is flat, unglazed and completely closed-in except for a small round hole centrally located.

It is interesting to note that the same form of base construction occurs on Minton animals modelled in the early 1830s (see nos. 18-23, 29-33 and 46), and as Edward Keys is known from the factory records to have been employed at Minton from a time prior to 1831, it is a reasonable inference to conclude that it was he who was responsible for introducing this form of construction and these animal models. The only realistic alternative candidate would be his younger brother Samuel, who is known from an isolated reference to him in June 1833 in the factory's wages book to have been there at least by that date. Moreover, he may well have been there earlier, for G.A. Godden has in his *Minton Pottery and Porcelain* drawn attention to the following entry appearing in the wages book in October 1831: 'Edward Keys & Co 2 men and 5 boys'   £7-9-9' and suggests that Samuel may have been one of the two men.

In any event by January 1850 Samuel Keys had joined in partnership with John Mountford to form the firm of 'Keys and Mountford', which received an honourable mention for their Parian ware in the Great Exhibition of 1851.[1]

In 1877, Lady Charlotte Schreiber found Samuel working at Tournai: 'Poor Mr Keys, a hearty old made of 72 or 73, had also been unsuccessful in business which occasioned his taking employment there. He had also worked for Blashfield of Stamford'.[2]

In 1842 Edward Keys started up on his own as a porcelain producer, but sadly the business failed.[3] It was, incidentally, in that same year that he gave evidence to the Royal Commission on the Employment of Children in Factories that he had been a potter for thirty-three out of his forty-four years, that he worked with one other modeller in a small room, that he thought his employment was healthy and that he was paid by the piece, his average earnings amounting to 30s per week. From 1845 to 1853 he was employed by the Wedgwood factory.

It is not known for certain whether the firm of Henry and Richard Daniel of Stoke, Staffordshire, for which Edward Keys worked from 1825/6 to sometime before October 1831, ever produced animals. However, the Derby pointer of figure 83 appears also in Staffordshire porcelain (together with a companion in reverse) and the possibility suggests itself that the Staffordshire model[4] might have originated at the hands of Edward Keys when he was working for the Daniels.[5] Other breeds of dogs are recorded with the same elaborate base. Perhaps they too are to be attributed to the same source.

---

1. See page 267.
2. Lady Schreiber's *Journals*, Vol. 2, p.11.
3. *Staffordshire Advertiser*, 14 May 1842.
4. This model must be distinguished from a version made by Samuel Alcock - no.13.
5. However, if Edward Keys was responsible for the Derby version, he must have executed it before 1826, but the neo-rococo base suggests a post-1830 origin.

THOMAS GRIFFIN (b.1797)

Haslem makes two references to Thomas Griffin, once as a modeller of 'Grimaldi as clown' in 'the list of models by Edward Keys' and secondly as Edward Keys' successor: 'Edward Keys left Derby in 1826, and Thomas Griffin, another of the modellers, was then appointed foreman, but only held the position for a short time.'

The researches of A. and A. Cox have revealed that in the militia list for 1827 (contained in the Swinton Parish documents) there appears the name of Thomas Griffin (where he is described as a potter then aged thirty),[1] so that he must on leaving Derby have gone straight to the Rockingham factory. Moreover, his name together with the date 'July 15th 1830' is inscribed on the base of a master mould for the Continental peasant figure 'No 138' (*Laitiere des environs d'Harlem*) excavated from the factory site at Swinton.[2] There is a further reference to Griffin in the *Yorkshire Gazette* of 14 April 1832 (again discovered by A. and A. Cox[3]) where, in connection with the famous Rockingham dessert service made for William IV, he is described as its 'modeller'. Presumably, Griffin was at Swinton from 1826/7 to at least 1832, and during this time he must have been responsible for many of the factory figures (notably the Continental peasants) and presumably many, if not most, of the animals.

In my *Rockingham Ornamental Porcelain* I pointed out the similarity between some Derby and Rockingham figures (including animals) and postulated the theory that Samuel Keys and George Cocker might be responsible for certain similar figures appearing at both factories. However, as regards Samuel Keys, a far more likely possibility, in the light of A. and A. Cox's discovery, is that the connection between the two factories is to be found in the presence of Thomas Griffin at both of them. His presence removes the need to try and identify a time, if any, when Samuel Keys could have been at Swinton.

1. *The Rockingham Works*, p.109.
2. See A. and A. Cox's *Rockingham Pottery and Porcelain 1745-1842*, p.189.
3. *The Rockingham Works*, p.79.

GEORGE COCKER (1794-1868)

George Cocker, who worked as a 'figure maker' at Derby and elsewhere, was apparently responsible for certain animal models. Haslem says of him:[1]

'George Cocker was apprenticed to figure making at the Derby factory early in the present [i.e. nineteenth] century, and left about 1817, a year or two after serving his apprenticeship. He afterwards worked at Coalport and also at Worcester, but only for a short period, as he returned to Derby in 1821, and was again employed at the old works until 1825, when he left, and in partnership with John Whitaker, sen., another of the workmen, commenced the making of china figures in Friar Gate, a short distance from where Coffee, about a quarter of a century before, had occupied premises for a similar purpose. Whitaker remained with Cocker little more than a year, and the latter afterwards carried on the small concern until 1840, where he removed to London. He resided in Chenies Street, Tottenham Court Road, where he also continued, in a small way,

1. *The Old Derby China Factory*, pp.159-60.

to make china figures and small ornaments. In 1853 he left London and went to reside in the Potteries, and was, for about two years, employed by the late Herbert Minton, at Stoke-upon-Trent. Afterwards he worked for John Mountford, and for several others in the Staffordshire Potteries, dying there in 1868, aged 74 years.

'The figures made by Cocker were in biscuit, and they are sometimes sold as genuine Derby. Although this may be, strictly speaking, correct, it is not true in the sense intended, in as much as they were not made at the old works. Cocker's figures possess some merit, but they are inferior to the old Derby figures in masterly modelling; and, being made in the same body as the ordinary china, have a dry and chalk-like appearance, which gives them altogether a different character from the genuine Derby biscuit statuettes.

'He published small busts of some of the celebrated characters of the day, and a few portrait statuettes, among them one of Hannah Moore. *He also made small animals of different kinds* [my italics], and numerous small baskets filled with raised flowers. His figures were of a rustic rather than of a classical character — as a boy with a birdcage, a boy at a well with a pitcher, and the like. On some of these his name is occasionally incised in the clay. A goodly quantity of articles of this sort were manufactured by Cocker, as he was assisted in making them by three daughters, two sons, and a nephew.'

Jewitt also gives an account of Cocker but does not add anything of importance. There is some connection between Cocker and the Rockingham factory. Thus, in the factory drawing book pattern number 684 (belonging to the 1826-30 period) is described as 'Gold hoops to match French cups sent by Cocker from Derby'. The shape of the cups has been identified — their distinctive feature is their horse's hoof-tail handles — and presumably Cocker sent the moulds. There are, moreover, certain Rockingham figure models for which Cocker was almost certainly responsible. However, it has not proved possible so far with any degree of certainty to identify any Derby or Rockingham independent animal model as being his work.

ROBERT BLORE (d.c.1866)

One of the Derby modellers of our period was Robert Blore. His name appears amongst the 'FIGURE MAKERS CALLED ORNAMENTAL REPAIRERS' recorded by Haslem as employed by the factory in 1832,[1] the others being: Whitaker, John, Overlooker; Goadsby, James; Hill, Thomas; Hopkinson, William; and, Perkins, John.

1. *The Old Derby China Factory,* p.35.

Haslem says of Robert Blore:

'Small articles in china, chiefly biscuit, were also made by Robert Blore, in Bridge Gate, Derby. These were animals and articles of an ornamental character, such as vases, ewers, &c, but mostly so small as to be little more than toys, and they resemble those made by Cocker. Blore served his apprenticeship at the Derby factory, but left soon afterwards, and worked at Messrs Minton's. About 1830 he returned to Derby, and, for a short period, manufactured the articles spoken of above. After a time he again went into the Potteries, and was employed at Messrs Mason's, Lane Delph. He afterwards removed to Middlesborough, Yorkshire, where he superintended a pot works until his death, about 1866. Blore was a clever workman, and understood the making of china and earthenware bodies and glazes.'[2]

Bearing in mind that Blore was employed in 1832 at the Derby factory itself, it is not altogether easy to identify the exact period when he was working on his own account. Once again it has not proved possible so far, with any degree of certainty, to attribute any particular animal model to the hand of Robert Blore.

---

1. *The Old Derby China Factory*, pp.159-60.
2. *The Old Derby China Factory*, p.160.

The Derby Factory (at King Street)

In 1848 the Derby factory in the Nottingham Road closed for ever. However, a year later William Locker, who had been the last manager there, founded, with the aid of five fellow employees from the old works including Sampson Hancock (who alone amongst them had not been apprenticed there), a new manufactory in King Street, trading under the name of the 'Old Crown China Works'. In 1859 Locker died. He was succeeded by Stevenson, a draper, when the bill-heads bore the title 'Stevenson & Co'. However, according to Haslem,[1] the firm in fact traded as 'Stevenson and Hancock'. In 1866 Stevenson died, after which the firm was taken over by Sampson Hancock as sole proprietor and traded as 'Sampson Hancock and Co'. This name continued in use after the death of Sampson Hancock in 1895. The factory's usual mark is in the form of the old Nottingham Road mark — a crown over dots and batons and a 'D' — but with the addition of the letter 'S' on one side and the letter 'H' on the other. According to Haslem,[2] the letters stood initially for 'Stevenson and Hancock' and later for 'Sampson Hancock'.

---

1. *The Old Derby China Factory*, p.217.
2. *The Old Derby China Factory*, p.219.

The mark was used from about 1863 onwards. The factory remained as a small concern throughout its existence but it survived until 1935 when it was taken over by the present Royal Crown Derby Porcelain Company Ltd. The latter factory was founded in 1876 and occupied premises in Osmanton Road about one mile from King St. and the Nottingham Road site. It was originally known as the 'Derby Crown Porcelain Company' but in 1891 it acquired the prefix 'Royal' when a crown was added to its mark.

However, the King St. factory, throughout its independent existence, turned out a few animal models. Fortunately, its sale catalogue for 1934/5 has survived[1] and thus reveals that it produced a variety of small animals including dogs, pigs,[2] cows, calves and lambs, a greyhound and a fox, each of the last two being on a base (does this suggest that the other animals were without bases?), stirrup cups in the form of dog or fox heads,[3] and the celebrated 'Peacock among Flowers' first modelled by John Whitaker. It is also to be presumed that all these animals were in fact produced in the nineteenth century as well as the twentieth century. Unfortunately none of these animals (apart from the peacock) is illustrated in the catalogue and identification has not yet proved possible. An example of a fox seated on a base bearing the Sampson Hancock mark c.1870 (actually it is a fox cub) is illustrated in plate 327 of *Ceramics of Derbyshire*. In plate 328 of the same book a group of kittens playing on a rectangular base with the Sampson Hancock mark is shown. It is dated c.1910, but conceivably the model was made in the nineteenth century. An interesting ewe lying on a mound base with scroll edges is illustrated in figure 23 of Gilhesby and Budd's *Royal Crown Derby China*. [4] Finally, a rare lion, free-standing, i.e. without a base, is to be seen in figure 166 of Gilhesby's *Crown Derby Porcelain*. It has the Sampson Hancock mark.

In a sale at Sotheby's held on 24 February 1987, seven Sampson Hancock animals in biscuit were included (lot 250). They comprised a pair of recumbent greyhounds, 5¼ in. (13.3cm), a pair of recumbent

1. See Twitchett and Bailey, *Royal Crown Derby*.
2. It is interesting to note that Gilhesby and Budd discovered an invoice from G.A. Robinson & Co, Church St, Longton 1874 for 'dogs, pigs...' Of this concern Jewitt in his *Ceramic Art in Great Britain* (Vol. 2, p.403) says:
'**Church St.**
These works for the production of Parian, jasper and majolica ware, belonging to Mr G.A. Robinson, were pulled down in 1876 for town improvements, Mr Robinson erecting new works in Sutherland Road.'
3. Such stirrup cups were also produced at the Nottingham Road factory, and for that matter, at Swinton, Yorkshire, throughout Staffordshire and elsewhere. These items are, however, essentially cups, and accordingly are not classified in this book as animals.
4. Another example on a green base was sold at Sotheby's on 25 February 1986, lot 321.

spaniels, 3¾in. (9.5cm), a recumbent mastiff, 4¾in. (12.1cm), a standing goat, 3½in. (8.9cm) and a recumbent doe, 3¼in. (8.3cm). The first five had the Sampson Hancock underglaze blue painted mark indicating an origin subsequent to 1862.

Chamberlain, Worcester

HISTORY AND MARKS

The history of the Chamberlain Worcester factory has been exhaustively set out in G.A. Godden's *Chamberlain Worcester Porcelain* and the reader is referred to that work for a full exposition of the origin, development and eventual decline of this factory. It is enough for our purposes to state as follows. Robert Chamberlain (1737-1798), reputedly the first apprentice at the original 'Dr Wall' factory, rose to become head of the decorating department of that concern (then under the control of John and Joseph Flight). In or about 1786 together with his son Humphrey he left to establish his own decorating business, seemingly undertaking contract work for the Flights and embellishing porcelain from Thomas Turner of Caughley. In June 1789 with the financial backing of Richard Nash and Thomas Turner he opened a retail shop at 33 High Street, Worcester, and from March 1791, or, at any rate, from the autumn of that year he added to his decorating activities the actual manufacture of porcelain.

The business prospered from its commencement and by the end of the eighteenth century the Chamberlain factory, now under the control of Humphrey Chamberlain, had attained a national and possibly an international reputation. On 3 August 1807 the Royal Warrant as porcelain manufacturer to the Prince of Wales was granted (an honour publicised in some of the subsequent factory marks). On 25 May 1814 the Chamberlain firm was also appointed porcelain manufacturers to the Princess Charlotte of Wales, and it may be that by then it had surpassed the original Worcester factory, at that time trading as 'Flight, Barr and Barr'. In June 1814 the Chamberlain concern opened its own London showrooms at 63 Piccadilly, and in July 1816 transferred from there to 155 New Bond St. These addresses are sometimes incorporated into the factory's mark, considerably facilitating the dating of specimens.

In 1840 the Chamberlain concern merged with its chief rival at Worcester still trading under the name of 'Flight, Barr and Barr'. Joseph Flight had died in 1838 and thereafter his firm under the exclusive control of Martin Barr and George Barr declined, so that when the merger took place the Chamberlains were the senior partners. It was resolved 'that the manufactory shall be styled The Worcester Royal Pavilion Works but that the business shall be carried on under the Firm of Chamberlain and

Co'. From 1840 onwards the old mark 'Chamberlain' or 'Chamberlains' printed, painted, or incised in script was replaced by the words 'Chamberlain and Co' similarly written. Evidently both the old and the new mark were frequently, but not always accompanied by the additional word 'Worcester', or very rarely 'Wor^s',[1] and sometimes by the address of Chamberlain's London Shop (taken over by the new amalgamated firm) until its sale in December 1845. (Very rarely the address of Flight Barr and Barr's showroom at No 1 Coventry Street was added until its eventual disposal in December 1844.) For the period from about 1847 to about 1852 the basic mark was changed again, this time to an impressed mark in the form of 'CHAMBERLAINS' in capital letters (sometimes with the word 'WORCESTER' similarly impressed).

Sadly, the amalgamation was not a success. By 1852 all the original partners in the merger had died or retired, and the concern had come into the hands of a new partnership, Kerr and Binns. Under the new management the factory re-established its old standing and in 1862 was formed into a company under the name 'Worcester Royal Porcelain Company', its subsequent products being known throughout the world as 'Royal Worcester'.

It is fortunate, for the purposes of identification, that many Chamberlain pieces, including animals, were frequently marked. We have already discussed the usual marks — at least as far as they are relevant to animals — but before leaving the subject three rare marks (clearly applicable to a period before the merger) should be mentioned.

Two are incised in script. They are: (i) 'H. Chamberlain and Sons Worcester', (ii) 'Chamberlains Royal Porcelain Manufacturers' and the third mark, which appears under the base of a poodle illustrated in Colour Plate XIII of G.A. Godden's *Chamberlain Worcester Porcelain,* is in the form of the elaborate printed Royal Arms mark together with the New Bond St. address.

PASTE

The Chamberlain Worcester paste is distinctive. It is somewhat grey in appearance, and this feature helps to identify an unmarked specimen or, for that matter, to prevent a misattribution. As can be seen from the biscuit examples, the paste is harsher than that of such factories as Rockingham, Derby or Minton.

---

1. Usually written in script underneath.

BASES

The bases vary in form. They are, for example, rectangular, usually with rounded corners (figures 26, 32 and 42a), but not invariably so (colour plate 7b), oval (figures 42b, 108a, 128, 129, 138, 139), stepped rectangular with canted corners (figures 89 and 132), circular, or in the form of a cushion (figures 40 and 41), and they are generally recessed underneath, although the underside of the cat and kitten group of colour plate 7b is flat and fully closed in, and the pair of cats of figure 12 are completely hollow, with no plinth at all. The Chamberlain cushion bases are distinguishable from those of the Rockingham, Derby and Minton factories. The contours and proportions are different, the tassels less pronounced and, most important of all, the underneath is recessed and not, as in the case of the other factories, flat and closed-in except for a small centrally located hole.

As for decoration, Chamberlain bases were left in the white or given a dry-blue, green or, very rarely, a pink ground colour, and were normally edged with a gilt-line.

MODELS

The range of animals turned out by the Chamberlain Worcester factory was considerable. Cats and dogs were, of course, produced, the former either lying recumbent (colour plate 7b) or sitting erect, and sometimes with a kitten (colour plate 7b). Various breeds of dogs were modelled including greyhounds (figure 26), pugs (figure 32), poodles (figures 39-42a), hounds (figure 89), and spaniels. As for farm animals, the factory modelled both sheep (figure 108a) and cows. Creatures of the countryside included deer (figures 128 and 129), squirrels, (figure 132) foxes, rabbits (figures 138 and 139), mice (figure 42b) and hedgehogs together with a variety of different birds — swans, peacocks (figure 161) and pea hens, finches, canaries, tomtits, linnets, pelicans, geese, parrots and kingfishers — although we are dependent for our knowledge of the factory's output of birds almost entirely on its records and not on surviving examples. The only animals from abroad known for sure to have been produced by the factory — again from its documents — were a lion and an elephant.

DATING

When the post-1840 marks were used on Chamberlain Worcester animals, they can be assigned to a reasonably narrow period, i.e. from 1840 to 1846 or from 1847 to around 1852, as the case may be. But the usual mark found on the factory's animals is in the form of 'Chamberlain' or 'Chamberlains', with or without the further word 'Worcester', all in script, printed, painted or incised. However, this particular mark was employed from about 1786 to 1839, a considerable time span, and the question immediately arises whether the factory's animals, when so marked, can be given a more precise date.

Many have a dry-blue base. G.A. Godden in his *Chamberlain Worcester Porcelain* states that a reference, dated 25 April 1821, to '2 Pairs stags, dry blue cushions 15-0' (which appears in the factory's records), is the first mention of this dry or matt-blue colour. However, there is an earlier reference in the papers to the inclusion, among items supplied in 1820 to certain Cheltenham dealers, of '1 box, dead blue and gold, birds &c 2-0-0', but in any event it would seem that this dry blue colour started about the beginning of the third decade of the century.

The other ground colours found on Chamberlain Worcester animals are green, and, more rarely, pink. There is no evidence to suggest that they were used otherwise than contemporaneously with the dry-blue ground.[1] Probably then, most of the Chamberlain animals marked in the way indicated above date from after 1820. This would correspond with the date from which interest in the production of animals would seem to have developed at other factories.

The Chamberlain records make frequent mention of animals during the 1820s, but according to the researches of G.A. Godden 'In the 1830s the demand for Chamberlain's animal models seems to have decreased and there appears to be no trace of any orders for them in the 1840s.' However, that animals were in fact produced during the 1840s is apparent from the poodle shown in figure 39b, and the dog sold at Sotheby's on 25 February 1986, lot 345, where the mark employed indicates a post-1840 origin. Nevertheless, the heyday for animals must have been between 1820 and 1840, and during this period the most frequent mark was 'Chamberlain' or 'Chamberlains' in script with or without the word 'Worcester'. Normally it is not possible to give a more precise date to an animal so marked. There may, of course, in a particular case be special circumstances enabling a certain model to be assigned to a narrower period e.g. in the case of the poodle of figure 42a where the wool is represented by moulding and not the application of individual china threads, a date later than 1830 is unlikely, but this is very much the exception.

---

1. At any rate there is a reference in a factory document originating in April 1826 to a pair of stags with green cushions. Query, incidentally, why stags, which are not domestic pets, should be sitting on cushions of any kind.

Grainger Lee & Co., Worcester

HISTORY AND MARKS

Just as Robert Chamberlain broke away from the old 'Dr Wall' factory and established a new concern, so similarly in 1801 Thomas Grainger, a painter at the Chamberlain works, and nephew of Humphrey Chamberlain, to whom he had been apprenticed, left his employers to found a new factory in St Martin's Street, Worcester. However, at first he and his partner, an accomplished artist called Wood, did little more than decorate porcelain purchased in white for re-sale. They traded as 'Grainger and Wood'. In 1812 the factory was rebuilt and a new partnership was formed between Thomas Grainger and his brother-in-law, Mr Lee. The new concern traded as 'Grainger Lee & Co'. It would seem that Lee retired in 1837 and that thereafter until his death in 1839 Thomas Grainger traded as 'Grainger & Co'. On his demise he was succeeded by his son George Grainger who added the initial 'G' to the trading name making it 'G. Grainger & Co'. The business lasted until 1889 when it was taken over by the Royal Worcester Company.

Although the Grainger Lee factory is generally considered to rank in importance below the Flight and Barr and the Chamberlain factories, it was nevertheless a natural survivor, and successfully withstood their competition. Its output was principally of useful ware, but it did manufacture some ornamental porcelain and a certain number of small animals identified by the impressed mark 'GRAINGER LEE & CO, WORCESTER' in capitals, or more rarely by the mark 'Grainger Lee & Co' in red script. So far no examples have come to light with the later 'GRAINGER & CO' or 'G. GRAINGER & CO' marks, so that presumably the factory ceased animal production after 1837. The commencement date is unknown, but as the factory was presumably in direct competition with Chamberlain, it probably began turning out animals around 1820.

FACTORY PATTERN BOOK

Examples which have survived are mostly white and gilt, though coloured specimens are recorded. Fortunately, the factory pattern book has survived, being now in the possession of the Dyson Perrins Museum. One sheet (page 233) illustrates five animals, a poodle with raised rump crouching on a rectangular cushion base supported on four bun feet — the porcelain threads applied to represent the animal's wool suggest a post-1830 origin — a cat, a rabbit and two separate models of a mouse, in each case lying recumbent on a rectangular base with rounded corners. Another sheet (page 234) shows a pair of greyhounds and two further dogs not easy to identify. The smaller appears to be some form of spaniel, the larger animal possibly an Esquimaux dog. The third sheet (page 235) depicts what seems to be the reverse of the last mentioned dog and also a Great Dane looking at a rat in a cage. The next sheet (page 236) illustrates two pointers in reverse, though one appears to have an uncharacteristically fluffy tail, and also a recumbent giraffe. The final sheet (page 237) shows a standing stag and a standing hind. Examples of the pair of greyhounds and of the giraffe are recorded (figures 27 and 152).

Animals not appearing in the pattern book are a sheepdog (figure 92), a Great Dane lying recumbent (figure 86), a Newfoundland (see pages 117, 118), a recumbent stag (see page 159) and a squirrel (see page 162).

PASTE

The paste is much whiter and less harsh than that of the Chamberlain animals and its glaze is much softer to the touch. The porcelain is more akin to that of the Rockingham and Derby factories. The gilding — there is usually a continuous line around the base — tends to be thin and is liable to wear. I have not yet seen a biscuit specimen.

BASES

As can be seen from the illustrations, Grainger Lee bases vary in form. Most can be broadly described as being rectangular with rounded corners, but this is only a rough indication of the shape. (Incidentally, note the attractive rope features shown in figure 86.) The underside of the base is recessed and glazed. When the mark occurs — it appears under the base — it is often very faintly impressed and can at a cursory glance sometimes be missed.

Reproduction of a page from the Grainger Lee & Co. factory pattern book showing a poodle, a cat, a rabbit and two mice. *(By courtesy of Royal Worcester Spode Ltd.)*

Reproduction of a page from the Grainger Lee & Co. factory pattern book showing a pair of greyhounds, an Esquimaux dog and a spaniel. *(By courtesy of Royal Worcester Spode Ltd.)*

Reproduction of a page from the Grainger Lee & Co. factory pattern book showing a Esquimaux dog and a Great Dane looking at a rat in a cage. *(By courtesy of Royal Worcester Spode Ltd.)*

Reproduction of a page from the Grainger Lee & Co. factory pattern book showing two pointers in reverse and a giraffe. *(By courtesy of Royal Worcester Spode Ltd.)*

Reproduction of a page from the Grainger Lee & Co. factory pattern book showing a standing stag and a standing hind. *(By courtesy of Royal Worcester Spode Ltd.)*

Royal Worcester

The Royal Worcester factory resumed the production of animal models, a speciality seemingly abandoned by the Chamberlain Worcester and Grainger Lee factories long before they became part of the new enterprise. Mr Henry Sandon, a former curator of the Dyson Perrins Museum, has in Appendix 1 of his *Royal Worcester Porcelain* extracted from the factory's records what purports to be the full range of its output and this includes for the period from 1862 to 1900 certain animal models, although they represent only a small fraction of the totality of the models produced at Worcester. The range of animals was limited, but it does include, among other models, cats, a kitten, a variety of different dogs — pugs, King Charles spaniels, greyhounds chained, a Skye-terrier, a mastiff, a spitz, a St Bernard, and a dachshund — a horse with panniers, mice with eggs, foxes, monkeys in caricature, elephants, a bear and drum and numerous birds such as a hawk, a dove, an owl, a parrot, a cock and hen group, various cockatoos, a stork, a falcon, several swans and a magpie. It is interesting to note that very few animal models were executed during the last quarter of the century. Some of these models were quite large, in fact on the Parian scale rather than the miniature scale of the small more collectable animals of the first half of the nineteenth century. Sometimes these animals were made in porcelain, sometimes in earthenware.

Royal Worcester animals of the period 1862-1900 are rarely encountered, but four of them are illustrated in figure 35, and a life size standing pug in figure 36.

From a period late in the nineteenth century (although not included in the lists compiled by Mr Sandon) are the two small but extremely attractive animals shown in colour plate 29. About 1870 the factory began to base its designs on Japanese prototypes. The Japanese style was at that time becoming fashionable in nearly all the decorative arts, and the factory showed products in this taste at the Vienna Exhibition of 1873, where it tied with Minton for the highest award. It is not, then, surprising to see the Japanese influence on the two models illustrated here. They must surely have been based on Japanese netsuke.

The mouse, which is nibbling a piece of cheese, measures only 2in. 5.1cm in length, and is finely modelled with its feet moulded *under* the base. It has the standard Royal Worcester mark printed underneath it together with the words (appearing anti-clockwise in a circle) 'Royal Worcester England' which were added to the standard mark in 1891. It bears the design registration number 1563?? (the last two figures are indecipherable), indicating that the design was registered in 1890. Between the letter 'R' of 'Royal' and the crown which surmounts the original circular mark are to be seen a number of dots, seemingly six in all, and a similar number of dots between the 'D' of 'England' and the Crown. Beneath the word 'Worcester' are seemingly seven more dots. I use the word 'seemingly' because they are minute and certainty is impossible. However, there would appear to be nineteen dots in all, each of which would signify one year after 1891 when the enlarged mark first came into use. Accordingly, the date of the animal would appear to be 1910. If this is so, then the model was produced from 1890 to at least 1910, twenty years in all. Manifestly, it was a popular model and examples must have been turned out throughout the remainder of the nineteenth century after the model first appeared.

The rabbit, also 2in. in length, is decorated in yellow, the rarest of all colours in porcelain. Its registered design number is 556159. Although like the mouse it is based on the Japanese netsuke, it was not registered as a design until 1910. The particular model shown in colour plate 29b would appear, from the number of dots used with the mark, to have been manufactured in 1913. Manifestly what started off as a late nineteenth century concept was continued into the early years of the following century.

The Royal Worcester factory also turned out animals in Parian (sometimes glazed and tinted). See Appendix B on Parian for examples.

The Minton Factory

HISTORY

In 1793 Thomas Minton (born in 1765) founded the famous factory that today still bears his name, albeit it would appear from its records that he did not actually commence business until 1796. He had been apprenticed to Thomas Turner at the Caughley porcelain factory where he had learnt the art of engraving for the purposes of printing on ceramics. In 1796, together with William Pownall (a Liverpool merchant, who for a few years as a sleeping partner provided capital to extend the firm's operations) and Joseph Poulson (a practical potter, reputedly a former manager of the neighbouring Spode works), he began to manufacture blue printed pottery at Stoke. In about 1797 he added porcelain production. In November 1808 Joseph Poulson died and his expertise was made good by the employment of John Turner from the firm of John and William Turner of Lane End. Porcelain production continued until about 1816, when the factory reverted to pottery manufacture only. However,

239

porcelain production was subsequently resumed. Although Jewitt speaks of the recommencement date as being 1821,[1] G.A. Godden has shown by reference to the factory records that a more likely date was 1824. It has continued to the present day. There is no evidence to suggest that any porcelain animals were turned out in the first period of porcelain manufacture. They would all seem to be post-1830.

In 1817 Thomas Minton took his two sons, Thomas and Herbert, into partnership and traded under the name 'Thomas Minton & Sons'. However, after a while Thomas, the elder brother, left to train for the church (he was ordained in 1825), and on 1 January 1823 the 1817 partnership was dissolved. The new partners were Thomas (the father) and Herbert Minton, and on the former's death in 1836 Herbert became sole owner. Born on 3 February 1793, he had been in the ceramics trade since 1808, having been employed by his father, first as a traveller and salesman, and later in the factory itself. By 1836 the business had grown to such an extent that Herbert felt obliged to take in a partner. His choice fell on John Boyle, an experienced and enthusiastic young man, and selected entries from Boyle's diary give us a vivid insight into the events of the partnership. However, the relationship between Minton and Boyle degenerated, and in 1841 the partnership was dissolved. The business thereafter traded under the style of 'Herbert Minton & Co'. In or before 1842 Michael Daintry Hollins, who had been employed in the business since at least December 1838, became a partner receiving one-sixth of the profits, and in 1849 Colin Minton Campbell, Herbert Minton's nephew, was also taken in, receiving a third share of the profits. The latter two carried on the business after Herbert's death in 1858, although for some years previously he had retired from the day-to-day management of the firm.

---

1. *Ceramic Art in Great Britain*, Vol. II, p.192.

PASTE

Minton animals appear in biscuit or glazed. In the latter case they are either white and gilt, or enamelled and gilt. The paste can best be judged from biscuit specimens. It is very similar in colour and texture to that of the Rockingham and Derby factories, and as in the case of these last mentioned factories, the glaze is soft to the touch. The paste is quite unlike that produced by the Chamberlain Worcester company.

BASES

Most of the Minton animals of our period were modelled shortly after

1830, and the structure of the underside of their base — flat and closed-in save for a small round hole occupying an approximately central position — is indistinguishable from that used under Rockingham and Derby animals. This method of construction was introduced from Derby by Edward Keys who was almost certainly responsible for modelling the early Minton animals (see page 221). As in the case of Derby, but not Rockingham bases, there is never an incised number. Moreover, whilst a factory mark appears more often than not under Rockingham animals and sometimes, albeit very rarely, under Derby animals, it never appears under the Minton counterparts.[1] In the case of later Minton animals (e.g. model nos. 119 and 120) the underside of the base is hollow, like the products of the minor Staffordshire factories.

Most of the early Minton animal bases (see model nos. 18-20, 22, 29 (alternative version), 32, 33 and 46) are in the form of cushions with tassels (figures 33 and 78). Some bases are, however, oval (model nos. 25 and 26) or rectangular with a moulded pattern around the edges (model no. 29 — colour plate 17), or in the form of an oval mound (model nos. 23 and 31, colour plate 18) and in the case of a Newfoundland dog (model no. 21), according to the drawing book, there is simply no base at all.[2]

---

1. The Minton mark is, however, often impressed under the differently constructed bases of late Parian animals.
2. But see p.118.

FACTORY DRAWING BOOK AND DATING

Fortunately, the factory's drawing book has survived, being now in the possession of the Minton Museum. With the aid of the illustrations which appear there, it has proved possible to identify the various animals that the factory turned out. Without these illustrations the task would have been far from easy, because, during the period when these animals were manufactured, it was not the factory's practice to mark its products, seemingly in deference to the pressure imposed by the London and other retailers.[1]

It is clear from the internal evidence of the drawing book that the animal models up to and including no. 46 were made in the period

---

1. The power and importance of the London retailers is vividly illustrated by the financial ability of John Mortlock, who owned a china shop in Oxford Street, to purchase in 1821 William Wilberforce's mansion Gore House in Kensington, and by his alleged willingness, after completion of the purchase, to offer back the title deeds to Wilberforce, who had been compelled to sell for financial reasons, as 'testimony of esteem due to your public character and talents' (Hare A.J.C. (ed.), *Life and Letters of Maria Edgeworth* (1894) II, p.57).

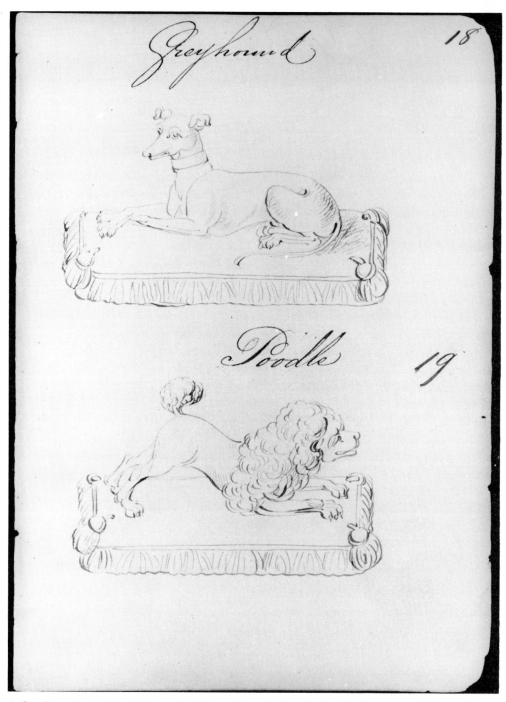

A Greyhound and a Poodle from the Minton factory's drawing book. *(By courtesy of Minton Museum, Royal Doulton Tableware Ltd.)*

1830/31. Accordingly, most examples will date from shortly afterwards, and few, if any, will have been produced after (say) 1840.

MODELS

The range of animals turned out by the Minton factory was narrow. The individual models, i.e. those which did not form part of a group, were, with two exceptions, exclusively dogs (leaving aside the late Parian

242

models). Most of these are illustrated in the factory's drawing book, and are generally (though not invariably) represented lying or standing on tasselled cushions. They comprise the following (the numbers being those assigned to them in the drawing book):

a greyhound (no. 18);

a poodle without a basket (no. 19) (also produced in reverse);

a pug (no. 20) (figures 33 and 34);

a Newfoundland, without a base (no. 21, see also figure 93), the same animal, albeit this time on an oval base with raised moulding, also appears with a boy sitting astride it with sword drawn, representing war (no. 25), and with a girl similarly positioned holding a crook, symbolic of peace (no. 26);

a recumbent spaniel (no. 22) (figure 61);

a setter (no. 29, but not illustrated in the factory book) (i) on a rectangular base with moulded edges (colour plate 17), (ii) on a cushion base with tassels (figure 78);

a standing greyhound ('Dog standing', no. 30, but not illustrated in the factory book) (colour plate 9a);

a trotting pointer (no. 31) (colour plate 18);

a begging spaniel (no. 32);

a poodle with a basket (no. 33) (this model was certainly produced in reverse — see page 71);

a Russian dog (no. 46).

The non-canine models are a horse rampant (no. 23) and produced much later, monkeys as caricatures of human beings (nos. 117 and 118). Late dogs are a large setter (no. 119) and two large greyhounds (nos. 120 and 130). It is interesting to note that model no. 119 was reissued in Parian as a Persian greyhound (figure 96).

Certain Minton animals appear, not as independent models, but as an integral part of a group. Thus, leaving aside designs nos. 25 and 26 already referred to; a goose accompanies 'Mother Goose' (no. 4); a donkey is ridden by Sancho Panza (no. 7) and a horse by Don Quixote (no. 8); another horse is modelled carrying Tom O'Shanter (no. 24); a dog appears with a boy who is represented playing with it on an oblong base (no. 49); a lamb is held by a young girl (no. 39); a dog accompanies a shepherd (no.79); and a sheep accompanies a shepherdess (no. 80); a sheep is shown being stripped of its wool by a seated shearer (no. 82); and a dog (possibly a pointer) and a cat accompany a man and a woman in a group from 'Tom Jones' (no. 87). There are also other later animals which are usually found in Parian (see Appendix B).

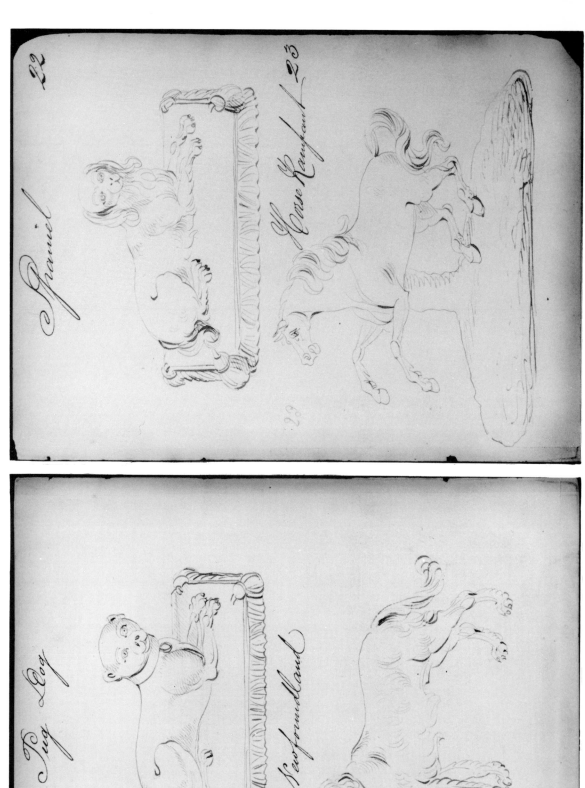

A Pug Dog, a Newfoundland, a Spaniel and a Horse Rampant from the Minton factory's drawing book. (*By courtesy of Minton Museum, Royal Doulton Tableware Ltd.*)

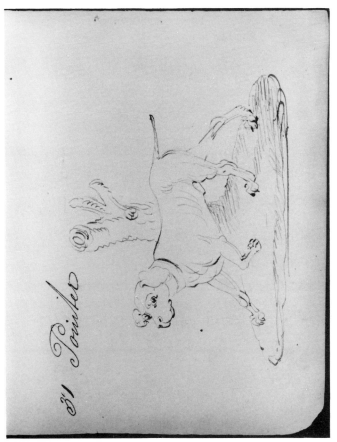

A Pointer, a Dog Begging and a Dog and Basket from the Minton factory's drawing book. (*By courtesy of Minton Museum, Royal Doulton Tableware Ltd.*)

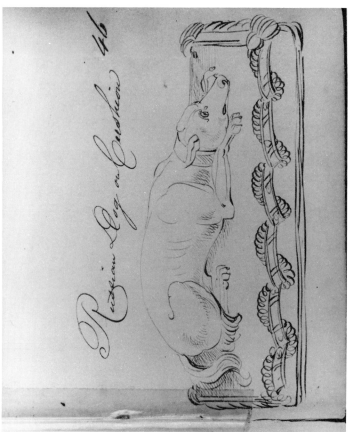

246

A Russian Dog on Cushion and a Setter from the Minton factory's drawing book. *(By courtesy of Minton Museum, Royal Doulton Tableware Ltd.)*

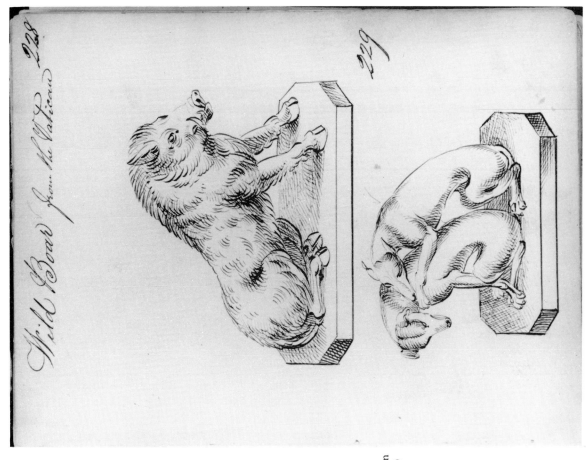

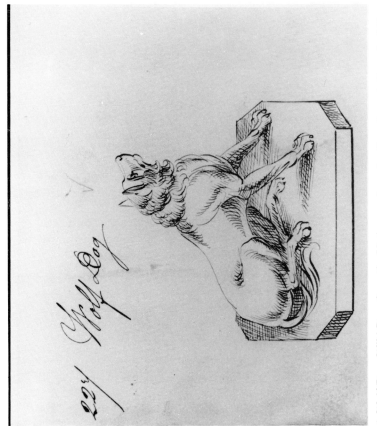

A Wolf Dog, Wild Boar from the Vatican and a pair of greyhounds from the Minton factory's drawing book. *(By courtesy of Minton Museum, Royal Doulton Tableware Ltd.)*

A Greyhound and a Large Greyhound from the Minton factory's drawing book. *(By courtesy of Minton Museum, Royal Doulton Tableware Ltd.)*

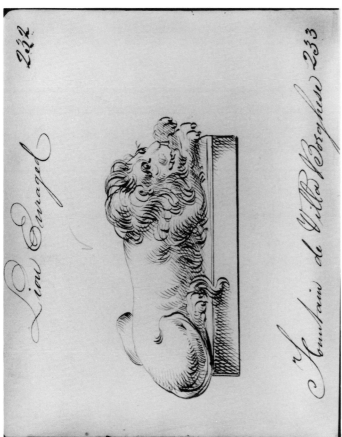

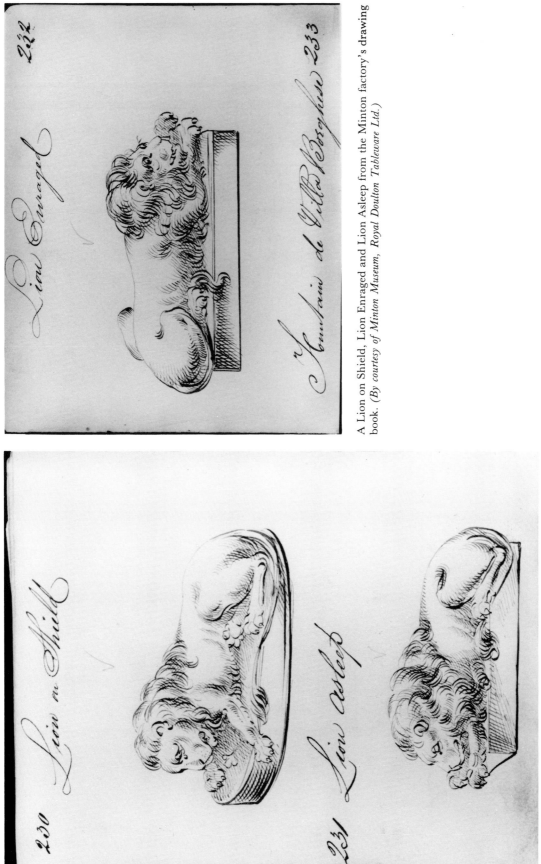

A Lion on Shield, Lion Enraged and Lion Asleep from the Minton factory's drawing book. *(By courtesy of Minton Museum, Royal Doulton Tableware Ltd.)*

238 Lion attacking Horse

239 Lion attacking Horse

286 French Horse

234 Lion reposing

235 Sow & Pigs from the Vatican

250

Lion reposing, Sow & Pigs from the Vatican, Lion attacking Horse and French Horse from the Minton factory drawing book. (By courtesy of Minton Museum, Royal Doulton

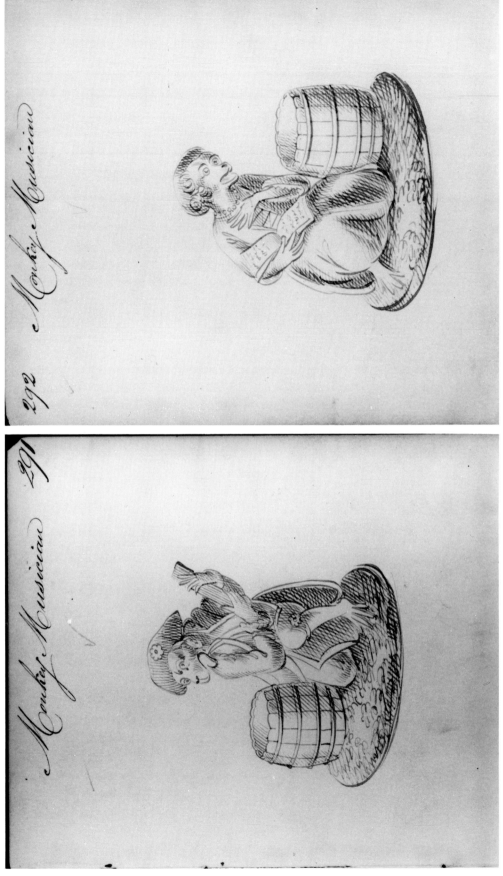

Monkey Musicians from the Minton factory's drawing book. (*By courtesy of Minton Museum, Royal Doulton Tableware Ltd.*)

The Swansea Factory

In 1814 William Billingsley and Samuel Walker, having left Nantgarw, where they had created a particularly fine porcelain both as to body and glaze (albeit too costly to produce on a truly commercial scale), moved to Swansea. There they resumed the manufacture of porcelain (after their original formula) for the benefit of Lewis Weston Dillwyn. However, Dillwyn soon dismissed them — they returned to Nantgarw — and for a time he continued the manufacture of porcelain, using a somewhat different body. In 1817 he discontinued the business altogether. Thereafter, for a period, porcelain production was carried on by T & J Bevington & Co. Isaac Wood, who had accompanied Billingsley and Walker from Nantgarw, remained at Swansea to work for the Bevingtons, and it was he who was responsible for modelling a fine biscuit ram impressed 'BEVINGTON & CO, SWANSEA' (figure 109).

Twelve of these rams are recorded, but no other animal has so far been identified with any certainty as being a product of the Swansea factory.

The Copeland and Garrett Factory

On the death of Josiah Spode III, in 1829, the famous factory, which had been founded by his grandfather in 1770 and carried on by his father (the latter had died only two years before Josiah III), was thereafter continued by his executors and William Taylor Copeland, an Alderman of the City of London. As well as producing earthenware the factory turned out porcelain of a high order. On 1 March 1833 Copeland purchased the concern and took into partnership Thomas Garrett, who had been Spode's principal traveller. The partnership lasted until the middle of 1847.

Copeland and Garrett, unlike the Spodes, included small porcelain animals in their output. These are of fine quality, as would be expected of a factory that was one of the largest and most important in Staffordshire, having, in 1840, according to John Ward, 800 employees and occupying an area of eight acres in the very centre of Stoke. The factory usually marked its products, so that identification is easy. However, the number of animal models actually produced would appear to have been very restricted. They included, however, dogs such as greyhounds (colour plate 10 and figure 28) and King Charles spaniels (colour plate 15), deer and monkeys. It was the practice of the factory, unlike that of the contemporary Derby and Minton factories, not to make the underside of the base of each animal flat, but instead to leave it recessed in a way similar to that normally adopted at the Chamberlain and Grainger Lee factories. The mark, when it appears under the base of coloured figures, usually takes the form of the partnership name, 'Copeland and Garrett' printed in a circle within a circular wreath surmounted by a crown. Whether the factory also produced biscuit animals is not known for certain. Undoubtedly, biscuit human figures were turned out, impressed with the name of the partners as the mark.[1] Presumably animals, similarly marked, were also produced, though no example has so far been recorded.

1. See H. Boswell Lancaster's *Talks on Pottery,* p.56.

The Copeland Factory

On the retirement of Thomas Garrett in 1847 the partnership of Copeland and Garrett came to an end and W.T. Copeland became sole proprietor. He thereafter traded as 'W.T. Copeland, late Spode' until 1867 when he took his four sons into partnership. The firm's name then became 'W.T. Copeland & Sons'.

Although Parian was in fact produced by the factory during the partnership of Copeland and Garrett, it was not until after the death of Garrett that this body was used on a substantial scale. Parian was employed principally in the representation of statuary, but occasionally animals also appear in this medium. They are, however, like the statuary apt to be large and, in consequence, wholly different in spirit from the small, highly collectable, animals of the first half of the nineteenth century. Examples, some of which have by way of a mark the name 'COPELAND' impressed, are described in Appendix B.

However, the Parian factory also manufactured animals which were glazed and coloured. An example in the form of a large cat sitting upright is illustrated in figure 22.

The Davenport Factory

The provenance of the delightful brown and white spaniel, lying on a green mound supported in turn by a black rectangular base, $2^1/_{16}$in. (5.3cm) long, banded with gold, which is illustrated in figure 62, gives rise to some uncertainty. So too does the factory of origin of the rare elephant, standing 2in. (5.1cm) high on a green rectangular base edged with a gilt line, shown in colour plate 35b. The underneath structure of the bases of both pieces is essentially the same — flat around the edges with an oval, concave centre. The distinctive characteristics of these animals, apart from the obvious high quality of their modelling, are their weight, the richness of the gilding, and in the case of the dog, the presence of crazing, all suggestive of the famous Davenport factory which operated at Longport in Staffordshire from 1794 to 1887. The difficulty about making a positive attribution in favour of Davenport is that so far no concrete evidence has come to light indicating that this particular factory ever made *any* animals. Certainly, no animals of any sort have been discovered bearing the factory mark.

However, against that, according to Alexander Brongniart in his *Traité des Arts Ceramiques* (Vol. II,1836, p.453 quoted in J.C. Wedgwood's *Staffordshire Pottery and Its History*) there was at the factory in 1836 a work-force of some 1,400 persons with an annual output of £100,000 worth of pottery and porcelain. The magnitude of such an output can be more readily comprehended if one bears in mind that in 1848 a dinner set of light blue printed earthenware with gilt knobs and handles, for twenty-four persons, (two hundred and twenty two pieces in all), was exported to India for a mere £16 less 10% discount.[1] There can be little doubt that in 1836 the Davenport factory was the largest concern in Staffordshire. Its activities covered pottery, porcelain (both useful and ornamental), and glass. It exported its products to India, Rio de Janeiro and throughout the world generally.

Now, in view of the range and magnitude of its activities, is it likely that it would have neglected figure production altogether? At least one marked figure has been discovered. It appeared at the 'Exhibition of Staffordshire Porcelain 1740-1851' held in 1979 and is illustrated in plate 119 of the exhibition catalogue. It consisted of a boy in biscuit pushing a glazed wheelbarrow containing a glazed barrel. The barrel held ink, whilst next to it stood a small receptacle for a quill. A particularly interesting feature was the rectangular base edged with a thick gilt line. However, no marked animal has so far been discovered. We know that from 1820 onwards porcelain animals were being turned out in quantity in this country to meet a ready market. It is difficult to believe that the Davenport factory chose to ignore such a market. It may be that its output of porcelain animals was small, and that very few have survived, but it would be surprising if none had ever been made at all.

The admitted absence of a mark is not particularly startling. Much, if not most, of the Davenport output is unmarked. Moreover, some of the contemporary factories, such as Minton and Samuel Alcock, appear never to have marked their animals. Presumably, the retail outlets preferred it this way.

If the Davenport factory did turn out small porcelain animals, we

1. See T.A. Lockett's *Davenport Pottery and Porcelain* 1794-1887, p.21.

would expect to find them well modelled, heavy in weight, finely gilded and subject to crazing. These criteria are satisfied by the King Charles spaniel of figure 62 and (save in respect of the crazing) by the elephant of colour plate 35b; and accordingly a tentative attribution has been made in favour of Davenport. A particular point to be noted is that the rectangular base of the animals illustrated, edged with a continuous gilt line, corresponds with the base of the marked figure appearing at the 1979 Exhibition.

The Samuel Alcock Factory

Samuel Alcock commenced production of porcelain in about 1822 at Cobridge. In 1834 he moved to the Hill Pottery at Burslem, and there developed one of the largest porcelain concerns of the early Victorian age. His output was voluminous, but the quality, though often of a high order, was not generally comparable with that of the really great contemporary factories. However, throughout Samuel Alcock's life the undertaking was a great commercial success. His business philosophy was attacked in a letter in William Evans' penny weekly, *The Potter's Examiner and Workman's Advocate,* written by someone using the pseudonym 'Mentor' (see the issue of Saturday, 11 May, 1844). The letter reveals that business was 'roaring' and that Alcock's products were inexpensive. Of them the writer says: '. . . cheap labour begets cheap goods; and he who can sell the cheapest will have the most orders. You have put this admirable practice into full operation, and have borne off the palm, for the present, for being the CHEAP SHOP of the Potteries. . .' (However, Samuel Alcock was not alone in being attacked for paying low wages for *The Potter's Examiner* was concerned with establishing unions in the industry and with assisting the emigration of workers to America.[1])

Samuel Alcock became a very prominent figure in local politics, but died in November 1848 at the early age of forty-nine. Thereafter the concern was carried on by his widow, Elizabeth, and her son, Samuel, and the researches of G.A. Godden have shown that in 1851, according to the Census, they employed a larger workforce than John Ridgway ('Potter to the Queen'). The comparative figures are as follows:

	Men	Women	Boys	Girls	Total
Alcock	249	187	135	116	687
Ridgway	230	162	154	74	620

However, in October 1859 the business became insolvent.

---

1. See *Staffordshire Porcelain,* ed. G.A. Godden, p.308.

The range of Samuel Alcock's products was considerable, including useful ware, fine quality biscuit busts and Parian statuary. However, the factory would never have been associated, in the mind of the present-day collector, with small animals, had it not been for the lucky chance that when, in April 1839, Samuel Alcock erected a new factory building, he arranged for a selection of the factory's products to be placed under the foundation stone, and these included a poodle and a sheep. These two animals (or more accurately the remnants of them), which in recent years have been excavated from the site, bear under their base the impressed numerals 36 and 86 (or 98 if the piece is turned the other way up) respectively.[1]

An animal base impressed 25 was also found on the site but there was no trace of the actual animal. Manifestly, the Samuel Alcock factory produced animals, and it was its usual practice to impress each model with an identifying numeral, usually difficult to read and sometimes indecipherable. A whole range of different animals, each impressed with a number identifying the model,[2] and sharing the characteristics of the examples found on the factory site, has been recorded, and all these animals are clearly Samuel Alcock products. However, some Samuel Alcock animals have been discovered where no impressed number appears, so that it is clear that the model number was not invariably employed. For example, only one of the pair of mastiffs illustrated in colour plate 21 and one of the pair of sheep in figure 112 has the appropriate number. Some Samuel Alcock animals carry under the base a small asterisk, either impressed or printed in red. The standard of modelling varies considerably, perhaps not surprisingly in view of 'Mentor's' reference to the factory as being the 'cheap shop' of the Potteries. However, whatever their technical shortcomings, some animals are modelled with great vigour and are as charming as any animals produced anywhere. The following are a small selection of the models produced by the factory:

No.

2	Cat and kitten group (The cat also appears as an individual model but the number is not recorded)	Figure 14 and 15a

1. Illustrated in the catalogue of the Northern Ceramics Society's *Exhibition of Staffordshire Porcelain, 1740-1851*, plate 132.
2. Unfortunately, as in the case of the Rockingham factory, the wrong number was sometimes used. Thus, an example of the ram of figure 112 exists where the numeral 13, instead of the correct number 8, has been impressed under the base. For completeness it should be mentioned that numbers were also impressed by the factory on items other than animals.

No.

No.		
6 or 9[1]	Pair of sheep lying on a craggy mound base	Figure 113
8	Pair of sheep lying on a rocky base	Figure 112
9 or 6[1]	Cat lying recumbent on an oval mound base	Figure 13
13	Recumbent pointer lying on a shaped base	
18 or 81[1]	Recumbent King Charles spaniel	Figure 64
22	Recumbent poodle on a rocky mound base	
36	Poodle with its hind quarters raised	Figure 43
38	Hind lying recumbent in front of a leafy tree; produced in two different sizes	
55	Pair of chained greyhounds lying on a tasselled cushion	Figure 30 for the parian version
86 or 98[1]	Pair of recumbent sheep	Figure 111
91 or 16[1]	Mouse eating cheese on a mound base	Colour Plate 28a
94	Miniature cat sitting upright on a high octagonal mound base	Figure 15b
108	Trotting pointer	
117	Monkey band, of which three members (all seated and in costume) are recorded, one blowing a trumpet, one playing a cello, and one holding cymbals, each incised with the number	

1. Unfortunately, the reading of the number depends on which way up the animal is held. The problem does not arise in the case of Rockingham figures because there the number is prefixed by the letters 'No' and it is obvious how the numeral should be viewed.

No.

120	Monkey in costume seated reading at a desk, the latter in the form of an ink-well	
121	Pair of spaniels seated on shaped mound bases	
125	Seated King Charles spaniel	Figure 63
135	Group of rabbits playing on a grassy mound in front of hollow tree trunks	Figure 44b
168	Group comprising a sheep and a lamb in front of a tree	
183	Pair of spaniels seated on oval mound bases	
236	Pair of recumbent leopards	Figure 146
239	Group comprising a cat playing with a seated poodle	Figure 16
305	Pair of mastiffs, lying recumbent on rocky bases	Colour plate 21
311	Seated Persian greyhound	Figure 95
329	Begging spaniel with a black hat	
Indecipherable		
	Pair of unclipped poodles, with pricked ears, each on a mound base	Figure 44a and c

In addition, the following models which are referred to in various sale catalogues (and sometimes wrongly attributed) are probably from the Alcock factory.

(i) 'A pair of English porcelain figures of a recumbent stag and hind, before leafy trees, on yellow bases — 5in. (12.5cm.) high — *impressed numbers* 34.' (Christie's, 28 June 1971, lot 75)

(ii) 'A pair of Staffordshire Figures of seated hounds, on yellow mound bases, their white bodies with grey markings, and with pointed noses, gilt edged rims, 3½ in, *impressed numerals 118*[1] and *252.'* (Sotheby's, 3 February 1970, lot 40.)

(iii) 'A Rockingham Figure of a Dalmatian, sleepily emerging from his kennel, surrounded by a border of green moss, gilt line-edged base, 2¼ *in., impressed numeral 142.* (Sotheby's, 3 October 1972, lot 35)

(iv) 'A Staffordshire Figure of a white Poodle... seated upon a pale yellow oval base, 3½ in *impressed numerals* 312.' (Sotheby's, 17 January 1978, lot 159)

(v) '...and a Smaller Figure of a Poodle seated on a buff-coloured base, 3⅜ *in., impressed no. 812* [clearly a misreading for 312]. (Sotheby's, 24 October 1972, lot 218)

(vi) 'A Rockingham Group of a Poodle and its Puppy lying on a green and cream-coloured cushion with tassels at the corner, 4¼ *in., impressed numeral 330...'* (Sotheby's, 3 October 1972, lot 28)

Where they are not simply left white, the colours applied to the bases of Samuel Alcock animals are light yellow (sometimes more aptly called beige), or a distinctive tone of green, and such bases are normally further embellished with a continuous gilt line around the edge. The mastiffs (model 305) are also recorded in biscuit.

---

1 This model is probably the Persian greyhound of figure 95, the number being a misreading for 311.

The Lloyd, Shelton Factory

John Lloyd, born around 1803, and Rebecca his wife (some two years his senior) ran a small pottery and porcelain factory at Marsh St., Shelton. The factory operated from about 1834 to 1852 and on John's death the business was carried on by Rebecca. They produced figures and toys generally, including animals.

It is doubtful whether the work of John and Rebecca Lloyd would ever have been identified or, for that matter, whether their very existence would have been anything to us other than a mere name, had it not been for the very unusual fact that, contrary to the general practice of Staffordshire manufacturers, they did occasionally impress the bases of their figures with the name-mark:

LLOYD
SHELTON

A bull marked in this way, in white standing on an oval base, appeared at Sotheby's sale of 27 May 1986, lot 220. Although so far no other animal has been discovered with this mark, various human figures have, and the characteristics of these figures have, to a limited extent, enabled us to identify other animals (see colour plate 13, and figure 45). Moreover, where a group consists both of a human figure and also of an animal and the former can confidently be attributed to the factory on the basis of its characteristics, the animal must necessarily be Lloyd Shelton in origin (see page 75). Further, if that same animal appears as an independent model, it too can be given a Lloyd Shelton provenance (see figure 46). The quality of the animals so far identified with the Lloyd Shelton factory has been high.

The Charles Bourne Factory

The work of Charles Bourne's factory is only known to us by the happy accident of his initials being found on a few pieces. The factory flourished at Foley, from about 1817 to 1830. Recorded animals include a cat,[1] a pug, a stag and hind, and a ram and ewe (figure 110), on matt-blue or green bases. When it first opened, the factory may conceivably have derived some advantage from the temporary cessation of porcelain production at Minton. It is possible, though there is no hard evidence to establish it, that Charles Bourne was in the happy position of being able to recruit part of the redundant Minton workforce, including painters and gilders.

---

1. Illustrated in G.A. Godden's *An Illustrated Encyclopaedia of British Pottery and Porcelain,* colour plate 1.

The Madeley Factory

In about 1828 Thomas Martin Randall established a small porcelain factory at Madeley in Shropshire. Initially, the factory functioned only as a decorating concern, and is particularly known for having decorated hard paste Continental porcelain and English soft paste porcelain bought in the white with Sèvres type designs. Only one animal, a small recumbent lion,[1] is known to have been produced at Madeley.

1. Illustrated in G.A. Godden's *An Illustrated Encyclopaedia of British Pottery and Porcelain*, plate 368.

The Minor Staffordshire factories

Staffordshire figures of the nineteenth century were for the most part manufactured in earthenware rather than porcelain. Nevertheless, from around 1830 to 1850 porcelain models were produced in quantity, particularly animals, and Staffordshire porcelain animals were especially prolific. However, after about 1850 they disappeared and the Staffordshire factories seem to have confined themselves to pottery figures only, and even these appear to tail away after about 1870 (by which time the competitive effect of 'Fairings' imported from Germany was being felt).

During the short period when Staffordshire porcelain animals were made, technically they were markedly inferior to the comparable products of the leading factories (i.e. as regards paste, glaze, decoration, and delicacy of modelling). However, from an artistic standpoint the difference is not so noticeable. The sheer verve of the modelling found at the various minor Staffordshire factories, coupled with the highly individual and attractive facial expressions given to their animals, frequently confers on them a higher artistic rating than on the corresponding products of the more sophisticated factories (see, for example, the cats of colour plates 8 and 9b and figures 17 to 21).

Unfortunately, the vast majority of Staffordshire porcelain animals simply cannot be assigned to any particular factory. So far the apparently universal practice of never marking goods, seemingly the result of pressure from retailers, has rendered identification impossible. Admittedly, some models show the same characteristics indicating that they originate from one common source, but to date it has proved impossible to identify any of these factories with any porcelain undertaking known to have existed at the relevant time.

The converse situation also obtains. We know the names of factories which produced china figures, including animals, but identification of their products has so far eluded us. Five such factories are examined below.

261

Allerton, Brough and Green

This concern operated from around 1832 to 1858 at Lane End. In 1840 it had four separate works. The Post Office directories for 1835, 1841 and 1853 indicate that porcelain as well as pottery was then in production. The 1851 Census return relating to the third partner, William Green — he was then sixty years of age — reveals that the factory at that time manufactured both china and earthenware, and had a considerable work-force consisting of 115 men, 133 women, sixty-six boys and thirty-four girls. Furthermore the researches of Roger Pomfret have shown that the business received a ton of bones every nine days for the manufacture of bone-china, which suggests a high porcelain output.

The evidence for the factory turning out figures comes from the *Report. . . on the Employment of Children in Factories* presented to Parliament in 1843. In that report there is a reference to a certain Walter Freeman, aged twelve, who earned four shillings per week as a figure maker at one of the five different works. Presumably, the factory turned out animals as well as figures generally. However, so far they have not been identified.

Hilditch and Hopwood

The firm of Hilditch and Hopwood, which manufactured porcelain at Longton in succession to Hilditch and Son, flourished from about 1832 to 1858. Some of its useful ware has been identified and it is of good quality. No animals have so far been attributed to the factory, and they would not have been associated with it at all, had it not been for the reference in the *Report. . . on the Employment of Children in Factories,* to a boy, Richard Moreton, aged nine, who worked at the factory. He said:

'I work by the piece and can make 40 dozen figures a day.'

If the factory made small figures in quantity, presumably some of them were in the form of animals. In view of the quality of the Hilditch and Hopwood useful ware, any animals turned out by the firm would be expected to be of a high standard.

Daniel Edge

Daniel Edge of Waterloo Road, Burslem who operated from about 1834 to 1842 appears as a china toy-maker in William White's *History, Gazetteer and Directory of Staffordshire,* 1834. It is to be presumed from this that he manufactured small animals, although no example has so far been attributed to him. It is interesting to note that his premises, comprising three hovels and buildings covering an area of 700 square yards and with a frontage of seventy-seven feet, were offered for sale in November

1842.[1] A printed letter-heading of his has survived depicting a table with figures, including animals, together with some vases. However it does not necessarily follow that the illustration was of actual articles produced by him. On the other hand he is described as 'china and earthenware ornament, figure and toy manufacturer'.

1. See *Staffordshire Advertiser*, 5 November 1842.

William Adams (and Sons)

It seems that William Adams, a firm which started around 1795 and continues today, was responsible for turning out small animals during our period. In certain surviving factory documents[1] concerned with the shipment of goods in 1837 and 1838 to Philadelphia, USA, there is a reference, *inter alia*, to china dogs and sheep, priced in each instance at 5/- per dozen. Whilst these animals could be bought-in items, there is no reason to suppose that this was the case. Nevertheless neither the dogs nor the sheep referred to have been identified with any surviving examples.

1. Reproduced in Appendix II to *Staffordshire Porcelain*, p.371.

James Dudson

James Dudson was born around 1813 in Shelton. Jewitt, after remarking that the business had been established in 1800, says: 'In 1835 Mr James Dudson entered upon the works, and they are still carried on by him. [He in fact died in 1882 but the concern still exists today, trading as Dudson Bros. at the original address, Hope St., Hanley]. At one time he manufactured ornamental china figures, vases and services... Mr Dudson, who received 'honourable mention' in the Exhibitions of 1851 and 1862, supplies both home and foreign markets'.[1]

The items entered in the 1851 Exhibition by James Dudson were 'ornamental china figures'.

Mrs Audrey Dudson has written a very informative book on the history and products of the factory, *Dudson: a family of potters since 1800,* and has pointed out that although the factory was predominantly a producer of earthenware — both a very white firing earthenware and also the common earthenware — some of its output was also porcelain. Indeed, the same figure model may be found in all three bodies. Moreover, it is thought that the later models were also made in Parian. In Appendices D and E of her book, Mrs Dudson has listed from the factory records the

1. *Ceramic Art in Great Britain*, Vol. II, p.336.

various animal models emanating from the factory, but has been unable to say positively that any particular model was, for certain, produced in porcelain.

All figure production declined after about 1850 and ceased altogether around 1865. Excavation of the factory site is currently taking place, but so far no animal has been unearthed save for a group of three red spaniels seated on a blue quill-holder base (figure 71). This particular item is in earthenware but Mrs Dudson believes that the model could just as well have appeared in porcelain. Doubtless much more will come to light about this very interesting factory.

Appendix A

FAKES AND FORGERIES

At the time of writing, fakes and forgeries present no particular problem for collectors of nineteenth century English porcelain animals. No serious attempt has so far been made to reproduce specimens from the great factories and such modern reproductions as there are, are directed to copying Staffordshire prototypes. The intention of the manufacturers is not, of course, to pass off their products as nineteenth century specimens. However, such copies will in the course of time pass into other hands, and then the possibility of deception exists.

There is no merit in trying to explain the differences between the original animals and their modern counterparts (or, for that matter, reproductions made earlier in this century). Words in themselves — and illustrations are little better — cannot really explain such subtleties as differences in glaze and paste and differences in colouring. Moreover, even if it were worthwhile to describe modern reproductions, there would be nothing to stop alterations to the formula, thereby rendering the description worthless as regards future reproductions. The answer is to approach the problem the other way round. First become thoroughly acquainted with genuine period items and anything that fails to correspond in respect of all crucial characteristics will not be 'right', and should be rejected.

The experienced collector will have no difficulty. It is the novice alone who is in jeopardy of being deceived. Novices should restrict their purchases to those from dealers of unquestioned expertise and integrity, and ensure that their receipt contains adequate particulars of what is being bought. If this is done, in the unlikely event of any purchase proving to be other than that which it purports to be, no difficulty will arise when it is taken back and the purchase price reclaimed. In the course of time the novice will become thoroughly familiar with the genuine and will have nothing to fear from any reproduction.

There are, however, two areas where even the experienced may find themselves deceived. First, Samson of Paris from around 1870 onwards reproduced porcelain items from virtually every factory that was collectable. Sometimes Samson's own factory mark was used, in which event there can be no question of deception, but often he forged the mark (frequently displayed conspicuously) of the particular factory whose product he was reproducing. An excellent example of his work can be seen in the dog of figure 59 where, for the reasons stated at pages 85 and 87, the Chelsea 'gold anchor mark' was employed instead of the Rockingham griffin mark. I have also seen an excellent facsimile by Samson of the Derby tiger and leopard of colour plate 32. Moreover in Christie's sale of 24 May 1971 there appeared Samson copies of a Derby pug (lot 72), a Derby sheep (lot 73), a pair of Derby deer (lot 74) and a Derby cat (lot 75). Samson's reproductions are of excellent quality and they are, incidentally, collected in their own right, but the 'give-away' feature is that they are invariably made of hard paste, whereas the items they purport to represent were of soft paste or bone-china.

The second danger area arises from the Sampson Hancock products turned out at the King Street factory, Derby. This concern commenced operations in 1848 and continued until 1935. A catalogue exists for the year 1934/35 and in it appear certain models initially belonging to the nineteenth century. Accordingly, such models, and others bearing a Sampson Hancock mark, could just as well belong to the twentieth century as the nineteenth. There is a reference in the 1934/35 catalogue, *inter alia*, to dogs, pigs, cows, calves and lambs, all seemingly without bases. It follows that any suggestion that a Sampson Hancock animal without a base (which could, of course, be unmarked) is nineteenth century in origin should be treated with grave suspicion.

Finally, a warning should be directed against the danger of finding an animal incised with the letters 'No' in script followed by the correct number, so as to suggest a Rockingham attribution, but which has in reality been incised by a modern-day forger with the aid of a dentist's drill or similar instrument. Fortunately, this fraud is of extremely rare occurrence.

Appendix B

PARIAN

The origin of Parian porcelain has been the subject of much dispute, but probably it was first produced, on a commercial scale at any rate, in the works of Copeland and Garrett in 1846. It was invented accidentally in the course of seeking to rediscover the composition of the eighteenth century biscuit porcelain that had been produced at Derby, the formula for which had been lost. The eighteenth century version was smoother to the touch and generally more pleasing than the chalky material of the nineteenth century found at the Derby, Rockingham and Minton factories. Original Parian was a highly vitrified form of biscuit porcelain, which usually had a delicate ivory tone suggestive of marble. It was smooth and silky in feel. However, a hard paste version was subsequently produced with a rougher and coarser surface, which was altogether less attractive. Its merit was that it was cheaper to manufacture.

Parian, with its suggestion of marble, was regarded as eminently suitable for statuary, and many well-known sculptors, although they did not really understand the material, were induced to model figures in this medium. The models were generally large, though the Minton factory reissued many of the figures that had originally been produced in biscuit in the new Parian body. Among the principal producers were Copeland, Minton, Coalport, Wedgwood, Worcester, Belleek, Samuel Alcock, Robinson and Leadbeater, Keys and Mountford[1] and William Brownfield and Son. In addition there were numerous smaller concerns turning out items in the Parian body.

Parian animals appear to have formed only a slight proportion of the total output of porcelain figures. However, they were normally large and as such quite out of keeping with the general run of porcelain animals produced in this country during the first half of the nineteenth century. Parian pieces are not amenable to collection on a large scale, for the obvious reason that they simply take up too much space in the average home. Lacking colour, they also appear dreary when viewed in quantity. However, Parian figures initially received an enthusiastic welcome from the critical press and new designs continued to be produced until about 1884. After this date the medium largely went out of fashion, though Robinson and Leadbeater carried on production into the twentieth century. However, when all is said and done, large statuary figures are not really suitable for the tactile charm of soft paste porcelain. Not surprisingly, Parian has in this century attracted little attention from serious collectors.

However, provided one is prepared to accept the scale of the modelling of Parian animals, they at least have a charm not shared by the heavy human figures produced contemporaneously. Examples shown here from the Minton factory are the Italian greyhound (figure 29) and Persian greyhound (figure 96) together with illustrations from the factory drawing book appearing in chapter 6. Also illustrated are a group comprising two chained greyhounds (figure 30); a shepherdess with a lamb (figure 115), from the Samuel Alcock factory; a group of rabbit and young from the Copeland factory (figure 140); a recumbent spaniel on a cushion from an unknown source (figure 70); a group of two cats playing with a bowl or vase (figure 23) made by William Brownfield & Son; and a pair of groups from the factory of Robinson and Leadbeater, one of a terrier puppy disturbing a sleepy recumbent Newfoundland (called 'Impudence'), the

---

1. At the 1851 Exhibition Keys and Mountford exhibited 'Group of two dogs, setter and pointer, with game; Group of three greyhounds'. There is no specific reference to these animals being in Parian. They could have been in glazed porcelain.

other of a terrier puppy receiving his just deserts from a now thoroughly roused Newfoundland (called 'Retribution') (figure 94).

A particularly attractive Copeland group, 12½ in. (38.1cm) long of three terriers after a rabbit, taken from the original bronze 'Chasse au lapin' by the French sculptor, P.J. Mêne, is illustrated in plate 45 of C. and D. Shinn's *Victorian Parian China*. That particular example is dated circa 1875. A pair of Copeland lions dating from around 1880, each on a shaped rectangular base, 4¾ in. (12.1cm) long, were sold at Sotheby's on 21 October 1986 (lot 525). A Copeland group consisting of a fox and terrier is recorded as having been produced in 1857. An example was given by Alderman W. Copeland MP to the Lichfield Museum at its opening in 1859. Also recorded is a large deerhound with the Copeland mark, measuring some 12in. (30.5cm) in length.

The Royal Worcester factory also turned out animals in Parian, sometimes glazed and tinted, such as the elephant with howdah and ceremonial cloth, 7¾ in. (19.7.cm) high shown in figure 158, and the camel with elaborate seat and cloth, 6¾ in. (17.1cm) high illustrated in figure 154. Both were modelled by Hadley, the former being registered on 19 November 1869 and the latter on 22 June 1870.

Appendix C

DATE OF MANUFACTURE OF ROCKINGHAM ANIMALS

As explained earlier, Rockingham figures consist of both animal and human subjects, and there is no reason to suppose that the period of production was significantly different in either case. Accordingly, in considering the question of the date to be assigned to Rockingham animals, it is appropriate to take into account any evidence that bears on the identification of the period to which the human figures are to be attributed.

Although, where the full mark appears on animals, it invariably takes the form appropriate to the red period (i.e. 1826-30) to the complete exclusion of the later mark, this is not universally the case with human figures. A single instance has been recorded where the impressed mark used on a biscuit figure of 'Femme de l'Andalousie' (No 119) incorporates the word 'Royal', thereby indicating a post-1830 origin. This, when coupled with certain other discoveries, has induced A. and A. Cox to conclude[1] that figure production continued until the factory's closure in 1842. However, it is my view that such a conclusion cannot stand in the face of the evidence taken as whole.

In addition to the isolated figure referred to above, A. and A. Cox rely on the following discoveries: the various purchases of figures made by the Fitzwilliam family after 1830, as recorded in the Wentworth papers; and the unearthing, during the course of excavating the factory site, of figure wasters mixed with wasters belonging to the 1831-42 period.

Although not specifically mentioned by A. and A. Cox, it is known, from the records of the auction sale of the factory's stock on its closure, conducted on 1, 2 and 4 May 1843 by Mr Edward Lancaster of Lancaster and Sons, Barnsley, that some four or five lots consisted of figures and one lot of a single bust (presumably biscuit). Moreover, it should also be mentioned that there exists in the Yorkshire Museum a bust of the second Earl Fitzwilliam, which because it records his death as being 'Feb 8, 1833' must have been produced after that date. It might be argued that the survival of some figures until 1842 and the production of at least one post-1830 bust lends support to the theory that figure production continued throughout the factory's life as a porcelain producer.

I will deal in turn with the various arguments that have been advanced in repudiation of the traditional view that figure production was, with a few exceptions, confined to the 1826-30 period.

---

1. A. and A. Cox, *The Rockingham Works,* pp.55, 56; *Rockingham Pottery and Porcelain* 1745-1842, p.184.

---

(1) The figure with a 'Royal' impressed mark

The case has been argued with force that the Rockingham mark containing the word 'Royal' was strictly confined to circa 1831 and, unlike the more frequent mark with the caption 'Manufacturer to the King' was not used throughout the whole of the later period up to 1842.[1] But whether this is correct or not, there is no reason to suppose that the 'Royal' mark was not at least sometimes employed on items made circa 1831. Accordingly, the existence of a single figure need indicate nothing more than the fact that one or two figures continued to be made for a few months after the end of the early red period. This in no way undermines the general thesis that figures were almost all produced within the 1826-30 period.

Figures were normally numbered, and there appears to be no break in the numbering series. Commonsense suggests that the models were produced in the order, or approximately in the order, indicated by their numbers, but in addition to commonsense there is some positive evidence

---

1. B. Bowden, *Royal Rockingham — in Regency and Neo-rococo Style, Collectors Guide,* March 1977 pp.70-74.

to support this conclusion. Those of the first eleven models that have so far been recorded are found (frequently or invariably, depending on the particular model concerned) with the early printed mark, whereas all the higher numbered models bear only the impressed mark. Towards the end of the series, the master model for the Continental peasant 'Laitière des environs d'Harlem', No 138, has been discovered on the factory site and is incised 'by T. Griffin/July 15th 1830', revealing not only the name of the modeller but, more important for our present purpose, the date when the model was actually produced. Unfortunately, there is no way of telling the rate at which the various master models were produced. It is uncertain whether model production proceeded at a regular tempo or whether a large number of different designs were turned out at the very beginning of porcelain manufacture, thereby ensuring that the factory could, in its early stages of figure production, call on a diversity of different models. There is some support for the latter view in the invoice sent to Wentworth House recording that in November 1826 the Fitzwilliam family purchased:

4 China Biscuit rabbits   £1-2-0

The only rabbits known to us, apart from the toys of figure 136 (in view of the price it is hardly likely that toys were meant), bear the numbers 78 (assuming this is not a hare rather than a rabbit) and 110 respectively. If the rabbits referred to in the invoice were examples of one of these models, then within a few months of the commencement of porcelain production at least seventy-eight different models had come to be completed. However, it is perhaps more likely that these rabbits were not examples of model Nos 78 or 110, but of an early unnumbered model. For it is known that the factory produced some early unnumbered animals printed with the red mark, e.g. the pugs of colour plate 11 and the cat of figure 5, and that sometimes such models appear never to have been incorporated in the numbered series (see page 210). Alternatively, the 'Fitzwilliam rabbits' may actually be examples of model No 78 or 110 but produced before they were brought into the numbered series (see the black cat No 77 referred to at page 20).

It is interesting to note that a biscuit example of the Continental peasant model 'Paysan Basque des environs de Bayonne,' No 115, has been discovered[1] incised under the base with the date 'November 5th 1829', presumably indicative of the date of manufacture rather than the date when the actual model was created. Manifestly, the model itself must have been made before 5 November 1829, but its numeral proximity to

1. See D.G. Rice, *Rockingham Ornamental Porcelain,* plate 133.

the Continental peasant 'Laitière des environs d'Harlem' No 138, suggests that it could nevertheless have been a fairly late production. It may well have been the case that the factory procured a large number of the lower numbered models to be turned out comparatively quickly and then allowed the tempo of production to slow down dramatically.

Although the researches of A. and A. Cox have shown that the factory produced models numbered 125, 126, 138, 146 and 148, all of which would appear to have been Continental peasants, no example has so far been discovered. The only examples of models higher than 120 that have been recorded are numbers 136 (one pair only), 139 (one specimen only) and 142 (three specimens). Now, if there was a slow-down in the factory's initial tempo of model production, so that those bearing a higher number than 120 were turned out (say) in 1830, it must necessarily follow that examples of these models were manufactured in 1830 or later. However, if the traditional view is correct, that all figure production ceased by or shortly after the end of 1830, an explanation for the dearth of figures with the highest numbers readily springs to mind. There was simply no time to produce the highest numbered figures in any quantity. Hence no survivors! The absence of figures with the highest numbers lends support to the view, based on the use of the early mark to the exclusion of the later version, that almost all figures were produced in the period 1826-30, with only a few exceptions following within the later 'Royal' period.

(2) Purchases by the Fitzwilliam family

The researches of A. and A. Cox into the Wentworth papers have brought to light certain purchases of various Rockingham figures made by the Fitzwilliam family after 1830. In 1835 Lady Anne took away in her carriage (in addition to two small tapers) '1 China small cat' (for a total of 5s 6d). Presumably, she had previously called at the factory showroom. Again, in 1838, '2 China dogs' (costing 2s. 6d.) were sent to the Earl's seat at Wentworth. Dr and Mrs. Cox have also been able to point to the purchase in 1839 by the Fitzwilliam family of

'1 Pair China Bis[t] French Shepd and Shep[s] - 11 -
1 Pair   "   Flower Boy and Girl -9 - 6

ordered by Confectioner to be used as ornaments for dress plates for Desserts'

Dr and Mrs Cox argue, on the basis of the above discoveries, that figures, including animals, were produced throughout the factory's life and not just during the period 1826-30.

However, in my view, the discovery of a few purchases made by the Fitzwilliam family after 1830 is not enough to rebut the inference that figure production virtually ceased shortly after 1830. The almost invariable employment on a figure, where the full mark is used, of the early rather than the late mark seems to make the inference virtually certain. It must be remembered that Earl Fitzwilliam and his family were in a privileged position in relation to the factory. If they wanted porcelain figures, the Bramelds would have done their best to oblige either by searching through the accumulated stock or, in the last resort, by producing what was wanted from existing moulds as a special order. It is significant that some of the figures referred to above as having been purchased by the Fitzwilliam family are specifically described as being 'biscuit' i.e. unglazed and undecorated. Now, if production of figures stopped shortly after 1830, it could well be the case that certain examples in the biscuit state (and perhaps others glazed with no further decoration) had been left lying around the factory. They could have been there for years, and it may be that it was these pre-1831 'left-overs' which were sold to the Fitzwilliam family in 1835, 1838 and 1839. Similarly, the figures appearing at the factory's 'closing-down sale' could also have been the remnants of a production long ago discontinued.

(3) Figure wasters mixed with post-1830 wasters

The third argument advanced by A. and A. Cox for the view that figures continued to be produced until 1842 is based on the discovery at the factory site of certain figure wasters mixed with wasters of items undoubtedly belonging to the post-1830 period. However, it is a *non sequitur* to infer from this that figures were necessarily made at the same time as the later ware. All that is proved by the juxtaposition of the two types of wasters is that discarded figures were thrown out at some time after 1830. Now it is only to be expected that the factory would from time to time jettison unwanted accumulations, and there is nothing remarkable in such accumulations including figures which were defective or on which the Bramelds had decided to do no further work.

On balance, therefore, I do not consider that the case has been made out that Rockingham animals were produced later than the end of 1830.

Appendix D

Extracts from the diary of Elizabeth Moulton-Barrett (later Browning) relating to her squirrel.

Sunday 2 Oct 1831
...*We* caught a squirrel; and *I* claimed it

Tuesday, 4 Oct 1831
...My squirrel very well

Saturday 15 Oct 1831
...By way of distraction Georgie and myself from Homer, I let out my squirrel. He leapt up into the air, and climbed my bookcase, and performed so many tight rope maneuvres (sic), that I was inclined to wish him to be tight again. Particularly in the evening, when Atalanta herself seemed to have no chance of catching him. Arabel & Bummy & Ann & I were about an hour at it. At last, he wisely ran into his cage, when he cd run no where else; and thus he was caught... Mr Deane & a goose for dinner... I played on the guitar; but my voice had gone away with my breath, in the squirrel chase.

Tuesday 18 Oct 1831
...We were much afraid, even I was, of the effect of this letter upon her; but she bore it as calmly as I should my squirrel running away...

Sunday 23 Oct 1831
...My squirrel has eaten three chestnuts out of my hand, and has tried to eat my hand besides. It did not bite much. I should grow very fond of it, if it wd but grow fond of me, & if I cd persuade it to become more odiferous. We have brought a myrtle tree into this room, for it to have leaping room upon Arabel's proposition.

Monday 24 Oct 1831
...My squirrel was found this morning asleep under the cushion of my chair. Suppose I had sate down upon him! — He is grown more and more civilized and has eaten out of my hand several times. I told Annie that she might have him, if she like it. Now that he has become so tame, I hope she wont like it...

Tuesday 1 Nov 1831
...Nobody was angry. Bummy only said that I required more looking after than my squirrel, and that I ought to have a cage made for me...

Sunday 6 Nov 1831
...Bro & A & I wasted some yards of time today, in watching my squirrel who ate two or three chestnuts on my knee and ran up Bro's shoulder...

Tuesday 15 Nov 1831

...In my absence off ran my squirrel. How provoking!

Wednesday 16 Nov 1831

...I sent off... a letter from me to Mr Boyd. In it I said that I missed both him and the squirrel very much indeed — tho' I was modest enough to believe in the possibility of its being best for both of them, that I shd...

Selected Bibliography
(Published in London unless otherwise indicated)

Barrett, F.A. and Thorpe A.L., *Derby Porcelain* (1971)

Bemrose, William, *Bow, Chelsea, and Derby Porcelain* (1898)
A Descriptive Catalogue of Porcelain and other Art Objects in the Collection of William Bemrose, privately printed (1898)

Bewick, Thomas, *A General History of Quadrupeds* (1790). Newcastle-upon-Tyne.

Bradley, H.G. (ed.), *Ceramics of Derbyshire 1750-1975* (1978)

Browne, Mary, *The Diary of a Girl in France in 1821* (1905)

Cox, Alwyn and Angela, *The Rockingham Works* (1974). Sheffield.
Rockingham Pottery and Porcelain 1745-1842 (1983)

Daniel, Rev. W.B., *Rural Sports* (1801-02)

Darton, F.J. Harvey (Ed.), *The Life and Times of Mrs Sherwood (1775-1851)* (c.1911)

Dudson, Audrey, *Dudson: a family of potters since 1800* (1985)

Gilhespy, F.B., *Crown Derby Porcelain* (1951). Leigh-on-Sea.

Gilhespy, F.B. and Budd, Dorothy M., *Royal Crown Derby China* (1964)

Godden, G.A., *An Illustrated Encyclopaedia of British Pottery and Porcelain* (1966)
Minton Pottery and Porcelain of the First Period 1793-1850 (1968)
The Illustrated Guide to Ridgway Porcelains (1972)
Chamberlain Worcester Porcelain 1788-1852 (1982)
Staffordshire Porcelain (ed.) (1983)

Grant, Elizabeth, of Rothiemurchus (afterwards Mrs Smith of Baltiboys), *Memoirs of a Highland Lady* (ed. Lady Strachey) (1911)

Hare, A.J.C. (ed.), *Life and Letters of Maria Edgeworth* (1894)

Harrison, William, *Description of England* (1586)

Haslem, John, *The Old Derby China Factory* (1876)

Hayden, Arthur, *Spode and his Successors* (1925)

Hughes, Bernard and Therle, *Collecting Miniature Antiques* (1973)

Hutchinson's, *Dog Encyclopaedia* (c.1938)

Ireland, Samuel, *Graphic Illustrations of Hogarth* (1799)

Jewitt, Llewellyn, *Ceramic Art in Great Britain* (1878) Two Vols.

Selected Bibliography (continued)

John, W.D., *Swansea Porcelain* (1958) Newport.

Lancaster, H. Boswell, *Talks on Pottery* (1949)

Lockett, T.A., *Davenport Pottery and Porcelain 1794-1887* (1972). Newton Abbot.

McClinton, Katharine Morrison, *Antique Cats for Collectors* (1974)

Nightingale, J.E., *Contributions towards the History of Early English Porcelain* (1881). Salisbury.

Oliver, Anthony, *The Victorian Staffordshire Figure* (1971)
Staffordshire Pottery (1981)

Owen, Hugh, *Two Centuries of Ceramic Art in Bristol* (1873). Privately printed. Gloucester.

Rice, Dennis G, *Rockingham Ornamental Porcelain* (1965)
The Illustrated Guide to Rockingham Pottery and Porcelain (1971)
Derby Porcelain The Golden Years (1750-70) (1983)

Richie, Carson, I.A., *The British Dog* (1981)

Sandon, Henry, *Royal Worcester Porcelain from 1862 to the Present Day* (1978)

Schreiber, Lady Charlotte, *Journals* (1911)

Shinn, C. and D., *The Illustrated Guide to Victorian Parian China* (1971)

Stables, Gordon, *Our Friend the Dog* (1895)

Taplin, William, *The Sportsman's Cabinet*. Two Vols. (1803)

Twitchett J. and Bailey B., *Royal Crown Derby* (1976)

Vivian, Margaret, *Antique Collecting* (1937)

Wedgwood, Josiah C., *Staffordshire Pottery and Its History* (1913)

Wood, Rev. J.C., *The Illustrated Natural History* (c.1850)

Worde de, Wynkyn, *The Treatise perteyning to Hawkynge, Huntynge, & c emprynted at Westmestre* (1496)

Youatt, William, *The Dog* (1854) [There were also earlier editions]
Sheep, their Breeds, Management and Diseases (1837)

Zoological Society, *The Gardens and Menageries of the Zoological Society, delineated.* Two vols. (1831)

Journals, Catalogues, Reports, Newspapers, Periodicals, etc.

Antique Collector (June 1961)

Apollo (November 1987)

Catalogue of the Great Exhibition 1851

Catalogue of the Exhibition of Minton 1798-1910 (held at Victoria and Albert Museum, 1976)

Catalogue of the Exhibition of Staffordshire Porcelain 1740-1851 (1979)

Collectors' Guide (March 1977)

The Connoisseur (September 1922 and April 1927)

The Connoisseur Year Book 1962

The Craftsman (5 December 1730)

Grainger Lee & Co Pattern Book

Minton Drawing Book

The Potter's Examiner and Workman's Advocate (11 May 1844)

Report on the Employment of Children in Factories (1843)

Sporting Annals (1824)

Staffordshire Advertiser (14 May and 5 November 1842)

Trans. E.C.C. Vol. 12, Part 3

William White's History and Gazetteer and Directory of Staffordshire (1834)

Yorkshire Gazette (14 April 1832)

Index

Note: numbers in italics refer to figure numbers and numbers in bold refer to colour plate numbers.